# Sports and Entertainment

# Sports and Entertainment

Shailendra Sengar

ANMOL PUBLICATIONS PVT. LTD.
NEW DELHI-110 002 (INDIA)

**ANMOL PUBLICATIONS PVT. LTD.**
*H.O.:* 4374/4B, Ansari Road, Darya Ganj,
New Delhi-110 002 (India)
Ph.: 23278000, 23261597
*B.O.:* No. 1015, Ist Main Road, BSK IIIrd Stage
IIIrd Phase, IIIrd Block
Bangalore - 560 085 (India)
Visit us at: www.anmolpublications.com

*Sports and Entertainment*



First Published, 2008
ISBN 978-81-261-3440-3

PRINTED IN INDIA

Printed at Mehra Offset Press, Delhi.

# Contents

# Preface

This Encyclopaedic Series of Career and Vocational Guidance Covers careers, describing jobs, places of employment, working conditions, qualifications, education and training. This has been developed to aid career and counsellors and job placement coordinators in planning activities for students and potential students about career vocational education programs. It contains a career and vocational guidance model which clarifies what career and vocational guidance services mean and what planners should include in their activities. The model shows an interrelatedness among major thrusts with career development being a central theme of vocational guidance. All of the thrusts depicted in the model represent essential services that should be available to students in career and vocational education programs. The encyclopaedia deals with various sections which correspond to the major thrusts identified in the model: (1) career development; (2) recruitment; (3) guidance and counselling; (4) placement; (5) follow-up and follow-through; and (6) consultation. Each section contains an outline of the perceived needs of the topic, an overview of the topic relative to career and vocational guidance, and some suggested activities and strategies that may be useful in meeting student needs.

It also contains current information about occupations, employment trends, and job searching. Materials on career decision-making, internships, and salaries are also located in each volume. This Series of Encyclopaedia helps students assess their potential for various careers.

*Shailendra Sengar*

1

# Career in Sports

If a career in sports holds your fancy, there are three main options you can choose from.

- Pursue the sport or game on a full time basis generally with sponsorship from an employer/promoter
- Become a trainer/instructor/coach for a game or sporting event
- Finally use the experience acquired over years as a sportsperson to work in a related field, such as, sports journalism, sports goods manufacture/marketing or as commentator.

To be a sports person one needs to be physically fit, energetic and enthusiastic. If aspiring to become a trainer or manager, a graduate degree in physical education can be pursued after Class XII (any stream with physical education).

## Career in Sports

***Industry Overviews:*** Industry Overviews provides detailed descriptions on the specific categories listed below. These descriptions will provide you with a better understanding of each industry category and what issues each faces on a daily basis.

***College Athletics:*** College athletics represents an enormous segment of the sport industry. Almost every college campus has an athletic department and there are over 3000 colleges and universities in the U.S. Athletic departments might have numerous departments such as tickets, sports information, facilities management, equipment, student-athlete affairs, marketing, fundraising and many more. Athletic departments are responsible for getting a team to the playing field an fans to the stadium. For many professionals working in the sport industry today, college athletics is where their career began. Athletic departments offer access for you to gain real life work experience, intimate knowledge of sport and an understanding of sport business.

***Health & Fitness:*** The Health and Fitness industry has experienced steady growth over the last two decades. Humans are staying healthy and living longer through enhanced Sports Medicine and Exercise Science. Sports Medicine provides career opportunities to work on prevention and rehabilitation of the human body either before or after sports injuries. Exercise Science conducts research, testing how the human body works under physical strain.

A health and fitness professional, such as personal trainer or aerobics instructor, will assist clients in physical education, personal training, or basic aerobics. If staying healthy or helping others maintain their health interests you, then a career in the health and fitness industry may be right for you.

***Recreation:*** Most everyone that works in the sports industry or those that are trying to begin a career in the sports industry probably fuelled their desire and passion for sports in childhood. Recreational leagues, be it Little League, Youth Soccer, Junior Hockey or Pop Warner Football, are prevalent in our society. A career in the recreation industry provides an opportunity to ensure that kids of today and adults too, have an opportunity to participate in sports.

***Professional Sports:*** Professional teams are the most widely recognized industry segment in sports. Professional teams and leagues include various sports teams, leagues and governing bodies for which individuals are compensated for performance.

Most notably are the NFL, NBA, MLB, NHL, WNBA and MLS and during the past two decades, more professional leagues have begun like the Arena Football and NFL Europe.

A career in this industry segment usually begins with an entry-level position as an account executive selling single, group and season tickets. It might be easier to access a career by working in one of the minor leagues. Like the players, you will need to get experience prior to making it to the big leagues. Most of the positions within an organization are filled from within. Once you have had the opportunity to demonstrate your abilities and commitment, promotions will follow.

***Associations & Organizations:*** Associations and organizations represent the governing bodies of sports. Almost every sport or industry segment has an official organization or association overseeing it. The main responsibility of these associations and organizations is to guide its members in areas of governing laws, business practices, competition, playoffs and championships.

Each association, for example, will represent its particular industry segment in political matters, protecting against unfair legal practices that might restrict business of its members. Examples of these associations or organizations include: The National Association of Sports Commission, The Sporting Goods Manufactures Association, The Professional Golfer's Association, The National Athletic Trainer's Association, the National Hockey League Player's Association, or The National Association of Collegiate Directors of Athletics.

### *High Schools*

***Sporting Goods:*** Sports apparel has become the attire of choice throughout much of the world. The impact and name recognition of the major companies in the sporting goods industry has increased tremendously.

The sporting goods industry includes Manufacturers, both suppliers and producers of finished goods and Retailers with either full-line stores or specialty stores and wholesalers/ distributors who manage mass merchandisers and mail orders. Companies that fall into the sporting goods segment include: NIKE Inc., Reebok International Ltd., Adidas America Inc., Converse Inc., Wilson Sporting Goods Company Inc., Rawlings Sporting Goods Company Inc., Taylor Made Golf Company, Sportsmart, The Sports Authority, Oshman's, Champs Sports and Footlocker.

If staying in touch with the latest fashion is your thing, then maybe a career in the sporting goods industry is right for you?

High School athletics represents a huge segment of the sports industry. There are over 17,000 high schools in the United States with athletic programmes. The National Federation of State High School Associations (NFHS) is the national service and administrative organization for high school athletics. The NFHS publishes playing rules and promotes programmes and services that can be used by the individual state associations governing their high school athletic programmes. Today, there are 16 sports and over 2.5 million young girls playing sports in every state. With an increasing number of young girls playing high school athletics, more and more women coaches are needed as well as women assistant coaches, women's athletic coordinators and women trainers. Many collegiate, professional and Olympic coaches began their careers coaching high school athletics. High school athletics gives you many tools that are used at every level in the sports business such as fundraising, marketing, budgeting and public relations.

### *Broadcasting & Media*

Sports Media is defined as the news and events surrounding the world of sport. Once the lone domain of newspapers, sports media has evolved into radio shows, television shows and now specialty sites on the Internet. Examples of companies in print media include: ESPN Magazine, Hockey News, Sports Illustrated and the sports page of your local newspaper. Examples of companies in electronic media include: CBS Sports, NBC Sports, ESPN, Fox Sports, ESPN Radio, KMVP (sports radio), KGME (sports radio) and SportsLine.com. Look into these companies or ones like them if sports media sounds interesting to you.

### *Sports Venues*

Wherever sports are played you are sure to find a facility designed for the enjoyment of sport or entertainment. It might be a simple field with small bleachers or quite possibly a

100,000 seat stadium. Other definitions of sports venues includes; city parks, natatoriums, tennis complexes, golf courses and multi-use entertainment venues.

Career opportunities exist within a particular facility itself, with companies and organizations that manage facilities, or with companies that supply products and services to facilities. Most individuals are familiar with well-known sports facilities including Madison Square Garden, The Rose Bowl, The "old" Boston Gardens, Yankee Stadium and the Los Angeles Coliseum.

***Sports Events***

The Olympic Games, The Super Bowl and World Cup Soccer; These are just a few of the thousands of sporting events held each year around the world. Millions of dollars are spent on these events which require large staffs to manage them. With a little research, you will find that most events are either run by an organizing committee or an event management company.

Overseeing an event is an enormous and challenging task. Event management includes executing the event, all the way to full service management, including sponsorship sales and promotional campaigns. Event managers within companies like International Management Group (IMG), SFX Entertainment and Mandalay Entertainment have oversee an event from concept to completion. This includes client services, marketing, sales, sponsorships and audio/video production. Events such as the Tostitos Fiesta Bowl, The College Football Classic, or The Tradition Presented by Countrywide, a Senior PGA golf tournament, have an existing staff that manages the event. The event staff usually includes directors and officers like; Executive Director, Marketing Director, Public Relations Director, Sales Managers, Director of Operations and Client Services Coordinator. Each has a role in implementing and overseeing the event. The Sales Manager might work with companies to secure advertising and promotional campaigns for the event, while the Client Services Coordinator coordinates needs of existing advertisers.

Volunteering for events aids in building a resume, developing a network base and exposes the inner working of event logistics. So remember, events such as the Rose Bowl, the Olympic Games and others need hundreds of volunteers to make them a success. Check with your local visitors and convention bureau or sports commission for information on events coming to your town and get out and volunteer. Who knows, you may be asked to stay permanently!

### *Professional Services*

The growth of the sports industry has required companies to employ more "business professionals", common to every industry, large or small. Some of these services include sports law specialists (both as in-house counsel or independent counsel), graphic designers, accountants, information system managers, mistakes made regarding the sports industry is the belief that if you are not an athlete, you will not have a chance to work in sports.

It is important to understand that employers need a lawyer to handle sports related law problems, or that it takes an accountant to handle the financial responsibilities of a sports company. In the professional services segment of sports, it takes all kinds of education's and backgrounds to handle some of the more job-specific responsibilities available. Do not limit yourself, sports is a 'big business" industry and there are numerous opportunities available to you.

### *Want a Career in Sports?*

The acceptability of sports and physical education as a career has gone up several times with the entry of prominent corporate bodies as sponsors of sports and events during the last decade. Some of them have also come forward to extend training facilities to sports persons. This shows the enormous potential that lies ahead for sportsmen.

Active sport careers are short. A few manage to find some work connected with their sport as managers, coaches or by promoting products. The majority have to look elsewhere for employment unless they are already employed with some organization by virtue of their sports prowess.

***Career in Sports:*** For a career in sports and physical education, you should have a keen interest in sports and games, a high level of physical fitness, mental and physical stamina, a competitive spirit, leadership qualities, organizing ability, resilience and will power to cope with injuries and setbacks, self-confidence, self-discipline, mental toughness, dedication and perseverance. Even hobbies such as sports, the performing arts and photography, if pursued with professional training, can be a worthwhile career.

***Job Opportunity:*** Some distinct career streams in sports and physical education may be as professional players or participants, or in teaching or coaching. You can find jobs in schools and colleges as Physical education teachers. As a physical education teacher, you should have the ability to instill in the young the importance of good health and fitness habits. Through the medium of sports, you have to teach children the meaning of leadership, aggression and competition.

***Sports Journalism:*** You can, as a player, engage yourself in writing or reporting sports events. Sports journalism can be taken up by those having a knowledge of various sports events and having a flair for writing. Sports Physiotherapy can be a specialization for a medically trained person or by a physiotherapist. You can be a sports nutritionist. A nutritionist who has trained to help sports persons according to the requirements of their life styles is called a sports nutritionist.

***Training in Sports and Games:*** The Sports Authority of India (SAI) organizes National Sports Talent Contest for identifying sports talent and providing adequate training in sports and games. Sports persons in schools/colleges/ universities who have secured first/second/ third positions in individual events or winners / runners-up positions in team events in international / national and state level competitions held during a calendar year may apply for scholarships.

## Professional Sports Career

There are several professional sports teams. You can visit many of the national leagues Internet pages. Check these links out on the interview page. Professional athletics require people who are highly talented and determined. This is an adventurous career and should be sought out by only the very ambitious.

***Earnings:*** If you are good, you can make a ton of money. This money will come not only from the team that you play for but also from endorsements. The national annual average is $10,000 to $100,000. Talent, skill and type of sport determines the starting salaries.

***Working Conditions:*** Working conditions vary according to what sport you play. There are several professional teams as well as self-employed professional athletics. The professional sports include baseball, hockey, soccer, basketball, tennis, golfing, boxers, skaters, bowlers and track athlethes. Whichever sport you decide to pursue, hard work, dedication and travel is required in order to compete.

***Hours:*** The hours are very long and include Saturdays, Sundays and some holidays. Again, depending on what sport you play, the hours vary. Most teams travel and train many hours of the day.

***Education and Training Needed:*** Most of the training begins at a very early age. You don't decide that you want to be a professional athlete all of a sudden. Skill is achieved through little leagues, high school teams and in the back yard. If you are serious about becoming a professional athlete, you should also play at the college level. The most important training is a self willed attitude. No one is going to push you to lift the weight and shoot the baskets or throw the ball everyday.

***Advantages:*** If you are good, fame and money are waiting for you. You are the center of attention and if not for you there would be many jobs lost. Because of professional athletes, there are ticket booth employees, coaches and numerous other jobs. You are always changing scenes, at a different gym, field, or court all the time.

***Disadvantages:*** The most obvious disadvantage is the fame. Fame can be an advantage or disadvantage depending on how you view it or how famous you are. You are always a role model and one wrong move and the whole world knows it. There is a lot of pressure working long, tough hours. You also have to work on Saturdays, Sundays and holidays since many games are played on those days. Being a professional athlete is not always fame and glory and has disappointments. Unlike many other careers, you not only disappoint yourself, but all the fans as well.

***Future in the Career:*** As long as the fans support you, there is a future in any professional sport. Baseball, football, basketball and other sports are American's pasttime. It will always be of interest and there will always be professional teams.

***How to Become a Professional Athlete:*** The best way to start is now! Most of the skills are learned easier at an earlier age. Let your kids sign up for every league that you are willing to drive them to in order to let them discover their talent. Most professional athlete careers start in the backyard. Join your high school team and plan to play while in college. If you're good enough, you'll know whether you'll be able to be a professional athlete. Good luck and keep practicing.

### *March Madness: Going Crazy for a Sports Career? Get One!*

***March Madness is Contagious:*** Capitalize on the thrills of this month's mania for tournament-style college hoops by pursuing a career that could put you in the middle of the Madness to come. Or simply give yourself a much-needed lifestyle change come spring with one of the jobs below.

***Health Careers:*** Helping Athletes Recover, Stay Healthy and Feel Their Best with Physical Therapy.

Even the world's top athletes fall victim to common sports injuries and they need help from physical therapists, physical therapy assistants and massage therapists to perform their best.

***Physical Therapist:*** Calling the Shots

As a physical therapist, you could be the one to get fallen players back on the court after surgery or an injury. Physical therapists help relieve pain, improve mobility, slowly restore a body to its pre-injury condition and minimize the long-term effects of physical trauma. A physical therapist devises a plan for a patient that typically includes exercises to increase flexibility and strength in specific muscle groups. They may also prescribe massage therapy or equipment like braces and cooling splints to help patients recover. Most collegiate and professional sports teams keep one or more physical therapists on duty throughout the year.

You will need to attend an accredited physical therapist education programme and pass the National Physical Therapy Examination before you can be licensed to soothe sore muscles and help today's brightest hoops stars recover from torn ligaments.

The job outlook for physical therapists is extremely promising. Experts at the U.S. Bureau of Labour Statistics (BLS) estimate that employment for physical therapists will increase much faster than the national average through 2014. The average salary of a physical therapist in the U.S. is $60,180.

***Physical Therapist Assistant:*** Ready to Relieve

Many professional therapists start their careers as physical therapist assistants. Under the supervision of a physical therapist, you could be helping athletes directly to perform their rehabilitation exercises, administer electrical stimulation or ultrasound and apply hot and cold packs. You may also gain experience with clerical and insurance work. The physical therapist assistant's job, in a nutshell, is to make the physical therapist more productive.

Physical therapist assistants are generally trained on the job, but they also typically earn as associate degree with academic courses in anatomy, physiology, biology and psychology from an accredited physical therapist assistant programme. Many states require licensure or registration to practice.

The job outlook for physical therapist assistants is rosy: The BLS projects employment of physical therapy assistants to grow much faster than average through 2014. Median annual earnings for this job were $37,890 in 2004.

***Massage Therapist:*** Muscles on the Rebound

Physicians have been recommending massage therapy for almost 2,400 years, going back to the Greek physician Hippocrates. After all, someone had to help the original

Olympians. Now, massage therapists work with athletes' muscles to decompress them and help remove waste products. Many athletes consider massage therapy crucial for their recovery from daily workouts and rehabilitation exercises.

Training standards for massage therapists vary widely across the country, but it's likely that you'll be required to complete a formal education programme and pass the national certification examination or a State exam in order to practice in your area.

The BLS projects employment for massage therapists to increase faster than average through 2014 because more people are learning about the benefits of massage therapy. The median earnings for massage therapists were $15.36 per hour in 2004.

***Taking Care of Business with Sports Finance:*** Most teams need business mangers to handle contracts for services such as hotels, insurance, travel and training supplies.

***Sports Administration:*** Teams always have bills to pay and arrangements to make for training camps, rookie tryouts and drafts. Most business managers start out as assistants, often through internship programmes. The most popular educational background is a four-year business administration degree, although marketing, finance and even liberal arts majors have all succeeded as business managers.

***Whatever Your Strength, Get in on the Action!:*** Even if you're not a star athlete, you can still be a part of the action with a career in the sports industry--helping athletes with physical therapy; promoting teams with advertising; PR and marketing; bringing the action to everyone through the media; or running the show from the back office. If you have a passion for sports, look beyond the court for a career that allows you to showcase your strong points--and be part of the Madness.

## Sports and Coaching Career

Athletic, Coaching and Umpire Career and Job Highlights:

- Requires irregular hours and extensive travelling.
- Athletes could get injuries that terminate their career.
- High school and amateur sports offer the best job

opportunities for coaches, sports instructors, umpires, referees and sports officials.

- There is intense competition for professional athlete jobs; therefore, athletes who seek to participate professionally must have amazing talent, passion and commitment to training.

## Sports (Athletic) and Coaching Career Overview

Being a nation full of avid sports fans and players, interest in watching sports and participating recreationally continues to expand at a rapid rate. Some amateur athletes dream of becoming paid professionals, such as players, coaches, or sports officials; but very little actually succeed at making a full-time living as a professional athlete. Those who do beat the odds, discover short careers and insecure jobs. Disregarding the small chance of getting a professional job, there are several options for part-time coaching, instructing, refereeing, or umpiring in amateur athletics and in educational systems.

Athletes and sports competitors entertain spectators by playing in officiated and controlled sports. Athletes must know the strategies of the game and abide by any rules and regulations as they play. Athletes can compete in a variety of team sports, such as baseball, basketball, football, hockey and soccer; and they can compete in individual sports, such as golf, tennis and bowling. Just as sports can be different, so can the degree of difficulty, varying from unpaid high school athletics to the professional level where the supreme athletes play on worldwide television.

On top of playing in games, athletes also spend numerous hours in hard practices every day, perfecting skills and learning teamwork under the direction of a coach or sports instructor. They also spend more time analyzing video tapes, so they may critique themselves on how they play and gain an advantage as they scrutinize their opponents' playing strategies and weaknesses. Some athletes receive strength training to build up muscle and endurance and prevent injuries. All levels of competition are very fierce and security in a job is always unstable. Consequently, several athletes must train consistently year round to keep exceptional form, technique and good physical condition. There are very few breaks for professional athletes. In accordance to physical training programmes, athletes may also be required to go on strict diets during the prime playing season. Several athletes push themselves as hard as they can during practices and games, increasing their risk for injuries that could end their career. Minor injuries are detrimental as well because the athlete could be replaced.

Coaches instruct and arrange amateur as well as professional athletes in essentials of individual and team sports. In individual sports, instructors might often have these same responsibilities. Coaches prepare athletes for a competitive season through directing practices where athletes perform drills to improve their abilities and endurance. Using their knowledge in the sport, coaches help the athlete with proper form and technique in beginning higher level exercises trying to make the most of the players' physical potential. In addition to supervising the improvement of athletes, coaches also are accountable for running the team during while practicing and competing and for instilling in their athletes good sportsmanship, the spirit of competition and working together as a team.

They may also choose, store, issue and stock equipment and supplies. During competitions, for example, coaches decide who will play to optimize fluid team work. Additionally, coaches conduct team strategy and impose certain plays during games to surprise and overpower opponents. To select the optimum plays, coaches assess or "scout" the opposing team before the competition, permitting them to decide on game strategies and certain plays. Several high school coaches mainly academic teachers who complement their income by being a part time coach. College coaches treat their jobs as full time; they travel frequently looking for potential players.

Sports instructors instruct professional and nonprofessional athletes individually. They arrange, teach, train and direct all types of athletes in sports such as bowling, tennis, golf and swimming. Because sports are so diverse (from weight lifting to gymnastics to scuba diving) and may involve self-defense sports such as karate, instructors usually specialize in one or two areas. In addition to coaches, sports instructors also may have daily practices and be in charge of equipment and supplies. Using their sporting, physiology and corrective technique expertise, they establish what the kind of exercises to use and how hard the exercises should be. They also give the athlete certain drills while correcting bad technique. A few instructors also give directions on using training apparatus like trampolines or weights, correct athletes' weaknesses and enhance their training. Sports instructors use their best knowledge to evaluate athletes and their opponents to devise a game strategy.

Because of their different focuses, coaches and sports instructors often approach athletes in various ways. For instance, coaches work with the team during a game to optimize their winning chances. On the other hand, sports instructors, like those who instruct professional tennis players, usually are not allowed to coach their athletes during competition. Sports instructors spend a lot of time working one-on-one with athletes, which gives them time to plan custom training programmes for individuals. It is challenging for coaches and instructors to encourage players; however, this is vital an athletes success. Several coaches and instructors get great satisfaction doing their job, helping children or young adults socially and physically to improve and learn skills that will promote achievement in their sport.

Umpires, referees and other sports officials officiate at competitive athletic and sporting events by examining the play, identifying infractions of rules and imposing penalties according to the sports' rules and regulations. They predict the plays and then place themselves in the best spot to see the action where they evaluate the situation and decide any violations. A few sports officials may work by themselves, such as those in boxing. Others such as umpires work in groups, such as baseball umpires. Officials' jobs are highly stressful in all sports because they are often have to make a quick decision, sometimes causing strong disagreements among players, coaches, or those watching.

Professional scouts assess the abilities of athletes, amateur and professional, to determine their talent and potential. The scout is a sports intelligence agent who primarily finds the best athletes that will qualify for his or her team and down the road, will bring success. Professional scouts usually work for scouting associations or do freelance work.

As scouts search out new talent, they perform their work in secret so their opponents won't know of their interest in particular players. A college-level head scout is usually an assistant coach; however, freelance scouts may assist colleges as they provide coaches information about outstanding players. These scouts look for gifted high school athletes through reading the newspaper, talking to high school coaches and alumni, going to high school games and reviewing videotapes of candidates' performances.

Athlete are known for having irregular hours. The coach, umpires, referees and other sports officials also share these hours. Athletes, coaches, umpires and related workers sometimes work weekends, evenings and even holidays. Through out most of the sports season and year, athletes and full-time coaches typically work more than 40 hours a week. A few coaches in educational systems, especially in high school, may coach several sports. Athletes, coaches and sports officials may be outside in different weather conditions for a lot for outdoor sports; those coaching indoor have the luxury of climate-controlled facilitates, such as arenas, indoor stadiums, or gymnasiums. Athletes, coaches and some sports officials travel regularly by bus, airplane, or car to scout out players at sporting events.

### *Training and Job Qualifications*

According to various levels and types of sports, education and training qualifications for athletes, coaches, umpires and other workers differ significantly. Every job requires a great deal of knowledge about the sport that is typically acquired after having years of experience at lower levels. Most athletes have played their whole life, starting in elementary school and continuing to play through high school and sometimes college. They compete in amateur competitions and on teams in high school and college, where professional scouts can observe them.

The majority of schools mandate athletes to obtain specific academic requirements to maintain eligibility to play. It takes years of effort to become a professional athlete. Those wanting to play professionally must obtain amazing talent, desire and devotion to training.

High schools typically prefer to hire teachers to be coaches and instructors that will work part-time. If they can't find someone suitable, they hire an outside coach. A few entry-level positions for coaches or instructors mandate merely experience resulting from participation in the activity or sport. Several coaches start out as assistant coaches to acquire the necessary knowledge and experience required for advancing to head coach. Head coaches working at bigger schools who endeavour to contend at the uppermost levels of a sport require considerable experience coaching as a head coach of a different school or as an assistant coach. To achieve professional coach status, it typically takes several years of coaching and winning at the lower levels. A bachelor's degree is required for all levels of public secondary school head coaches and sports instructors. It is required for those who are not teachers to meet specific State qualifications in order to certify to become a head coach. Private school coaches and sports instructors may not have to reach these same standards to certify. Course in degree programmes include the following: exercise and sports science, physiology, kinesiology, nutrition and fitness, physical education and sports medicine.

For sports instructors wanting to instruct tennis, golf, karate, or anything else, certification is highly recommended. Sometimes, an individual must be CPR certified as well as 18 years old. Different certifying organizations particular to a sport have various requirements and training according to their expectations. One must participate in a clinic, camp, or school in order to certify. Those working part-time and in smaller places have a lower chance of needing formal education or training.

Umpires, referees and other sports officials have certain requirements for each sport. They usually volunteer for intramural, neighborhood and recreational league competitions to start out their career. College referee candidates have to be certified through an officiating school and be assessed during a trial period. A few bigger college leagues mandate officials to be certified with further qualifications, such as being a resident in or near the league's boundaries and having prior experience that usually includes numerous years refereeing at high school and college level conference games.

Qualifications for professional sport officials are even stricter. For example, an umpire for professional baseball must have a high school diploma or an equivalent plus perfect vision (20/20) and fast reflexes. However to certify for a professional position, it required that potential candidates go to professional umpire training school. At this time, the Professional Baseball Umpires Corporation (PBUC) has approved two schools curriculums for training. Leading graduates are chosen for additional assessment as they officiate in a rookie minor league. Umpires, prior to being considered for major leagues, frequently need 8 to 10 years of experience in different minor leagues. In football candidates are required to obtain a minimum 10 years of officiating experience, with 5 of them at a collegiate varsity or minor professional level. Prospects for the NFL must be cross-examined by clinical psychologists to evaluate intelligence level and capability of handling tremendously stressful situations. Additionally, the NFL's security department carries out detailed background checks. Potential candidates are probably interviewed by a board from the NFL officiating department and take a comprehensive test about the association's rules and regulations.

A scout's requires experience playing professional or college sports. This knowledge allows them to recognize young players who have astonishing athletic talent and skill. The majority of starting scouts jobs include spotting talent in a certain area or region. Working hard and having success can lead to full-time jobs in charge of bigger regions. A few scouts proceed to scouting director positions or different sport executive positions.

Athletes, coaches, umpires and related workers possess developed skills in communication and leadership as well as being able to relate to others. To successfully instruct and encourage individuals or groups of athletes, coaches also must be creative and adaptable.

### *Employment Opportunities*

Through the year 2012, employment of athletes, coaches, umpires and related workers is projected to rise about as fast as the average for all occupations. Employment will grow due to the general public persisting to participate more and more in formal sports for entertainment, recreation and exercise. Job expansion will also be pushed by the growing numbers of baby boomers about to retire, during which they are projected take part in leisure-time activities, like tennis and golf and need instruction. Active participants in high school athletics will be the posterity of the baby boomers, requiring more coaches and instructors.

Increasing opportunities are estimated for coaches and instructors because physical fitness is becoming more important in our society. All ages of Americans are participating in extra young and lower-levelled athletic competitions, are becoming members of athletic clubs and are being motivated to engage in physical education. Coaches and instructor employment also will expand with increasing programmes for athletes in school and college and rising need for private sports training. Job expansion relating to sports among education will be determined by local school board decisions. Population expansion commands the building of more schools, especially in the developing suburbs. Nevertheless, when budgets become tight, financial support for athletic programmes is usually cut first. Because team sports are so popular, they are able to compensate by assistance from fund-raisers, booster clubs and parents.

State-certified academic and physical education teachers are likely to be optimum candidates for becoming coaches and instructors. Coaching opportunities will arise from the need to change several high school coaches.

Professional athlete jobs will persist to be highly competitive. Opportunities to have a career in professional sports, such as golf or tennis may increase as novel tournaments are founded and participant receive more prize money. The majority of professional athletes' careers are relatively short because of incapacitating injuries as well as age. As a result, a large fraction of the athletes in these jobs are changed each year, opening a few job opportunities. However, far more gifted young men and women have hopes of becoming a sports celebrity and will be competing for a restricted number of job openings. Persons seeking part-time umpire, referee and other sports high school level official jobs will have the optimum job opportunities; however, competition is probable for college level jobs with higher salaries and additional competition professional level jobs. Competition is expected to be very intense for scouts, certainly for professional teams who have limited positions.

## Athletes, Coaches, Umpires and Related Workers

***Significant Points:*** Work hours are often irregular; travel may be extensive.

Career-ending injuries are always a risk for athletes.

Job opportunities will be best for part-time coaches, sports instructors, umpires, referees and sports officials in high schools, sports clubs and other settings.

Competition for professional athlete jobs will continue to be extremely intense; athletes who seek to compete professionally must have extraordinary talent, desire and dedication to training.

***Nature of the Work:*** We are a nation of sports fans and sports players. Some of those who participate in amateur sports dream of becoming paid professional athletes, coaches, or sports officials, but very few beat the long and daunting odds of making a full-time living from professional athletics. Those athletes who do make it to professional levels find that careers are short and jobs are insecure. Even though the chances of employment as a professional athlete are slim, there are many opportunities for at least a part-time job as a coach, instructor, referee, or umpire in amateur athletics or in high school, college, or university sports.

*Athletes and sports competitors* compete in organized, officiated sports events to entertain spectators. When playing a game, athletes are required to understand the strategies of their game while obeying the rules and regulations of the sport. The events in which they compete include both team sports—such as baseball, basketball, football, hockey and soccer—and individual sports—such as golf, tennis and bowling. The level of play varies from unpaid high school athletics to professional sports, in which the best from around the world compete in events broadcast on international television.

Being an athlete involves more than competing in athletic events. Athletes spend many hours each day practicing skills and improving teamwork under the guidance of a coach or a sports instructor. They view videotapes to critique their own performances and techniques and to learn their opponents' tendencies and weaknesses to gain a competitive advantage. Some athletes work regularly with strength trainers to gain muscle and stamina and to prevent injury.

Many athletes push their bodies to the limit during both practice and play, so career-ending injury always is a risk; even minor injuries may put a player at risk of replacement. Because competition at all levels is extremely intense and job security is always precarious, many athletes train year round to maintain excellent form and technique and peak physical condition. Very little downtime from the sport exists at the professional level. Athletes also must conform to regimented diets during their sports season to supplement any physical training programme.

*Coaches* organize amateur and professional athletes and teach them the fundamentals of individual and team sports. (In individual sports, *instructors* sometimes may fill this role.) Coaches train athletes for competition by holding practice sessions to perform drills that improve the athletes' form, technique, skills and stamina.

Along with refining athletes' individual skills, coaches are responsible for instilling good sportsmanship, a competitive spirit and teamwork and for managing their teams during both practice sessions and competitions. Before competition, coaches evaluate or scout the opposing team to determine game strategies and practice specific plays. During competition, coaches may call specific plays intended to surprise or overpower the opponent and they may substitute players for optimum team chemistry and success. Coaches' additional tasks may include selecting, storing, issuing and taking inventory of equipment, materials and supplies.

Many coaches in high schools are primarily teachers of academic subjects who supplement their income by coaching part time. College coaches consider coaching a full-time discipline and may be away from home frequently as they travel to scout and recruit prospective players.

*Sports instructors* teach professional and nonprofessional athletes individually. They organize, instruct, train and lead athletes in indoor and outdoor sports such as bowling, tennis, golf and swimming. Because activities are as diverse as weight lifting, gymnastics, scuba diving and karate, instructors tend to specialize in one or a few activities. Like coaches, sports instructors also may hold daily practice sessions and be responsible for any needed equipment and supplies. Using their knowledge of their sport and of physiology, they determine the type and level of difficulty of exercises, prescribe specific drills and correct athletes' techniques. Some instructors also teach and demonstrate the use of training apparatus, such as trampolines or weights, for correcting athletes' weaknesses and enhancing their conditioning. As coaches do, sports instructors evaluate the athlete and the athlete's opponents to devise a competitive game strategy.

Coaches and sports instructors sometimes differ in their approaches to athletes because of the focus of their work. For example, while coaches manage the team during a game to optimize its chance for victory, sports instructors—such as those who work for professional tennis players—often are not permitted to instruct their athletes during competition. Sports instructors spend more of their time with athletes working one-on-one, which permits them to design customized training programmes for each individual. Motivating athletes to play hard challenges most coaches and sports instructors but is vital for the athlete's success. Many coaches and instructors derive great satisfaction working with children or young adults, helping them to learn new physical and social skills, improve their physical condition and achieve success in their sport.

*Umpires, referees and other sports officials* officiate at competitive athletic and sporting events. They observe the play, detect infractions of rules and impose penalties established by the rules and regulations of the various sports. Umpires, referees and sports officials anticipate play and position themselves to best see the action, assess the situation and determine any violations. Some sports officials, such as boxing referees, may work independently, while others such as umpires work in groups. Regardless of the sport, the job is highly stressful because officials are often required to make a decision in a split second, sometimes resulting in strong disagreement among competitors, coaches and spectators.

*Professional scouts*evaluate the skills of both amateur and professional athletes to determine talent and potential. As a sports intelligence agent, the scout's primary duty is to seek out top athletic candidates for the team he or she represents. At the professional level, scouts typically work for scouting organizations or as freelance scouts. In locating new talent, scouts perform their work in secrecy so as not to "tip off" their opponents about their interest in certain players. At the college level, the head scout often is an assistant coach, although freelance scouts may aid colleges by reporting to coaches about exceptional players. Scouts at this level seek talented high school athletes by reading newspapers, contacting high school coaches and alumni, attending high school games and studying videotapes of prospects' performances. They also evaluate potential players' background and personal characteristics, such as motivation and discipline, by talking to the players' coaches, parents and teachers.

***Working Conditions:*** Irregular work hours are the trademark of the athlete. They also are common for coaches, umpires, referees and other sports officials. People in these occupations often work Saturdays, Sundays, evenings and holidays. Athletes and full-time coaches usually work more than 40 hours a week for several months during the sports season, if not most of the year. Some coaches in educational institutions may coach more than one sport, particularly in high schools.

Athletes, coaches and sports officials who participate in competitions that are held outdoors may be exposed to all weather conditions of the season; those involved in events that are held indoors tend to work in climate-controlled comfort, often in arenas, enclosed stadiums, or gymnasiums. Athletes, coaches and some sports officials frequently travel to sporting events by bus or airplane. Scouts also travel extensively in locating talent, often by automobile.

Umpires, referees and other sports officials regularly encounter verbal abuse by fans, coaches and athletes. The officials also face possible physical assault and, increasingly, lawsuits from injured athletes based on their officiating decisions.

***Training, Other Qualifications and Advancement:*** Education and training requirements for athletes, coaches, umpires and related workers vary greatly by the level and type of sport. Regardless of the sport or occupation, jobs require immense overall knowledge of the game, usually acquired through years of experience at lower levels. Athletes usually begin competing in their sports while in elementary or middle school and continue through high school and sometimes college. They play in amateur tournaments and on high school and college teams, where the best attract the attention of professional scouts. Most schools require that participating athletes maintain specific academic standards to remain eligible to play. Becoming a professional athlete is the culmination of years of effort. Athletes who seek to compete professionally must have extraordinary talent, desire and dedication to training.

For high school coaching and sports instructor jobs, schools usually prefer to hire teachers willing to take on the jobs part time. If no one suitable is found, schools hire someone from outside. Some entry-level positions for coaches or instructors require only experience derived as a participant in the sport or activity. Many coaches begin their careers as assistant coaches to gain the knowledge and experience needed to become a head coach. Head coaches at large schools that strive to compete at the highest levels of a sport require substantial experience as a head coach at another school or as an assistant coach. To reach the ranks of professional coaching, a person usually needs years of coaching experience and a winning record in the lower ranks.

Head coaches at public secondary schools and sports instructors at all levels usually must have a bachelor's degree. Those who are not teachers must meet State requirements for certification to become a head coach. Certification, however, may not be required for coaching and sports instructor jobs in private schools. Degree programmes specifically related to coaching include exercise and sports science, physiology, kinesiology, nutrition and fitness, physical education and sports medicine.

For those interested in becoming a tennis, golf, karate, or other kind of instructor, certification is highly desirable. Often, one must be at least 18 years old and certified in cardiopulmonary resuscitation (CPR). There are many certifying organizations specific to the various sports and their training requirements vary. Participation in a clinic, camp, or school usually is required for certification. Part-time workers and those in smaller facilities are less likely to need formal education or training.

For example, there are two organizations that certify tennis instructors and coaches—the Professional Tennis Registry, an international organization and the U.S. Professional Tennis Association. Both organizations offer three levels of certification, but the requirements are slightly different. Each level of certification is based on the candidate's National Tennis Rating Programme rating, teaching experience and score on the organization's written and practical certifying exams. There are also minimum age requirements for each level.

Each sport has specific requirements for umpires, referees and other sports officials. Umpires, referees and other sports officials often begin their careers by volunteering for intramural, community and recreational league competitions. To officiate at high school athletic events, officials must register with the State agency that oversees high school athletics and pass an exam on the rules of the particular game. For college refereeing, candidates must be certified by an officiating school and be evaluated during a probationary period. Some larger college sports conferences require officials to have certification and other qualifications, such as residence in or near the conference boundaries, along with several years of experience officiating at high school, community college, or other college conference games.

Standards are even more stringent for officials in professional sports. Whereas umpires for high school baseball need a high school diploma or its equivalent, 20/20 vision and quick reflexes, those seeking to officiate at minor or major league games must attend professional umpire training school. Currently, there are two schools whose curriculums have been approved by the Professional Baseball Umpires Corporation for training. Top graduates are selected for further evaluation while officiating in a rookie minor league. Umpires then usually need 8 to 10 years of experience in various minor leagues before being considered for major league jobs.

Becoming an official for professional football also is competitive, as candidates must have at least 10 years of officiating experience, with 5 of them at a collegiate varsity or minor professional level. For the National Football League (NFL), prospective trainees are interviewed by clinical psychologists to determine levels of intelligence and ability to handle extremely stressful situations.

In addition, the NFL's security department conducts thorough background checks. Potential candidates are likely to be interviewed by a panel from the NFL officiating department and are given a comprehensive examination on the rules of the sport.

Scouting jobs require experience playing a sport at the college or professional level that makes it possible to spot young players who possess extraordinary athletic ability and skills. Most beginning scouting jobs are as part-time talent spotters in a particular area or region. Hard work and a record of success often lead to full-time jobs responsible for bigger territories. Some scouts advance to scouting director jobs or various administrative positions in sports.

Athletes, coaches, umpires and related workers must relate well to others and possess good communication and leadership skills. Coaches also must be resourceful and flexible to successfully instruct and motivate individuals and groups of athletes.

***Employment:*** Athletes, coaches, umpires and related workers held about 212,000 jobs in 2004. Coaches and scouts held 178,000 jobs; athletes, 17,000; and umpires, referees and other sports officials, 16,000. Nearly 37 percent of athletes, coaches, umpires and related workers worked part time, while 20 percent maintained variable schedules. Many sports officials and coaches receive such small and irregular payments for their services— occasional officiating at club games, for example—that they may not consider themselves employed in these occupations, even part time.

Among those employed in wage and salary jobs, 30 percent held jobs in private educational services. About 15 percent worked in amusement, gambling and recreation industries, including golf and tennis clubs, gymnasiums, health clubs, judo and karate schools, riding stables, swim clubs and other sports and recreation facilities. Another 9 percent worked in the spectator sports industry.

About 1 out of 4 workers in this occupation was self-employed, earning prize money or fees for lessons, scouting, or officiating assignments. Many other coaches and sports officials, although technically not self-employed, have such irregular or tenuous working arrangements that their working conditions resemble those of self-employment.

***Job Outlook:*** Employment of athletes, coaches, umpires and related workers is expected to increase faster than the average for all occupations through the year 2014. Employment will grow as the general public continues to participate in organized sports for entertainment, recreation and physical conditioning. Increasing participation in organized sports by girls and women will boost demand for coaches, umpires and related workers. Job growth also will be driven by the increasing number of baby boomers approaching retirement, during which they are expected to participate more and require instruction in leisure activities such as golf and tennis. The large number of children of baby boomers also will be active participants in high school and college athletics and will require coaches and instructors.

Employment of coaches and instructors also will increase with expansion of school and college athletic programmes and growing demand for private sports instruction. Sports-related job growth within education also will be driven by the decisions of local school boards. Population growth dictates the construction of additional schools, particularly in the expanding suburbs, but funding for athletic programmes often is cut first when budgets become tight. Still, the popularity of team sports often enables shortfalls to be offset somewhat by assistance from fund-raisers, booster clubs and parents. Persons who are State-certified to teach academic subjects in addition to physical education are likely to have the best prospects for obtaining coaching and instructor jobs. The need to replace the many high school coaches who change occupations or leave the labour force entirely also will provide some coaching opportunities.

Competition for professional athlete jobs will continue to be extremely intense. Opportunities to make a living as a professional in individual sports such as golf or tennis may grow as new tournaments are established and as prize money distributed to participants increases. Because most professional athletes' careers last only a few years due to debilitating injuries and age, annual turnover in these jobs is high, creating some job opportunities. However, the talented young men and women who dream of becoming sports superstars greatly outnumber and will compete aggressively for these openings.

Opportunities should be best for persons seeking part-time umpire, referee and other sports official jobs at the high school level. Competition is expected for higher paying jobs at the college level and will be even greater for jobs in professional sports. Competition should be very keen for jobs as scouts, particularly for professional teams, because the number of available positions is limited.

***Earnings:*** Median annual earnings of athletes were $48,310 in May 2004. However, the highest paid professional athletes earn much more. Median annual earnings of umpires and related workers were $21,260 in May 2004. The middle 50 percent earned between $16,870 and $31,390. The lowest paid 10 percent earned less than $14,160 and the highest paid 10 percent earned more than $44,140.

In May 2004, median annual earnings of coaches and scouts were $26,350. The middle 50 percent earned between $17,230 and $40,460. The lowest paid 10 percent earned less than $13,320 and the highest paid 10 percent earned more than $57,800. However, the highest paid professional coaches earn much more. Median annual earnings in the industries employing the largest numbers of coaches and scouts in May 2004 are shown below:

| | |
|---|---|
| Colleges, universities and professional schools | $36,610 |
| Other amusement and recreation industries | 26,340 |
| Other schools and instruction | 22,560 |
| Elementary and secondary schools | 21,970 |
| Civic and social organizations | 19,020 |

Earnings vary by level of education, certification and geographic region. Some instructors and coaches are paid a salary, while others may be paid by the hour, per session, or based on the number of participants.

### *Historical Earnings Information*

In 2002, median yearly earnings of athletes were $45,320. The lowest 10 percent received less than $14,090, while the highest 10 percent received than $145,600. Still, professional athletes receiving the highest pay earn millions of dollars a year. Factors such as level of education, certification and geographic region may cause earnings to differ. A few instructors and coaches receive a salary, while those remaining may receive earnings per hour, per session, or according to the number of athletes.

## Sports Marketing Careers Abroad

As the director of marketing partnership for the NBA, Jennifer Hemmer worked with country managers around the world from her office in New York. "One minute I was talking to Moscow and two minutes later, Istanbul," says Hemmer. "It was very international.

International sports marketing may sound glamorous and it can be. But there is also a lot of hard, behind-the-scenes work that gets Visa, Nike or Coca-Cola out on the playing field at a major sporting event. The jobs not only involve event management, but also athlete representation, TV rights, sales and distribution and licensing and promotion.

*What's a Typical Day Like?*

Someone in this field might spend the day coordinating the details of contracts or negotiating with an athlete for an appearance or commercial. There is also time spent meeting with your peers in advertising or PR and promotion to strategize about how to best leverage sponsorships or assist with event planning and coordination. The job is demanding, multifaceted and requires creativity and attention to detail.

*Where are the Jobs?*

Professionals in international sports marketing can work through a variety of venues. You might work for a league, like the NBA or a soccer federation, or maybe a team, like the LA Lakers.

Corporations like Pepsi, Budweiser and UPS hire individuals to manage their promotional campaigns and sponsorship of domestic and international sporting events. Hemmer, for example, now works for Visa as its director of event and sponsorship marketing, where she manages relationships with the sports and entertainment properties Visa has deals with. She also directs the company's integrated marketing platform to leverage each of its sponsorships.

There are also jobs available with agencies hired by corporations to do this type of work. ISL, now headquartered in Switzerland, or Octagon, which operates globally in more than 20 countries, are two well-known examples.

Nella McMonigal, Octagon's HR coordinator, notes that the organization tends to hire sports agents, administrative assistants and candidates with sports marketing, financial services and accounting experience. She also noted Octagon has a job hotline for athlete representation and marketing positions (703-905-4326), but it only lists current employment opportunities throughout the United States.

*What Skills are Required?*

Hemmer's biggest piece of advice, which she admits she didn't follow, is to come in with brand marketing or advertising experience. The field has a lot of MBAs and individuals with traditional brand marketing backgrounds.

"Basically, sports is another brand; it is just sexier than soap," says Hemmer. The ability to put together an integrated marketing plan is critical, as the work often involves planning around a huge event like the World Cup or Nascar, large sporting events that have many components and often last several days or weeks.

Managing and negotiating contracts are also a big part of the job and while a legal background could be helpful, most of this is learned through experience. Hemmer has a master's in international affairs with a focus on international business. This, combined with six years of relevant client experience, helped her land the job at the NBA. They valued both her industry background as well as her ability to understand and effectively relate in a multicultural environment.

## Athletic Trainers

***Significant Points:*** Job prospects should be good in the health care industry; however, competition is expected for positions with sports teams.

Long hours, sometimes including nights and weekends, are common.

About one-third of athletic trainers work in the health care industry.

About 7 out of 10 athletic trainers have a master's or higher degree.

***Nature of the Work:*** Athletic trainers help prevent and treat injuries for people of all ages. Their clients include everyone from professional athletes to industrial workers. Recognized by the American Medical Association as allied health professionals, athletic trainers specialize in the prevention, assessment, treatment and rehabilitation of musculoskeletal injuries. Athletic trainers are often one of the first heath care providers on the scene when injuries occur and therefore must be able to recognize, evaluate and assess injuries and provide immediate care when needed. They also are heavily involved in the rehabilitation and reconditioning of injuries.

Athletic trainers often help prevent injuries by advising on the proper use of equipment and applying protective or injury-preventive devices such as tape, bandages and braces. Injury prevention also often includes educating people on what they should do to avoid putting themselves at risk for injuries. Athletic trainers should not be confused with fitness trainers or personal trainers, who are not health care workers, but rather train people to become physically fit.

Athletic trainers work under the supervision of a licensed physician and in cooperation with other health care providers. The level of medical supervision varies, depending upon the setting. Some athletic trainers meet with the team physician or consulting physician once or twice a week; others interact with a physician every day. The extent of the supervision ranges from discussing specific injuries and treatment options with a physician to performing evaluations and treatments as directed by a physician.

Athletic trainers also may have administrative responsibilities. These may include regular meetings with an athletic director or other administrative officer to deal with budgets, purchasing, policy implementation and other business-related issues.

***Working Conditions:*** The work of athletic trainers requires frequent interaction with others. This includes consulting with physicians as well as frequent contact with athletes and patients to discuss and administer treatments, rehabilitation programmes, injury-preventive practices and other health-related issues. Many athletic trainers work indoors most of the time; others, especially those in some sports-related jobs, spend much of their time working outdoors. The job also might require standing for long periods, working with medical equipment or machinery and being able to walk, run, kneel, crouch, stoop, or crawl. Some travel may be required.

Schedules vary by work setting. Athletic trainers in non-sports settings generally have an established schedule with nights and weekends off; the number of hours differs by employer, but usually are about 40 to 50 hours per week. Athletic trainers working in hospitals and clinics spend part of their time working at other locations on an outreach basis. Most commonly, those outreach programmes include secondary schools, colleges and commercial business locations.

Athletic trainers in sports settings, however, deal with schedules that are longer and more variable. These workers must be present for team practices and games, which often are on evenings and weekends and their schedules can change on short notice when games and practices have to be rescheduled. As a result, athletic trainers in sports settings regularly may have to work 6 or 7 days per week, including late hours.

In high schools, athletic trainers who also teach may work at least 60 to 70 hours a week. In NCAA Division I colleges and universities, athletic trainers generally work with one team; when that team's sport is in season, working at least 50 to 60 hours a week is common.

Athletic trainers in smaller colleges and universities often work with several teams and have teaching responsibilities. During the off-season, a 40-hour to 50-hour work week may be normal in most settings. Athletic trainers for professional sports teams generally work the most hours per week. During training camps, practices and competitions, they may be required to work up to 12 hours a day.

There is some stress involved with being an athletic trainer, as there is with most health-related occupations. Athletic trainers are responsible for their clients' health and sometimes have to make quick decisions that could affect the health or career of their clients. Athletics trainers also can be affected by the pressure to win that is typical of competitive sports teams.

***Training, Other Qualifications and Advancement:*** A bachelor's degree from an accredited college or university is required for almost all jobs as an athletic trainer. In 2004, there were more than 300 accredited programmes nationwide. Students in these programmes are educated both in the classroom and in clinical settings. Formal education includes many science and health-related courses, such as human anatomy, physiology, nutrition and biomechanics.

A bachelor's degree with a major in athletic training from an accredited programme is part of the requirement for becoming certified by the Board of Certification (BOC). In addition, a successful candidate for board certification must pass an examination that includes written questions and practical applications. To retain certification, credential holders must continue taking medical-related courses and adhere to standards of practice. In the 43 States with athletic trainer licensure or registration or both in 2004, BOC certification was required.

According to the National Athletic Trainers' Association, 70 percent of athletic trainers have a master's or doctoral degree. Athletic trainers may need a master's or higher degree to be eligible for some positions, especially those in colleges and universities and to increase their advancement opportunities. Because some positions in high schools involve teaching along with athletic trainer responsibilities, a teaching certificate or license could be required.

There are a number ways in which athletic trainers can advance or move into related positions. Assistant athletic trainers may become head athletic trainers and, eventually, athletic directors. Athletic trainers might also enter a physician group practice and assume a management role. Some athletic trainers move into sales and marketing positions, using their athletic trainer expertise to sell medical and athletic equipment.

Because all athletic trainers deal directly with a variety of people, they need good social and communication skills. They should be able to manage difficult situations and the stress associated with them—for example, when disagreements arise with coaches, clients, or parents regarding suggested treatment. Athletic trainers also should be organized, be able to manage time wisely, be inquisitive and have a strong desire to help people.

***Employment:*** Athletic trainers held about 15,000 jobs in 2004 and are found in every part of the country. Most athletic trainer jobs are related to sports, although many also work in non-sports settings. About one-third of athletic trainers worked in health care, including jobs in hospitals, offices of physicians and offices of other health practitioners. Another one-third were found in public and private educational services, primarily in colleges, universities and high schools. About 20 percent worked in fitness and recreational sports centres.

***Job Outlook:*** Employment of athletic trainers is expected to grow much faster than the average for all occupations through 2014. Job growth will be concentrated in health care industry settings, such as ambulatory heath care services and hospitals. Growth in sports-related positions will be somewhat slower, as most professional sports clubs and colleges, universities and professional schools already have complete athletic training staffs. Job prospects should be good for people looking for a position in the health care industry. Athletic trainers looking for a position with a sports team, however, may face competition.

The demand for health care should grow dramatically as the result of advances in technology, increasing emphasis on preventive care and an increasing number of older people who are more likely to need medical care. Athletic trainers will benefit from this expansion, because they provide a cost-effective way to increase the number of health professionals in an office or other setting. Also, employers increasingly emphasize sports medicine, in which an immediate responder, such as an athletic trainer, is on site to help prevent injuries and provide immediate treatment for any injuries that do occur.

Athletic trainers' increased licensure requirements and regulation has led to a greater acceptance of their role as qualified health care providers. As a result, third-party reimbursement is expected to continue to grow for athletic training services. As athletic trainers continue to expand their services, more employers are expected to use these workers to realize the cost savings that can be achieved by providing health care in-house. Settings outside the sports world, especially those that focus on health care, are expected to experience fast employment growth among athletic trainers over the next decade. Continuing efforts to have an athletic trainer in every high school reflect concern for student-athletes' health as well as efforts to provide more funding for schools and may lead to growth in the number of athletic trainers employed in high schools.

Turnover among athletic trainers is limited. When dealing with sports teams, there is a tendency to want to continue to work with the same coaches, administrators and players when a good working relationship already exists. Because of relatively low worker turnover, the settings with the best job prospects will be the ones that are expected to grow most quickly, primarily positions in heath care settings. There will also be opportunities in elementary and secondary schools as more positions are created. Some of these positions also will require teaching responsibilities. There will be more competition for positions within colleges, universities and professional schools as well as professional sports clubs. The occupation is expected to continue to change over the next decade including more administrative responsibilities, adapting to new technology and working with larger populations and job seekers must be able to adapt to these changes.

***Earnings:*** Most athletic trainers work in full-time positions and typically receive benefits. The salary of an athletic trainer depends on experience and job responsibilities and varies by job setting. Median annual earnings of athletic trainers were $33,940 in May 2004. The middle 50 percent earned between $27,140 and $42,380. The lowest 10 percent earned less than $20,770, while the top 10 percent earned more than $53,760. Also, many employers pay for some of the continuing education required of ATCs, although the amount covered varies from employer to employer.

## Careers in Physical Education

### *Career Possibilities*

***Activities Director:*** Responsible for a recreation program's daily operation, primarily organize and direct participants. Starting Salary: $15.72/hr.

***Athletic Coach:*** Organize, instructs and teaches amateur and professional athletes in fundamentals of individual and team sports. Starting Salary: $13,370.

***Cardiovascular Fitness Instructor:*** Conduct group exercise sessions that involve aerobic exercise, stretching and muscle conditioning. Starting Salary: $11.51/hr.

***Community/Commercial Recreation:*** Organize and direct leisure activities and athletic programmes for employees of all ages. Starting Salary: $8.69/hr.

***Corporate Fitness Instructor:*** Help clients to assess their level of physical fitness and help them to set and reach fitness goals. Starting Salary: $15.72/hr.

***Nutrition Specialist:*** Plan food and nutrition programmes and supervise the preparation and serving of meals. They help to prevent and treat illnesses by promoting healthy eating habits and recommending dietary modifications. Starting Salary: $25,520.

***Personal Trainer:*** Work with clients on a one-on-one basis in either a gym or the client's home. Starting Salary: $11.51/hr.

***Rehabilitation Specialist/Physical Therapist:*** Provide services that help restore function, improve mobility, relieve pain and prevent or limit permanent physical disabilities of patients suffering from injuries or disease. Starting Salary: $40,200.

***Social Director:*** Organize and lead group activities. Starting Salary: $15,420.

***Teacher; Physical Education:*** Help students delve more deeply into physical education and expose them to the world of physical fitness. Starting Salary: $30,719.

In most educational systems, physical education (PE), also called physical training (PT) or gym in less progressive settings, is a course in the curriculum which utilizes learning in the cognitive, affective and psycho motor domains in a play or movement exploration setting. In the United States, it is almost always mandatory for students in elementary schools and often for students in middle schools and high schools.

The primary aim of physical education is to equip students with the knowledge, skills, capacities and values along with the enthusiasm to maintain a healthy lifestyle into adulthood. Some schools also require physical education as a way to promote weight loss in students. Activities included in the programme are designed to promote physical fitness, to develop motor skills, to instill knowledge and understanding of rules, concepts and strategies and to teach students to work as part of a team, or as individuals, in a wide variety of competitive activities.

### *What is Health Education?*

Health education is defined as the process by which individuals and groups of people learn to behave in a manner conducive to the promotion, maintenance or restoration of health.

Education for health begins with people as they are, with whatever interests they may have in improving their living conditions. Its aim is to develop in them a sense of responsibility for health conditions, as individuals and as members of families and communities. In communicable disease control, health education commonly includes an appraisal of what is known by a population about a disease, an assessment of habits and attitudes of the people as they relate to spread and frequency of the disease and the presentation of specific means to remedy observed deficiencies.

### *Related Career Titles*

Some positions are entry level, while others require advanced degrees and experience:

| *Activities Director* | *Cruise Recreation Director* | *Personal Trainer* |
|---|---|---|
| Adventurer/Risk | Dance-/Aerobics | Prison Recreation |
| Trainer | Instructor | Specialist |
| Aquatic Management | Emergency Medical Tech. | Recreation Specialist |
| Athletic Coach | Exercise Physiology | Rehabilitation Specialist |
| Athletic Trainer | Health/Fitness Consultant | Sporting Goods Sales |
| Cardiac Rehabilitation | SPA/Health Club Manager | Social Director |
| Cardiovascular | Nutrition Specialist | Strength-Conditioning |
| Fitness Instructor | | Coach |

*Contd...*

| *Activities Director* | *Cruise Recreation Director* | *Personal Trainer* |
|---|---|---|
| Community Recreation | Occupational Exercise | Swimming Pool Manager |
| Corporate Fitness Instructor | Park Manager | Teacher; Physical Education |
| Country Club manger | Occupational Therapy Asst. | Physical Therapist |
| Camp Director | Sports Medicine | Physical Therapist Assistant |
| Dietitian | Sports Medicine | Sports-Fitness Nutritionist |
| Chiropractor | Sports Psychologist | Professional Sports Scout |
| Sports Agent | PE/Sport/Research Instructor | Professional Sports Umpire |
| Athletic Director | Commercial Recreation | |
| Related Major Skills | | |
| Interest in Coaching | Interest in Teaching | |
| Motor Skills | Knowledge of Proper Nutrition | |
| Motivational Skills | Planning Skills | |
| Discussion Skills (*i.e.*, human sexuality) | | Patience |
| Oral & Visual Communication Skills | | Athletically inclined |
| Demonstration Skills (physical activities) | | Interest in Physical Activities |

Interest in Health Issues Interest & Knowledge in the mechanics and general health of human body.

## Health, Physical Education and Recreation

***Description of Major:*** The School of Health, Physical Education and Recreation (HPER) offers majors and prepares students to be professionals in the fields of health, kinesiology and recreation. The HPER school has three departments: Department of Applied Health Science, Department of Kinesiology and Department of Recreation & Park Administration.

The Department of Applied Health Science at IU is one of the oldest and most respected professional preparation programmes in the United States. The department offers study in dietetics, health secondary teacher education, human development/family studies, nutrition science, public health education and safety management.

The Department of Kinesiology offers a Bachelor of Science major in Kinesiology, with concentrations in athletic training, athletic training/teacher education, exercise science, fitness specialist, sport communication-broadcast, sport communication-print, sport marketing and management and physical education teacher education.

The undergraduate programmes offered by the Department of Kinesiology are interdisciplinary, providing coursework and practicum experience that are excellent preparation for specific careers or for preprofessional and graduate school opportunities.

The Department of Recreation & Park Administration offers a Bachelor of Science in Recreation with specializations in outdoor recreation and resource management, park and recreation management, recreational sport management, therapeutic recreation and tourism management.

### *Skills & Knowledge Developed in this Field of Study*

***Applied Health Sciences:*** Dietetics offers the student the opportunity to study the role of nutrition in disease prevention and treatment in clinical and community settings. The health secondary teacher education programme prepares students to teach in junior and senior high schools. Human development/ family studies examines the growth and development of human beings throughout their lifespan. Nutrition science integrates the basic and applied principles of nutrition and related sciences such as anatomy, physiology, biochemistry and medicine. Students learn to apply nutrition to health promotion.

The major in occupational safety explores the promotion of safety and health in the workplace through education, inspection, hazard control and risk management. The public health education major helps students acquire the background for developing, implementing and evaluating health education programmes in the community, with most occurring in clinical, educational and occupational settings.

***Kinesiology:*** The athletic training major focuses on prevention, recognition, evaluation and immediate care of injuries and rehabilitation and reconditioning, as well as health care administration. Athletic training also offers the course work required to obtain teaching certification.

The exercise science programme is a science-based undergraduate curriculum designed to provide a background in the exercise sciences for those who wish to further their education at the graduate level. Special emphasis is placed upon the disciplines of anatomy, biomechanics, exercise physiology, sport psychology and motor learning. Sport communication (broadcast and print) combines the study of kinesiology and communication (telecommunication or journalism). Sport marketing and management is an interdisciplinary approach to the study of sport management and includes courses in business and sport. The physical education teacher education programme leads to a Bachelor of Science degree in kinesiology with a provisional teaching certificate.

***Recreation and Park Administration:*** The focus of the outdoor recreation and resource management major is to educate the student about outdoor recreation resources and their users as well as to provide knowledge and skills required for this field in areas including outdoor recreation, environmental education, interpretive techniques, outdoor adventure education, outdoor leadership, nature study and recreational resource management and organized camping.

The park and recreation management major offers students the opportunity to learn about the provision of health enhancing leisure services for communities. The major in recreational sport management prepares students to assume leadership positions in all types of participatory sports programmes and focuses on management of people and resources in recreational sports. Therapeutic recreation involves the use of recreational activities as therapeutic interventions to improve health, functional ability and quality of life. The major in tourism management prepares students to work in such diverse sectors of the travel and tourism industry as tour operations, resort management, convention management, meeting planning and commercial recreation management.

***Minors and Second Majors that Expand Career Options with this Major:*** Biology, business, chemistry, communication and culture, computer science, psychology, public and environmental affairs, sociology, telecommunications.

## Other Career Possibilities

In all of the applied health, kinesiology and recreation fields, bachelor degree graduates may go into careers in sales, marketing and business management in the related fields of services or products. Students may go on for graduate study in the related academic field or in fields such as medicine or law. HPER students are well prepared for many career fields that require leadership skills.

***Careers that Normally Require a Graduate Degree:*** Many management and supervisory positions, research positions, clinical positions and education positions in the fields related to the HPER majors may require an advanced degree.

## Employment Opportunities

***Job Outlook:*** Positions in public health, extended care and human services are generally expected to increase. School health education positions well remain stable or increase slightly with teacher retirement. Competition is keen in many of the kinesiology related career fields. Flexibility in regard to job location and entry level position will enhance marketability. Job prospects are good for all of the recreation fields in municipal settings, non-profit recreation and service agencies and the private sector.

***Salary Information:*** Starting salaries in the Applied Health Science field range from $25,000 to $35,000. Kinesiology graduates generally obtain starting salaries in the $23,000 - $30,000 range. Recreation majors find salaries starting at $20,000 - $30,000.

***Potential Career Growth:*** Career growth opportunities are excellent for most of the HPER related career fields in areas such as management, research and college teaching. Some growth opportunities may require an advanced degree.

***Placement Statistics for IU Graduates with this Major:*** With the wide range of majors and career fields in the School of Health, Physical Education and Recreation, placement statistics vary in availability. Check with each HPER department career center for specific information.

***High School Preparation:*** In addition to meeting the regular IU Admission requirements, a strong background in math, biology and chemistry is recommended for many HPER programmes. Courses in psychology, sociology, writing and speech will also help prepare students.

***Special Opportunities:*** IU's School of Health, Physical Education and Recreation is internationally recognized as a leader in human development, public health, nutrition, sport management, physical education teacher preparation, exercise science, athletic training, therapeutic recreation and outdoor resource management.

HPER's three accredited departments all offer innovative and highly respected programmes of study. Few institutions can compete with HPER's educational, athletic and professional service facilities.

The Student Recreational Sports Center offers Olympic size swimming and diving pools, an elevated indoor jogging track, three multipurpose gyms and racquetball and squash courts. The extensive strength and conditioning rooms are staffed with consultants who orient students to the equipment and provide fitness tips and guidance.

Other facilities include research laboratories, library, seminar rooms, gardens, outdoor centres, sports fields, 18 hole golf course, driving range and tennis courts. IU's 2,300 acre Bradford Woods Outdoor Leadership Development Center is nationally acclaimed for residential outdoor/environmental education, challenge education and executive development programmes.

## Physical Education Jobs

This section provide Physical education jobs information including various aspects of what a Physical Education professional does, their specializations and where they get employed.

*What is Physical Education?*

Physical Education is the study and practice of recreational activities, physical fitness, healthy lifestyle issues and sports and interpersonal skills.

*What is a Physical Education Professional and what do they do?*

A Physical Education (PE) professional may be a teacher, a trainer, a sports specialist or scientist whose primary responsibilities address health and physical fitness. PE teachers lead or coach students in sports and recreational activities, often with an emphasis on developing life-long leisure skills that will promote healthy lifestyles and physical fitness.

*What qualifications do Physical Education Professionals need?*

A PE professional is good at physical activities and interested in many sports and has a strong commitment to personal health and physical fitness. Personal qualities of enthusiasm, patience, tact and good communication skills along with good organizational skills are valuable. Most PE professionals enjoy working with young people.

Some positions require an undergraduate degree while others expect a higher level of professional training such as a Masters or PhD level. There are many universities with viable PE graduate programmes.

*What subjects do Physical Education professionals include in their coursework?*

Basic undergraduate preparation in the areas of biology, physical fitness, sports and physical education teaching and coaching strategies are part of the foundation for a PE professional. Advanced skills and leadership in athletics and physical fitness are essential. Areas of training include education, advising, coaching, recreation, leisure and nature activities.

*What types of tasks do Physical Education professionals do in their job?*

The most familiar PE professional is the PE teacher who serves at the secondary school. PE teachers are usually qualified to teach at least one other subject or coach a specific sports team or perform guidance counsellor services as part of their working contract. While specialists have different work requirements, common tasks are noted here.

The primary task of the PE teacher is teaching. This is accomplished by preparing a sequential year-long programme of learning experiences designed to link physical activities with health and fitness and to promote and develop healthy life-long leisure skills and interests. Instruction includes the basic techniques and skills of team and individual sports, track and field, gymnastics, aquatics and a variety of recreational activities. Maintaining a safe learning atmosphere and environment facilitates teaching students about safety in such areas as swimming pools, athletic fields, gymnasiums.

Students often learn about community and personal health issues including nutrition, sexuality, drug use and HIV/AIDS from their health and PE teachers as a part of their planned curriculum.

PE professionals are often responsible for leading and coordinating special events, sports programmes and special seminars or study days on pertinent health issues such as stress management or sexually transmitted diseases.

## Areas of Specialization

**Areas of specialization for Physical Education specialists include Health and Physical Education Teacher, Personal Development Teacher, Education Aide, Athlete, Fitness Instructor, Outdoor Adventure Leader, Teacher - Primary or Secondary, School Principal, Fitness Instructor, Physiotherapist, Recreation Officer, Sports Coach, Sports Scientist, Recreation Therapist.**

*What types of companies employ Physical Education professionals?*

Schools, colleges and other educational institutions are significant employers of PE teachers. Sports and outdoor recreation and leisure industries such as white-water rafting or skiing or golf are also likely to employ PE professionals. Many government agencies have specialists in the area of maintaining fitness for their staff. Defense and military agencies also value the skills and fitness of PE professionals. Sports physiologists and sports scientists are emerging in therapeutic recreation, rehabilitation and medical facilities.

## Alternative Career Paths

During the past 20 years, alternative professional preparation and certification programmes have expanded within the field of physical education. Societal trends, the media and demographics have dictated these changes. For example, a decline in the number of students attending grades K-12 has decreased the need for physical education teachers (Freeman, 1987). Fewer school systems today require physical education (Newell, 1990), yet Americans are increasingly interested in maintaining health and fitness into adulthood. Even the term "physical education," has gone through a transformation. Newell (1990) identified almost 70 different academic department labels in the area of physical education, including exercise and sport sciences, kinesiology, health promotion and human performance and sport fitness and leisure studies. This Digest will examine the factors which lead to an increase in the scope of career opportunities for physical education professionals and look at future trends, including a move back toward traditional teaching positions.

## Development of Career Paths

Prior to the 1970s, physical education professionals were primarily channeled into the traditional roles of physical education teacher and/or coach. In 1970, Kenneth H. Cooper introduced The Aerobics Way to the general public, addressing the benefits of exercise as a lifetime activity. Jackie Sorenson (aerobic dance) and Jim Fixx (running) were also physical activity pioneers in the early 1970s and helped to further that idea. Within the next few years, jobs began to emerge in health clubs and corporate fitness facilities (Jacoby, 1990).

With the advancement of technological resources and time-saving devices, available time for leisure and recreation increased from an average of 34 hours per week in 1965 to an average of 41 hours per week for males and 40 for females in 1985 (Cutler, 1990). Facilities opened that gave the public a means and place to recreate.

Organizations such as the President's Council on Physical Fitness and Sport helped encourage the American population to spend leisure time pursuing lifetime physical fitness. Corporations and health maintenance organizations (HMOs) discovered the link between fitness and health and employer-sponsored facilities began to proliferate (Seefeldt & Vogel, 1986). Hospitals began to conduct wellness programmes.

This growth of fitness facilities and programmes resulted in additional jobs for exercise and sport professionals as exercise specialists, corporate fitness directors, wellness consultants and coordinators (Jacoby, 1990; Nieman, 1990). A need for additional physical education professionals in these alternative career areas was created.

The media also had a profound influence on the broadening of physical education career opportunities. With the advent of satellite capabilities and the increase in cable television stations such as Home Team Sports, ESPN and local cable networks, the media has become a major factor in shaping and molding America's increased acceptance of exercise and physical activity (Spears, Swanson, & Smith, 1978). The media has given the public an entirely new perspective on exercise and physical activity in terms of acceptability and job possibilities.

## Emergence of Professional Preparation

As job opportunities expanded, knowledge increased and equipment became more sophisticated, there was a greater need for specialists who could put theory into practice. The ability to draw knowledge from strong scientific foundations continues to be paramount as students prepare for careers in exercise and sport.

Courses such as anatomy and physiology, exercise physiology, kinesiology and other courses in the study of human movement have provided these scientific foundations. In addition, students began to need specialization in a specific aspect of exercise and sport such as cardiac rehabilitation and sports marketing (Nieman, 1990).

Due to the variety of academic programmes available, in 1988 the National Association for Sport and Physical Education (NASPE), an association of the American Alliance for Health, Physical Education, Recreation and Dance (AAHPERD), developed specific academic standards for students preparing for careers in exercise and sport. These standards provide students "with entry level skills and knowledge to competently function in a wide range of fitness employment opportunities" (Arnold et al., 1988). In addition to the Standards for Programmes Preparing Undergraduate Students for Careers in Fitness, NASPE has compiled a listing of academic programmes in exercise and sport (Blanke & Rice, 1991).

Along with college and university-based professional preparation programmes, many professional organizations now provide exercise and sport credentialing opportunities (Nieman, 1990; Summerfield, 1991). Examples of such organizations are:

American College of Sports Medicine (ACSM) Box 1440, Indianapolis, IN 46206-1440

American Council on Exercise (ACE, formerly IDEA) 2431 Morena Boulevard, Suite 2-D, San Diego, CA 92110

Association for Fitness in Business (AFB) 965 Hope Street, Stamford, CT 06907

National Athletic Trainers Association (NATA) 1001 East 4th Street, Greenville, NC 27834

National Recreation and Park Association (NRPA) 3101 Park Center Drive, Alexandria, VA 22302

National Strength and Conditioning Association P.O. Box 81410, Lincoln, NE 68501

## Renewed Interest in Teacher Certification

As with most occupations, projections for physical education career opportunities are largely dependent upon future trends and national economic forecasts. The increase in nonteaching job opportunities coupled with a decrease in the number of available teaching positions has resulted in a movement away from the traditional physical education teaching major. This trend, in conjunction with cuts in physical education programmes due to budget constraints, meant that large numbers of physical education teachers left teaching.

However, even though there is still a shift away from the traditional physical education major, it is important to note that students who have already earned a degree are beginning to return to school for teacher education certification. There appear to be three reasons.

First, the nonteaching exercise and sport job market has become so heavily saturated that job opportunities are not as plentiful today.

Second, physical education teachers who have been teaching for 20 or 30 years are beginning to retire and there will be a gradual increase in the number of physical education teaching positions available.

And third, in some non-teaching careers there is no career ladder. There is potential for a shortage of physical educators as a result of the small pool of students being certified to teach physical education (Gerald & Hussar, 1990), although this shortage may be keener in specific geographic areas.

There are additional factors influencing the return to traditional teaching positions. In 1990 the Public Health Service of the U.S. Department of Health and Human Services established 16 health and fitness objectives for the year 2000. One of the objectives is to "increase to at least 60% the proportion of people age 6 and older who participate in moderate physical activities...3 or more days per week for 20 minutes or more per occasion" (Public Health Service, 1990). This may have a positive impact on the number of school systems requiring physical education. Because the largest growing segment of the American population is adults over the age of 65 (Public Health Service, 1990), there will be an ever increasing need to provide people with opportunities to exercise throughout the life span (Nieman, 1990).

***Conclusion***

The challenge for physical education professionals and those who prepare them is to provide the knowledge necessary to be at the forefront of change. Emphasis must be placed on continued study of present trends and forecasts and their relationship to physical activity careers. The public's pursuit of a healthy lifestyle through physical activity will be best served if exercise and sport professionals are leading, rather than reacting to, the latest trends. Examples of some present trends that may have an impact on curriculum development include: aging of the population, more at-risk children in the school system, increased use of computers. While emphasis has been placed on nontraditional physical education careers, it is also important to continue a focus on traditional teaching and coaching opportunities.

## Physical Education Training Courses

In this fast developing world, health is increasingly becoming the concern of the masses and the importance of physical education is rising all over the world. Moreover physical education training courses have also emerged as a promising career course in India.

At present, different colleges and institutes offer various Physical education courses such as Bachelor in Physical education, Masters in Physical Education, Certificate in Physical Education (CPED) and Diploma in Physical Education (DPED). These courses in Physical Education is generally inter disciplinary in nature and transmits physical knowledge and skill through both theory and practice.

On this page, we have tried to cover various physical education training courses in India. So far as we are concerned all the information regarding the physical education training courses in India are correct. However, if you encounter any discrepancy please do feel free to inform us as we strive to become the best site on physical education in India.

Below mentioned are the institutes offering various courses in Physical Education across India.

***Certificate Course in Physical Education***

- CPED Institutes in Gujarat
- CPED Institutes in Jammu & Kashmir
- CPED Institutes in Karnataka
- CPED Institutes in Kerala
- CPED Institutes in Maharashtra
- CPED Institutes in Orissa
- CPED Institutes in Rajasthan

***Diploma Course in Physical Education***

- DPED Institutes in Madhya Pradesh
- DPED Institutes in Rajasthan
- DPED Institutes in Uttar Pradesh
- DPED Institutes in Gujarat

***CPED Institutes Gujarat***

Physical education training courses are increasingly becoming popular and the institutes offering these courses are available in most of the Indian states. On this page, we have attempted to list state wise all those institutes that are providing physical education training courses to students.

Here, on this page, we have tried our best to provide as authentic information as possible regarding physical education training courses and physical education colleges in India, but incase there is some discrepancy, then please do write to us about it. We would appreciate any kind of effort that would improve the quality of this page, a page that focuses on physical education training courses in India.

***CPED Institutes Jammu & Kashmir***

Physical education training courses are increasingly becoming popular and the institutes offering these courses are available in most of the Indian states. On this page, we have attempted to list state wise all those institutes that are providing physical education training courses to students.

Here, on this page, we have tried our best to provide as authentic information as possible regarding physical education training courses and physical education colleges in India, but incase there is some discrepancy, then please do write to us about it. We would appreciate any kind of effort that would improve the quality of this page, a page that focuses on physical education training courses in India.

### *CPED Institutes Karnataka*

Physical education training courses are increasingly becoming popular and the institutes offering these courses are available in most of the Indian states. On this page, we have attempted to list state wise all those institutes that are providing physical education training courses to students.

Here, on this page, we have tried our best to provide as authentic information as possible regarding physical education training courses and physical education colleges in India, but incase there is some discrepancy, then please do write to us about it. We would appreciate any kind of effort that would improve the quality of this page, a page that focuses on physical education training courses in India.

### *CPED Institutes Kerala*

Physical education training courses are increasingly becoming popular and the institutes offering these courses are available in most of the Indian states. On this page, we have attempted to list state wise all those institutes that are providing physical education training courses to students.

Here, on this page, we have tried our best to provide as authentic information as possible regarding physical education training courses and physical education colleges in India, but incase there is some discrepancy, then please do write to us about it. We would appreciate any kind of effort that would improve the quality of this page, a page that focuses on physical education training courses in India.

### *CPED Institutes Maharashtra*

Physical education training courses are increasingly becoming popular and the institutes offering these courses are available in most of the Indian states. On this page, we have attempted to list state wise all those institutes that are providing physical education training courses to students.

Here, on this page, we have tried our best to provide as authentic information as possible regarding physical education training courses and physical education colleges in India, but incase there is some discrepancy, then please do write to us about it. We would appreciate any kind of effort that would improve the quality of this page, a page that focuses on physical education training courses in India.

### *CPED Institutes Orissa*

Physical education training courses are increasingly becoming popular and the institutes offering these courses are available in most of the Indian states. On this page, we have attempted to list state wise all those institutes that are providing physical education training courses to students.

Here, on this page, we have tried our best to provide as authentic information as possible regarding physical education training courses and physical education colleges in India, but incase there is some discrepancy, then please do write to us about it. We would appreciate any kind of effort that would improve the quality of this page, a page that focuses on physical education training courses in India.

### *CPED Institutes Rajasthan*

Physical education training courses are increasingly becoming popular and the institutes offering these courses are available in most of the Indian states. On this page, we have attempted to list state wise all those institutes that are providing physical education training courses to students.

Here, on this page, we have tried our best to provide as authentic information as possible regarding physical education training courses and physical education colleges in India, but incase there is some discrepancy, then please do write to us about it. We would appreciate any kind of effort that would improve the quality of this page, a page that focuses on physical education training courses in India.

### *DPED Institutes Madhya Pradesh*

Physical education training courses are increasingly becoming popular and the institutes offering these courses are available in most of the Indian states. On this page, we have attempted to list state wise all those institutes that are providing physical education training courses to students.

Here, on this page, we have tried our best to provide as authentic information as possible regarding physical education training courses and physical education colleges in India, but incase there is some discrepancy, then please do write to us about it. We would appreciate any kind of effort that would improve the quality of this page, a page that focuses on physical education training courses in India.

### *DPED Institutes Rajasthan*

Physical education training courses are increasingly becoming popular and the institutes offering these courses are available in most of the Indian states. On this page, we have attempted to list state wise all those institutes that are providing physical education training courses to students.

Here, on this page, we have tried our best to provide as authentic information as possible regarding physical education training courses and physical education colleges in India, but incase there is some discrepancy, then please do write to us about it. We would appreciate any kind of effort that would improve the quality of this page, a page that focuses on physical education training courses in India.

### *DPED Institutes Uttar Pradesh*

Physical education training courses are increasingly becoming popular and the institutes offering these courses are available in most of the Indian states. On this page, we have attempted to list state wise all those institutes that are providing physical education training courses to students.

Here, on this page, we have tried our best to provide as authentic information as possible regarding physical education training courses and physical education colleges in India, but incase there is some discrepancy, then please do write to us about it. We would appreciate any kind of effort that would improve the quality of this page, a page that focuses on physical education training courses in India.

### *DPED Institutes Gujarat*

Physical education training courses are increasingly becoming popular and the institutes offering these courses are available in most of the Indian states. On this page, we have attempted to list state wise all those institutes that are providing physical education training courses to students.

Here, on this page, we have tried our best to provide as authentic information as possible regarding physical education training courses and physical education colleges in India, but incase there is some discrepancy, then please do write to us about it. We would appreciate any kind of effort that would improve the quality of this page, a page that focuses on physical education training courses in India.

### *Physical Education Career Options*

*What Can You Do With a Degree in Physical Education?*

The Exercise and Sport Science option provides a general education about the body and movement. The Exercise Science degree is a Renaissance type preparation: natural sciences, applied sciences, socio-cultural aspects, practical experience and physical activity. Graduates in Exercise and Sport Science have a variety of career options depending upon specialization within the major. Graduates of the Fitness and Exercise Science option may become employed in health clubs, hospital and workplace settings, or work in sales of fitness and health products (such as equipment, braces, pharmaceuticals, among others), or with further training may work in careers such as physicians assistants, allopathic medicine practioners, nutritionists, chiropractors, or biomedical imaging. Graduates of the Pre-Physical Therapy option generally pursue post-baccalaureate study in a physical therapy programme, or other allied health programmes (*e.g.*, occupational therapists, physicians assistants, allopathic medicine practioners, nutritionists, or chiropractors). Our Sport Psychology graduates pursue practical application of psychology to sport and exercise settings. Graduates representing all four areas of specialization may go on to pursue graduate study in their area of interest.

*Which Line Of Work Is For You?*

Probably the best way to figure out the "right fit" in a job is to clarify what interests you the most. Do your research. Think about the kinds of work you are interested in and learn everything you can about your top two or three areas of interest. What inspires you most? Also think about your own natural strengths and abilities, as well as your values. How do you see yourself and where do you see yourself working? How do you really want to spend your time? What specific goals do you wish to achieve? What type of company or organization would you like to work with? What kinds of people do you wish to work with?

Look through the resources listed in this web site and use all the resources available to you at Western's Career Services Center. The Center is the best resource for assistance with career planning, assessments, internships, job market information, job search services and alumni services. The Career Center offers individual counselling as well as a wide variety of workshops.

## Job Search Strategies

Use the resources available to you through Western's Career Services Center, Old Main 280

As early as your junior year, attend job search workshops. Learn how to research companies, promote your skills and experience and identify the hidden job market. The Career Services Center offers several workshops throughout each quarter to help students with every topic you can think of:

- Job Search Strategies
- Resume writing
- Cover letter writing

- Interviewing techniques
- Developing an internship
- Getting into graduate school

Attend career fairs and other events. Several career fairs and other events are offered throughout the year to help students and alumni research employers and job opportunities. Check the special events schedule to see what events are scheduled for this quarter.

During your senior year, register with the Career Services Center to take full advantage of job search services, including on-campus interviews and the candidate referral programme.

Also participate in on-campus recruiting. Business, industry and government organizations recruit during fall, winter and spring quarters. School districts recruit primarily during winter and spring quarters.

Here are several other Job Search Strategies:

- Contact agencies, companies or organizations you would like to work for and see if they're hiring
- Check with the state employment opportunity office
- Talk with parents and others about job possibilities in their companies
- Check local newspaper classified ads--especially on Sunday
- Consider volunteer or internship positions (these sometimes lead to paid positions)
- Call employment/temporary placement agencies
- Check the internet for job posting web sites--several are listed below:

### *Job Listings*

***Job Hotlines:*** The Career Services Center maintains a list of job hotline numbers. Many employers use automated telephone listings to announce current openings and provide application information. Stop by the Center for a copy.

Job Search Websites. When you register with the Career Services Center, you'll have online access to a weekly Job Opportunity Bulletin which lists regional openings.

### *Considering Graduate School?*

Many undergraduate physical education majors pursue graduate training in physical education or exercise science. A master's degree or doctorate will be essential for higher education teaching and advanced research or applied careers. Others choose graduate work in professional fields such as physical therapy, physicians assisantship, or other allied health professions.

### *Choosing a Graduate School*

Here are some excellent resources to help you search for and learn about, graduate programmes.

- Graduate School Search Engine.
- National Academic Advising Association Graduate School Information

Preparing for Graduate School. During your junior year, or early in your senior year, you should begin talking with WWU faculty about how to prepare for graduate school. You should also begin contacting the schools you wish to consider. To apply to graduate school you will need to begin planning at least a year before the fall in which you intend to enter. Most schools only accept students in the fall and expect to have all of your materials in hand by the end of the previous December. Most departments require you to fill out an application form, including a personal statement on why you want to pursue graduate work. You will probably be asked to supply a transcript and at least three letters of reference. It is therefore to your advantage to get to know faculty by taking small classes, writing papers, serving as a teaching assistant, or getting involved in faculty research projects. Many departments also require applicants to take the Graduate Record Exam (GRE).

The Graduate Record Exam (GRE). Be sure to look through the "GRE Free Publications section". This site contains a description of test content, sample test questions.

Western's Graduate Programme in Human Movement and Performance.

Information on the WWU graduate programme in Exercise Science or Sport Psychology.

## Guide to College Majors

*What is Physical Education and Health?*

A physical education and health major prepares undergraduate and graduate students for a career in teaching and coaching classes related to:

- general exercise,
- recreation,
- games,
- sports,
- fitness,
- nutrition and
- hygiene.

Basic instruction, both on campus and through distance learning, prepares teachers and coaches for grades K-12. Graduate degrees provide the credentials for teaching on a college level.

Though some of the programme content quite literally involves "fun and games," students seeking a physical education and health degree also enrol in serious academic courses on subjects such as kinesiology, morphology and physiology (studies related to motion, body structure and function). The science and art of teaching also play an important role in the curriculum for a physical education and health degree.

Students considering this path can take advantage of online education, e-learning or distance learning opportunities as part of the programme in many colleges, cutting down on campus commutes and residency requirements. Graduates can count on strong career growth, since physical education and health degrees carry increasing importance in school curricula.

## Trends for Physical Education

Given current societal trends, a physical education and health degree provides graduates with the opportunity to help improve the wellness of a sedentary generation plagued with increasing obesity. Although academic demands once appeared to devalue physical education and health studies, statistics incite the current generation of children and adolescents to buck the trend and to develop a more active, healthy lifestyle.

As a result, a physical education and health degree will grow in importance. Educators will place an increasing emphasis on integrating these disciplines more directly into their curriculum. In addition, leisure time for early retirees and senior citizens - a growing segment of the population - increases demand for graduates holding a physical education and health degree.

Online education in this field has expanded in recent years, offering more flexibility and lower residency requirements. E-learning or distance learning will grow, even in this hands-on, face-to-face discipline.

## Preparing for Physical Education

Before launching into a physical education and health degree programme, a student should consider as many aspects of this career as possible. For instance, a prospective student can ask coaches and physical education/health teachers about the satisfaction they enjoy in their work.

In addition to hearing the positive side of the career, students should seek to understand the more challenging parts of the vocation, especially the time required of professionals who coach teams in various sports. Coaches work very long hours, both during the competitive season and the off-season, constantly preparing for the next cycle in the athletic calendar.

The curriculum will surprise some students contemplating a physical education and health degree. Beyond the expected course subjects, classes on the science of motion and function and body structure will challenge students. The details on fitness, nutrition and hygiene for health classes receive critical support through more complex courses in various sciences.

In other words, to teach children, adolescents, or young adults the basics in health classes, the scientific studies for teachers will be demanding preparation beyond what might be expected by the aspiring coach or physical education teacher. The same will hold true for studies of the skeletal and muscular intricacies of the human body. Students considering the physical education and health degree need to take into account some of these scholastic rigours.

It helps to be a "people person" when a student seeks a career after earning a physical education and health degree. Instructing pupils in gym classes or on a ball field requires interpersonal skills like good communication, leadership and discipline. While teachers in other subject areas may focus on a text or an abstract idea, instructors in physical education and health engage their students in an intense, dynamic way that cannot be scripted completely.

Prospective students should also consider the amount of public attention in the community that coaches often attract. Physical education and health majors should develop a level of comfort in the spotlight, especially when dealing with the news media, sports fans, booster clubs and other pressure points. Some professionals see these challenges as benefits, if not as job perks. Physical education and health graduates enjoy opportunities to make a difference in a community while teaching values of sportsmanship, leadership, teamwork, discipline and courage.

Before beginning their degree programmes, prospective physical education and health majors should investigate potential career paths and specialty options. Internet resources abound and candidates can pursue a surprising number of courses in this subject area online, with distance learning or e-learning.

## Physical Education and Health Degree Programmes

The variety of paths offered in this subject area continues to expand, thanks to a growing fitness industry. A number of national certification programmes enable multiple points of entry toward a physical education and health degree.

### *Certificate Programme*

A certificate programme provides a course or a series of courses designed to qualify the recipient in a prescribed field. For physical education and health, those holding a bachelor's degree, for example, in another area of study may gain the requisite background to teach health education by entering a certificate programme after completing courses on:

- curriculum planning,
- mental health,
- disease,
- sexuality and
- various other health issues.

In the burgeoning fitness industry, certificate programmes play an essential role in qualifying trainers for gyms - even for those not wishing to pursue a physical education and health degree. For teachers who received their degrees in other fields, a certificate programme can qualify them to assist a school's athletic department in certain team sports or classes.

***Associate Degrees:*** Two-year degrees in physical education and health remain an option in a number of states, with some of the course work available as online education, e-learning or distance learning. Community colleges often provide means for gaining an associate degree for students who will transfer later to another school for a bachelor's degree. This route may also prove practical for students who want to postpone the pursuit of a four-year degree. Such situations would apply to trainers seeking further qualifications or certifications, gym instructors and fitness leaders of various programmes. Some venues for health-education instructors may also accept associate degrees as sufficient qualification for teaching.

***Bachelor's Degree Programmes:*** Although each institution seems to offer a different title for this type of programme, the bachelor's degree in physical education and health equips graduates with the necessary tools to teach these subjects in K-12 classes. Experienced coaches qualify for employment in college athletic departments with this degree alone. Teaching academic courses at the college level still requires a master's or a doctorate, however.

Beyond the core curriculum required of students in most subject areas, the programme for the physical education and health degree focuses on:

- learning how to analyze human performance,
- the effects of muscular and skeletal functions on performance,
- kinesiology (human movement studies) and
- related subjects.

Successfully completing the requirements of the physical education and health degree will qualify the graduate for state certification to teach classes from kindergarten through twelfth grade. Some high-demand school districts even seek signed letters of intent from final-semester students prior to graduation.

In some institutions, students may pursue a specialization in recreation, a category growing in demand over the past decades as municipalities hire workers to coordinate recreational activities in parks and other facilities.

Online education offers a number of e-learning courses or distance learning for students seeking a physical education and health degree. Many online degree programmes allow students to complete necessary residency and teaching requirements at nearby campuses or other facilities.

***Master of Science in Physical Education and Health Degree***

Depending on the institution, this degree may focus on physical education, on heath, or on both elements combines. Online education programmes offer busy teachers and coaches access to this career-advancing coursework. Distance learning plans allow teachers to work at their own pace in completing degree requirements without the costly and timely commute to a physical campus.

For teachers and coaches desiring to work at the high school level or beyond, as well as those wishing to keep open the option of administrative work later (as a principal or administrative staff leader), the master's degree makes qualification easier for openings each school year.

At this level, kinesiology - the study of human movement - becomes a key part of the curriculum. In addition to completing thirty or more credit hours of coursework over a year or more, degree candidates also develop a thesis. Teaching certification plays a major role in all of a master's level student's studies.

***Doctorates in Physical Education, Sport Management & Kinesiology:*** Within the Schools of Education in various universities, graduate students may pursue a doctoral degree in physical education and health. Some institutions call this a Ph.D. in kinesiology, the study of human movement. Doctorate level students perform a dissertation during their pursuit of this degree.

Studies include:

- biomechanics,
- biochemistry,
- anatomy,
- systems of human motor control and
- performance analysis.

*What can you do with a physical education and health major?*

***Teaching:*** From kindergarten all the way through doctoral programmes, a physical education and health degree qualifies graduates to teach. Instruction involves not only gym or field time but also classroom instruction. Demand for online teaching grows every semester, affording talented instructors the opportunity to expand their scope by producing webcasts and videos of their lectures.

***Coaching:*** At one time or another, many teachers with a physical education and health degree find themselves coaching. While coaches enjoy many rewards, the hours are long. Often, teachers who coach receive supplemental pay for their extra time. At the college level, coaches can receive significant compensation packages and job perks.

***Training:*** Beyond the training required in both individual and team sports, graduates possessing a physical education and health degree may work as trainers in private gyms, aerobic centres, recreation centres and many other establishments. Their education in performance analysis and movement study provides invaluable aid to trainees in any locale.

***Performance Analysis:*** Athletes search for an instructor or mentor or trainer who can break down their performance into its various components and analyze how they can increase speed or find more efficiency in their movements. A physical education and health degree can supply the required skills for this function.

***Sports and Recreation Management:*** With a physical education and health degree, a graduate can coordinate of the myriad activities at a sports or recreation center, as well as in a municipal recreation programme.

***Research:*** Especially at the doctoral level, a physical education and health degree can launch a research career. This career track appears most often in the field of kinesiology, or study of human movement.

***Other specialties:*** These include activities director, camp director, nutrition specialist, occupational exercise scientist, spa/health club manager, corporate fitness instructor, rehabilitation specialist and many more.

## Salary Expectations

Salaries for graduates with a physical education and health degree run the gamut from basic kindergarten teachers' earnings, which vary from state to state, to professional sports coaches who receive salaries commensurate with stars in the entertainment business.

The average physical education and health teacher earns a salary set by a local school district and state government. Cost of living in a given area plays a major role in determining compensation. Since the tax base of a region greatly affects school budgets, affluent districts often pay their teachers a higher salary while hiring additional athletic staff. Teachers holding a master's or doctorate may earn more than their peers holding only bachelor's degrees.

Gym trainers, instructors and mentors may earn less on the average than schoolteachers, depending on the locale. Other specialists may find that their work is seasonal.

***Certification and Licensure:*** Before they can teach at the K-12 level, physical education and health majors must still participate in the usual certification processes required in their state and district. In addition, they may be required to receive special certification for some teaching or coaching jobs related to health or sports.

In addition to earning general teaching certification, physical education and health majors can earn certifications in a variety of specialized areas. For example, if a student minors in athletic coaching, he or she would meet requirements to take the American Coaching Effectiveness Programme Level-I Certification Exam. Whenever possible, students should cover all the possible courses providing the prerequisites for certification or licensure exams or processes.

***Professional Associations***

Many states have professional associations for teachers specializing in physical education and health. These and other associations provide teachers with all the information and encouragement necessary to endure the challenges of their profession on an ongoing basis.

Some of the national organizations for coaches and trainers with a degree in physical education and health include:

- National Association for Sport and Physical Education
- National Athletic Trainers Association .

2

# Career in Entertainment

## Performing Arts

The entertainment industry is driven by a team of producers, directors and talented performers. The prime entertainer/ performer is one who showcases the effort of the whole team. Although the performer may appear spontaneous, he goes thorough rigorous rehearsals - as an actor, musician or a dancer.

The performing arts provides opportunities for not only the frontmen (the actors, dancers and musicians), but also to specialists like VJs, RJs, choreographers and even critics.

### *Acting*

Shakespeare wrote, “all the world's a stage”—and that means you'll have to step up on one to get noticed in the acting profession. In order to take your passion and talent for acting to a new level, consider learning the art of acting from skilled professionals at an acting school near you. At acting schools, you'll take classes in theatre, drama, speech, movement, direction, playwriting and other acting-related coursework. In addition, you'll learn a variety of performance skills and liberal arts to help arm you with a well-rounded knowledge for future roles.

Acting careers are very competitive, as you've no doubt, heard, however, you don't necessarily have to find work on stage, in film, or on television. Before you land a big break, acting careers can vary from doing voice work on an animated short, to performing cabaret acts, to local TV programming.

Because of the proliferance of entertainment options, from cable and satellite TV and radio, to the vastness of the Internet, more and more acting career opportunities will become available. The key is to hone your skills and network at acting schools so when your big break comes around, you'll be ready for action. Start by researching acting schools and then take center stage in your career.

## Film, TV, Radio Productions

Believe it or not, it is reckoned that by the year 2005, India would be producing even more television programmes than the US. After all, the swelling number of channels spurred by the satellite revolution, has generated a sharp demand for television professionals, both behind and in front of the camera. And thanks to the craze for India-led programming, the money and the work which this industry has to offer is truly phenomenal.

An interesting feature of this industry is the sheer diversity which lures people from diverse areas with no specific training in this field. It is not just trained media professionals who are heading for the nearest production house, but all types of professionals like press journalists, engineers, architects, even doctors.

### *The Work*

***Director:*** A director in television is the creative controller. He is the one who gives the programme its shape and character. He takes care of all creative inputs — selecting the music and graphics, supervising the 'edit' or deciding the camera angles. Creativity and the ability to think in perspective are essential for the Director.

The Programme Director in television is in charge of the shooting of a programme and provides direction to performers and technical crew. Once the shooting is completed, it is time to supervise the post-production work *i.e.* such as editing and sound dubbing.

### *Floor Manager*

The work of a Floor Manager falls into two main areas: liaison between the Producer/Director and people on the studio floor and responsibility (as the name suggests), for studio floor management. Safety is an important part of the work; checking sets to make sure they are safe, ensuring that everything and everyone is in the right place at the right time. Leadership qualities and a high degree of stamina are essential.

### *Music Composer*

Almost every programme on TV, irrespective of its nature or content, leans on musical scores. If you are an original who can churn out compositions with versatility, there should be no stopping you. Join an established, well-known orchestra for starters and watch out for better avenues.

### *Production Manager*

Production Manager makes arrangement for procuring the technical and other equipment, fixes the editing schedules in consultation with the Producer-Director, books studios and arranges for every logistical detail. The responsibility of a Production Manager is immense. An active, resourceful and capable manager qualifies as a Production Manager. As with most of the jobs we have seen earlier, you could start as an assistant working with a senior professional and later graduate to a full-fledged role upon attaining professional maturity.

### *Researcher*

The researcher is responsible for information management. He is expected to provide facts and figures for television scripts, graphics, etc. News, current affairs programmes, quizzes, infotainment shows and documentaries require extensive collaboration from Researchers who are expected to contribute ideas for the programme and prepare material for particular items.

Researchers need to be creative and enthusiastic to contribute ideas for programmes. They should be inquisitive and resourceful, yet methodical and painstaking in their research. They must be able to organise their material logically and be capable of expressing themselves clearly in writing. They should have a good knowledge of reference sources and production processes. Excellent interpersonal skills are called for as researchers need to be outgoing to draw out information from people.

### *Script Writer*

Script Writer writes scripts for a television serial, a documentary, a soap opera, or adapts a novel or a story for television or radio. He must be an ace wordsmith to add punch and meaning to the plot while taking care not to duplicate the visual. If you don't have a flair for writing, steer clear of this one.

Ever in demand and yet in short supply, the job is open for the best talent and promises a celebrity status and lots of money for the gruelling hard work and long hours of toil.

The way to go about becoming a Scriptwriter is to undergo formal training and then assist an established professional before taking on a project. Alternatively, you could latch on to a senior Scriptwriter straight off and pick up the skills on the job.

### *Cameraperson*

Cameraperson contributes immensely toward a programme's success by capturing the specific feeling or mood that sells products, highlight news stories and brings back memories. Painting pictures with visuals, s/he translates an abstract idea or a story or programme into a live, tangible, pulsating array of visuals flowing in a meaningful sequence. It calls for seeing the uncommon in commonplace situations and the extraordinary within the ordinary. Naturally, then, acuteness of perception and artistic ability are as important as an extensive technical knowledge of lights and filters. If you want to be one of those intrepid ones who chronicle events as they happen. A News Cameraman has to combine courage and speed with all the qualities detailed above.

After you've got the basic training, your best bet would be to assist the best professional cameraperson or cinematographer who is ready to accept you. He in turn will slowly give you work bits and pieces to shoot and once you grow sufficiently, you can pitch yourself as a pro.

### *Videotape Editor*

It is the Videotape Editor who puts together a film or a programme. Wading through the reels of footage shot by the crew, the Videotape Editor arranges it in a sequence to make a coherent, crisp programme. A good editor combines strong technical knowledge with a sense of meticulous detail and a style of e delivery that is sensitive to visuals and sound.

### *Visual Mixer*

A television programme is made up of pictures that come from a number of sources; for instance, from cameras in the studio, prerecorded footage or slides (transparencies). The Visual Mixer receives a signal from the Director to cut from one picture source to another producing a smooth sequence of images. The job calls for quick reflexes and an excellent sense of timing.

### *Production Assistant*

Look for the people carrying walkie-talkies around the set and you have found a Production Assistant (PA). PAs are the troops who work under the supervision of the Producer or the Production Manager. They make sure that everyone is where they need to be, transport actors and crew to the sets, get the reams of paperwork signed by the right people, distribute the calls to announce costume fittings, or last minute changes and so on. While some people make a good career out of working as a Production Assistant, this position is considered a perfect hands-on entry-level job for those who have the ambition to move into the production end of the business.

### *What it takes?*

Ideas hold supreme in this profession. You are constantly expected to churn out original and viable ideas, though it is not necessary that they are accepted each time. Commenting on the essentials for making it in this industry, Raghav Bahl of TV Eighteen suggests, "You've got to be good at communication and therefore good with words, figures or ideas. You must be able to look at circumstances or ideas in a slightly different perspective. You must have the ability to work hard because at the end of the day, this is as much a physical medium as a mental one".

For serious aspirants who want to plan their way into the electronic media, a degree in the field of Mass Communications is a good starting point. A diploma need not necessarily give you a job but it definitely does give you the chance of being considered for selection.

Of course, there are those who insist that there is no substitute for on-the-job training. Still a large number of those who join this field typically are either graduates or come in straight after school. In most of the companies you would start off as a Production Assistant. However, once you get your foot in the door, you can feel your way around, explore the options and zero-in on the particular area that interests you the most.

Work in this field means long hours - no fixed timings - you could be working for several days at a stretch without a break. You need to be 100% alert -anything can go wrong, at anytime. You also need to be able to think on your feet and plan in advance for any emergency.

The best bit is the feeling of complete charge from beginning to end. The immediate reward of seeing your well-orchestrated and polished production on screen. Completing a project is a new and satisfying feeling each time.

A question often asked by young people is whether they really need to be trained to be a designer. Most young people who are

***Employment Opportunities***

Work activities will vary depending on the type of programmes involved. Producers in news and current affairs will have a different set of activities to those working in the area of drama or music and light entertainment. In addition, those working as freelance producers or for independent production companies may spend more of their time generating ideas for programmes and making programme bids than, say, a staff producer working for British Broadcasting Corporation (BBC) news and current affairs. Producers working in current affairs tend to stay with the same programme for longer and work with a team of several producers under the supervision of an editor and possibly a senior editor.

Typical work activities include:

- Generating and researching programme ideas, selling these to commissioning editors, finding and interviewing contributors;
- Researching stories, archive material and music;
- Writing scripts and designing the structure of programmes in line with budgets;
- Location interviewing using portable recording equipment;
- Editing recorded material using digital (computer-based) equipment and operating studios, particularly in local and commercial radio;
- Attending planning meetings;
- Liaison with and briefing presenters;
- Solving production problems like timing and editing;
- Eliciting and responding to listeners' comments;
- Managing other staff, including broadcast assistants and researchers.

### *Radio Production*

How to spot a good story for radio, how to research and find suitable contributors and book guests, what you can and cannot say on radio, Copyright Law, Mechanical Copyright, Intellectual Copyright and Performance Rights, are some of the things one must know before embarking on the job of a radio professional.

Writing for radio broadcast is very different from writing for print or television. Radio professionals teach you the skill set to enable you to write radio scripts for news, adverts, live shows and plays.

Producers are the unsung heroes of radio. They are charged with the job of making the presenter sound superb on air. They supply the content for a radio show, whatever kind of show it may be and every producer learns that 'content is king.' During the course you will learn how to produce features and how to organise a busy radio show; how to generate creative ideas and how to write treatments to pitch to radio broadcasters.

Having a basic understanding of how the technical equipment works will enable you to be creative with your work.

You should also be able to negotiate contracts with radio stations, independent production companies and in multimedia. Develop an individual voice in your work (original approaches to radio and multimedia formats). Analyse and appraise your own work, with appropriate references to historical and theoretical context and benefiting from group critics. Show independence and self-management in your private research and projects; radio studio skills; project planning; technical ability, knowing when to seek guidance.

***What you'll make?***

PAs and Researchers start out with a token stipend of Rs.4,000-5,000 to begin with. Only a few outfits will pay better.

As a Producer, Sr/Exec Producer, you would be paid Rs.35,000 p.m. Independent professionals earn much more depending on the projects handled - as much as Rs.50,000 to Rs.80,000 p.m.

***TV & Film Production***

Runner, researcher, floor manager or production coordinator. You could be anything if you have the right personality coupled with energy and enthusiasm, in the TV and Film industry.

There are good opportunities for experienced production managers and as this can be a very well paid post, many stay in this field. Some move on to assistant producer or producer posts. You will need to be a good communicator and organiser, with effective people management skills, able to motivate others and resolve disputes. A reasonable standard of numeracy, in order to keep accounts, is necessary. You also need to be self-reliant, able to promote yourself by networking and 'pitching' for contracts.

***The Work:*** The producer is responsible for initiating ideas, selling these to commissioning editors and managing the technical and creative team to produce the final programme. With production teams becoming ever smaller the producer will do much of the research, interviewing, scriptwriting and technical production themselves. In local and commercial radio there is an emphasis on journalistic skills - many producers will have a broadcast journalism background. Producers are also responsible for the budget of the programme, negotiating contracts, paying for services/facilities and bringing the programme in line with budget. In some instances, typically in local radio, the producer also doubles as presenter.

***Where to train?***

Since the field is so vast and varied, so are the courses and levels at which they are offered. Starting with umbrella courses in mass communication, an array of courses in cinematography, sound recording, TV & film production are offered separately by mostly private and some government institutes. Since only a handful are accredited or recognised. You are advised to check out their bonafides before enrolling.

## Artists and Related Workers

***Significant Points:*** About 63 percent of artists and related workers are self-employed.

Keen competition is expected for both salaried jobs and freelance work; the number of qualified workers exceeds the number of available openings because the arts attract many talented people with creative ability.

Artists usually develop their skills through a bachelor's degree programme or other postsecondary training in art or design.

Earnings for self-employed artists vary widely; some well-established artists earn more than salaried artists, while others find it difficult to rely solely on income earned from selling art.

***Nature of the Work:*** Artists create art to communicate ideas, thoughts, or feelings. They use a variety of methods—painting, sculpting, or illustration—and an assortment of materials, including oils, watercolors, acrylics, pastels, pencils, pen and ink, plaster, clay and computers. Artists' works may be realistic, stylized, or abstract and may depict objects, people, nature, or events.

Artists generally fall into one of four categories. *Art directors* formulate design concepts and presentation approaches for visual communications media. *Craft artists* create or reproduce handmade objects for sale or exhibition. *Fine artists,* including *painters, sculptors and illustrators* create original artwork, using a variety of media and techniques. *Multimedia artists and animators* create special effects, animation, or other visual images on film, on video, or with computers or other electronic media.

*Art directors* develop design concepts and review material that is to appear in periodicals, newspapers and other printed or digital media. They decide how best to present the information visually, so that it is eye catching, appealing and organized. Art directors decide which photographs or artwork to use and oversee the layout design and production of the printed material. They may direct workers engaged in artwork, layout design and copywriting.

*Craft artists* hand-make a wide variety of objects that are sold either in their own studios, in retail outlets, or at arts-and-crafts shows. Some craft artists may display their works in galleries and museums. Craft artists work with many different materials—ceramics, glass, textiles, wood, metal and paper—to create unique pieces of art, such as pottery, stained glass, quilts, tapestries, lace, candles and clothing. Many craft artists also use fine-art techniques—for example, painting, sketching and printing—to add finishing touches to their art.

*Fine artists* typically display their work in museums, commercial art galleries, corporate collections and private homes. Some of their artwork may be commissioned (done on request from clients), but most is sold by the artist or through private art galleries or dealers. The gallery and the artist predetermine how much each will earn from the sale. Only the most successful fine artists are able to support themselves solely through the sale of their works. Most fine artists have at least one other job to support their art careers. Some work in museums or art galleries as fine-arts directors or as curators, planning and setting up art exhibits. A few artists work as art critics for newspapers or magazines or as consultants to foundations or institutional collectors. Other artists teach art classes or conduct workshops in schools or in their own studios. Some artists also hold full-time or part-time jobs unrelated to the art field and pursue fine art as a hobby or second career.

Usually, fine artists specialize in one or two art forms, such as painting, illustrating, sketching, sculpting, printmaking and restoring. *Painters, illustrators, cartoonists and sketch artists* work with two-dimensional art forms, using shading, perspective and colour to produce realistic scenes or abstractions.

*Illustrators* typically create pictures for books, magazines and other publications and for commercial products such as textiles, wrapping paper, stationery, greeting cards and calendars. Increasingly, illustrators are working in digital format, preparing work directly on a computer.

*Medical* and *scientific illustrators* combine drawing skills with knowledge of biology or other sciences. Medical illustrators draw illustrations of human anatomy and surgical procedures. Scientific illustrators draw illustrations of animal and plant life, atomic and molecular structures and geologic and planetary formations. The illustrations are used in medical and scientific publications and in audiovisual presentations for teaching purposes. Medical illustrators also work for lawyers, producing exhibits for court cases.

*Cartoonists* draw political, advertising, social and sports cartoons. Some cartoonists work with others who create the idea or story and write the captions. Most cartoonists have comic, critical, or dramatic talents in addition to drawing skills.

*Sketch artists* create likenesses of subjects with pencil, charcoal, or pastels. Sketches are used by law enforcement agencies to assist in identifying suspects, by the news media to depict courtroom scenes and by individual patrons for their own enjoyment.

*Sculptors* design three-dimensional artworks, either by molding and joining materials such as clay, glass, wire, plastic, fabric, or metal or by cutting and carving forms from a block of plaster, wood, or stone. Some sculptors combine various materials to create mixed-media installations. Some incorporate light, sound and motion into their works.

*Printmakers* create printed images from designs cut or etched into wood, stone, or metal. After creating the design, the artist inks the surface of the woodblock, stone, or plate and uses a printing press to roll the image onto paper or fabric. Some make prints by pressing the inked surface onto paper by hand or by graphically encoding and processing data, using a computer. The digitized images are then printed on paper with the use of a computer printer.

*Painting restorers* preserve and restore damaged and faded paintings. They apply solvents and cleaning agents to clean the surfaces of the paintings, they reconstruct or retouch damaged areas and they apply preservatives to protect the paintings Restoration is highly detailed work and usually is reserved for experts in the field.

*Multimedia artists and animators* work primarily in motion picture and video industries, advertising and computer systems design services. They draw by hand and use computers to create the large series of pictures that form the animated images or special effects seen in movies, television programmes and computer games.

Some draw storyboards for television commercials, movies and animated features. Storyboards present television commercials in a series of scenes similar to a comic strip and allow an advertising agency to evaluate commercials proposed by the company doing the advertising. Storyboards also serve as guides to placing actors and cameras on the television or motion picture set and to other details that need to be taken care of during the production of commercials.

***Working Conditions:*** Many artists work in fine- or commercial-art studios located in office buildings, warehouses, or lofts. Others work in private studios in their homes. Some fine artists share studio space, where they also may exhibit their work. Studio surroundings usually are well lighted and ventilated; however, fine artists may be exposed to fumes from glue, paint, ink and other materials and to dust or other residue from filings, splattered paint, or spilled fluids. Artists who sit at drafting tables or who use computers for extended periods may experience back pain, eyestrain, or fatigue.

Artists employed by publishing companies, advertising agencies and design firms generally work a standard workweek. During busy periods, they may work overtime to meet deadlines. Self-employed artists can set their own hours, but may spend much time and effort selling their artwork to potential customers or clients and building a reputation.

***Training, Other Qualifications and Advancement:*** Postsecondary training is recommended for all artist specialties. Although formal training is not strictly required, it is very difficult to become skilled enough to make a living without some training. Many colleges and universities offer programmes leading to the bachelor's or master's degree in fine arts. Courses usually include core subjects such as English, social science and natural science, in addition to art history and studio art.

Independent schools of art and design also offer postsecondary studio training in the craft, fine and multimedia arts leading to a certificate in the specialty or to an associate's or bachelor's degree in fine arts. Typically, these programmes focus more intensively on studio work than do the academic programmes in a university setting. The National Association of Schools of Art and Design accredits about 250 postsecondary institutions with programmes in art and design; most award a degree in art.

Formal educational programmes in art also provide training in computer techniques. Computers are used widely in the visual arts and knowledge and training in computer graphics and other visual display software are critical elements of many jobs in these fields.

Medical illustrators must have both a demonstrated artistic ability and a detailed knowledge of living organisms, surgical and medical procedures and human and animal anatomy. A bachelor's degree combining art and premedical courses usually is required. However, most medical illustrators also choose to pursue a master's degree in medical illustration. This degree is offered in five accredited schools in the United States.

Art directors usually begin as entry-level artists in advertising, publishing, design and motion picture production firms. Artists are promoted to art director after demonstrating artistic and leadership abilities. Some art schools offer coursework in art direction as part of postsecondary training. Depending on the scope of their responsibilities, some art directors also may pursue a degree in art administration, which teaches nonartistic skills such as project management and communication.

Those who want to teach fine arts at public elementary or secondary schools must have a teaching certificate in addition to a bachelor's degree. An advanced degree in fine arts or arts administration is necessary for management or administrative positions in government or in foundations or for teaching in colleges and universities.

Evidence of appropriate talent and skill, displayed in an artist's portfolio, is an important factor used by art directors, clients and others in deciding whether to hire an individual or to contract out work. The portfolio is a collection of handmade, computer-generated, photographic, or printed samples of the artist's best work. Assembling a successful portfolio requires skills usually developed through postsecondary training in art or visual communications. Internships also provide excellent opportunities for artists to develop and enhance their portfolios.

Artists hired by firms often start with relatively routine work. While doing this work, however, they may observe and practice their skills on the side. Many artists freelance on a part-time basis while continuing to hold a full-time job until they are established. Others freelance part time while still in school, to develop experience and to build a portfolio of published work.

Freelance artists try to develop a set of clients who regularly contract for work. Some freelance artists are widely recognized for their skill in specialties such as cartooning or children's book illustration. These artists may earn high incomes and can choose the type of work they do.

Craft and fine artists advance professionally as their work circulates and as they establish a reputation for a particular style. Many of the most successful artists continually develop new ideas and their work often evolves over time.

***Employment:*** Artists held about 208,000 jobs in 2004. Sixty-three percent were self-employed. Employment was distributed as follows:

| | |
|---|---|
| Multimedia artists and animators | 94,000 |
| Art directors | 71,000 |
| Fine artists, including painters, sculptors and illustrators | 29,000 |
| Artists and related workers, all other | 8,500 |
| Craft artists | 6,100 |

Of the artists who were not self-employed, many worked in advertising and related services; newspaper, periodical, book and software publishers; motion picture and video industries; specialized design services; and computer systems design and related services. Some self-employed artists offered their services to advertising agencies, design firms, publishing houses and other businesses on a contract or freelance basis.

***Job Outlook:*** Employment of artists and related workers is expected to grow about as fast as average for all occupations through the year 2014. However, the competition for jobs is expected to be keen for both salaried and freelance jobs in all specialties, because the number of qualified workers exceeds the number of available openings. Also, because the arts attract many talented people with creative ability, the number of aspiring artists continues to grow. Employers in all industries should be able to choose from among the most qualified candidates.

Art directors work in a variety of industries, such as advertising, public relations, publishing and design firms. Despite an expanding number of opportunities, they should experience keen competition for the available openings.

Craft and fine artists work mostly on a freelance or commission basis and may find it difficult to earn a living solely by selling their artwork. Only the most successful craft and fine artists receive major commissions for their work. Competition among artists for the privilege of being shown in galleries is expected to remain acute and grants from sponsors such as private foundations, State and local arts councils and the National Endowment for the Arts should remain competitive.

Nonetheless, studios, galleries and individual clients are always on the lookout for artists who display outstanding talent, creativity and style. Among craft and fine artists, talented individuals who have developed a mastery of artistic techniques and skills will have the best job prospects.

The growth in computer graphics packages and stock art Web sites is making it easier for writers, publishers and art directors to create their own illustrations. As the use of this technology grows, there will be fewer opportunities for illustrators. One exception is the small number of medical illustrators, who will be in greater demand to illustrate journal articles and books as medical research continues to grow.

Salaried cartoonists will have fewer job opportunities because many newspapers and magazines are increasingly relying on freelance work. In addition, many cartoonists are opting to post their work on political Web sites and online publications. As online posting of cartoons increases, many are creating animated or interactive images to satisfy readers' demands for more sophisticated cartoons.

Multimedia artists and animators should have better job opportunities than other artists, but still will experience competition. Demand for these workers will increase as consumers continue to demand more realistic video games, movie and television special effects and 3D animated movies. Additional job openings will arise from an increasing demand for Web site development and for computer graphics adaptation from the growing number of mobile technologies. Job opportunities for animators of lower-technology, two-dimensional television cartoons could be hampered as these jobs continue to be outsourced overseas.

***Earnings:*** Median annual earnings of salaried art directors were $63,840 in May 2004. The middle 50 percent earned between $47,890 and $88,120. The lowest 10 percent earned less than $35,500 and the highest 10 percent earned more than $123,320. Median annual earnings were $66,900 in advertising and related services.

Median annual earnings of salaried craft artists were $23,520 in May 2004. The middle 50 percent earned between

$17,950 and $32,980. The lowest 10 percent earned less than $14,740 and the highest 10 percent earned more than $44,490.

Median annual earnings of salaried fine artists, including painters, sculptors and illustrators, were $38,060 in May 2004. The middle 50 percent earned between $25,990 and $51,730. The lowest 10 percent earned less than $17,390 and the highest 10 percent earned more than $68,860. According to the Association of Medical Illustrators, the median earnings in 2005 for salaried medical illustrators were $59,000.

Median annual earnings of salaried multimedia artists and animators were $50,360 in May 2004. The middle 50 percent earned between $37,980 and $70,730. The lowest 10 percent earned less than $29,030 and the highest 10 percent earned more than $94,260. Median annual earnings were $67,390 in motion picture and video industries and $46,810 in advertising and related services.

Earnings for self-employed artists vary widely. Some charge only a nominal fee while they gain experience and build a reputation for their work. Others, such as well-established freelance fine artists and illustrators, can earn more than salaried artists. Many, however, find it difficult to rely solely on income earned from selling paintings or other works of art. Like other self-employed workers, freelance artists must provide their own benefits.

## Painting and Coating Workers

***Significant Points:*** About 70 percent of jobs are in manufacturing establishments.

Most workers acquire their skills on the job; for most operators, training lasts from a few days to several months, but becoming skilled in all aspects of automotive painting usually requires 1 to 2 years.

Overall employment is projected to grow more slowly than average; transportation equipment painters are expected to grow about as fast as average, while coating, painting and spraying machine setters, operators and tenders are expected to decline.

***Nature of the Work:*** Millions of items ranging from cars to candy are covered by paint, plastic, varnish, chocolate, or some other type of coating solution. Often, the protection provided by the paint or coating is essential to the product, as with the coating of insulating material covering wires and other electrical and electronic components. Also, many paints and coatings have dual purposes; for example, the paint finish on an automobile heightens the visual appearance of the vehicle while providing protection from corrosion.

Coating, painting and spraying machine setters, operators and tenders control the machinery that applies these paints and coatings to a wide range of manufactured products. Perhaps the most straightforward technique is simply dipping an item in a large vat of paint or other coating. This is the technique used by *dippers*, who immerse racks or baskets of articles in vats of paint, liquid plastic, or other solutions by means of a power hoist. Similarly, *tumbling barrel painters* deposit articles made of porous materials into a barrel of paint, varnish, or other coating; the barrel is then rotated to ensure thorough coverage.

Another familiar technique is spraying products with a solution of paint or some other coating. *Spray machine operators* use spray guns to coat metal, wood, ceramic, fabric, paper and food products with paint and other coating solutions. Following a formula, operators fill the machine's tanks with a mixture of paints or chemicals, adding prescribed amounts of solution. Then they adjust nozzles on the guns to obtain the proper dispersion of the spray and they hold or position the guns so as to direct the spray onto the article. Operators also check the flow and viscosity of the paint or solution and visually inspect the quality of the coating. When products are drying, these workers often must regulate the temperature and air circulation in drying ovens. Individuals who paint, coat, or decorate articles such as furniture, glass, pottery, toys, cakes and books are known as *painting, coating and decorating workers.*

Painting and coating workers use various types of machines to coat a range of products. Frequently, their job title reflects the specialized nature of the machine or of the coating being applied. For example, *enrobing machine operators* coat, or "enrobe," confectionery, bakery and other food products with melted chocolate, cheese, oils, sugar, or other substances. *Paper coating machine operators* spray "size" on rolls of paper to give it its gloss or finish. *Silvering applicators* spray silver, tin and copper solutions on glass in the manufacture of mirrors.

In response to concerns about air pollution and worker safety, manufacturers increasingly are using new types of paints and coatings, instead of high-solvent paints, on their products. Water-based paints and powder coatings are two of the most common. These compounds do not emit as many volatile organic compounds into the air and can be applied to a variety of products. Powder coatings are sprayed much as are liquid paints and then are heated to melt and cure the coating.

The adoption of new types of paints often is accompanied by a conversion to more automated painting equipment that the operator sets and monitors. When using these machines, operators position the automatic spray guns, set the nozzles and synchronize the action of the guns with the speed of the conveyor carrying articles through the machine and drying ovens. The operator also may add solvents or water to the paint vessel, thereby preparing the paint for application. During the operation of the equipment, these workers tend painting machines, observe gauges on the control panel and check articles for evidence of any variation from specifications. The operator then uses a spray gun to "touch up" spots where necessary.

Although the majority of painting and coating workers are employed in manufacturing, the best known group refinishes old and damaged cars, trucks and buses in automotive body repair and paint shops. *Transportation equipment painters*, or *automotive painters*, are among the most highly skilled manual spray operators, because they perform intricate, detailed work and mix paints to match the original colour, a task that is especially difficult if the colour has faded.

To prepare a vehicle for painting, painters or their helpers use power sanders and sandpaper to remove the original paint or rust and then fill small dents and scratches with body filler. They also remove or mask parts they do not want to paint, such as chrome trim, headlights, windows and mirrors. Automotive painters use a spray gun to apply several coats of paint. They apply enamel or water-based primers to vehicles with metal bodies and flexible primers to newer vehicles with plastic body parts. Controlling the spray gun by hand, they apply successive coats until the finish of the repaired sections of the vehicle matches that of the original, undamaged portions. To speed drying between coats, they may place the freshly painted vehicle under heat lamps or in a special infrared oven. After each coat of primer dries, they sand the surface to remove any irregularities and to improve the adhesion of the next coat. Final sanding of the primers may be done by hand with a fine grade of sandpaper. A sealer then is applied and allowed to dry, followed by the final topcoat.

***Working Conditions:*** Painting and coating workers typically work indoors and may be exposed to dangerous fumes from paint and coating solutions. Although painting usually is done in special ventilated booths, operators typically wear masks or respirators that cover their noses and mouths, even in such booths. In addition, Federal legislation has led to a decrease in workers' exposure to hazardous chemicals by regulating emissions of volatile organic compounds and other hazardous air pollutants. This legislation also has led to the increasing use of more sophisticated paint booths and fresh-air systems that provide a safer work environment.

Operators have to stand for long periods and when using a spray gun, they may have to bend, stoop, or crouch in uncomfortable positions to reach different parts of the article. Most operators work a normal 40-hour week, but self-employed automotive painters sometimes work more than 50 hours a week, depending on the number of vehicles customers want repainted.

***Training, Other Qualifications and Advancement:*** Most painting and coating workers acquire their skills on the job, usually by watching and helping other, more experienced workers. For most setters, operators and tenders, as well as for painting, coating and decorating workers, training lasts from a few days to several months. Coating, painting and spraying machine setters, operators and tenders who modify the operation of computer-controlled equipment while it is running may require additional training in computer operations and minor programming.

Similarly, most transportation equipment painters start as helpers and gain their skills informally on the job. Becoming skilled in all aspects of automotive painting usually requires 1 to 2 years of on-the-job training. Beginning helpers usually remove trim, clean and sand surfaces to be painted, mask surfaces they do not want painted and polish finished work. As helpers gain experience, they progress to more complicated tasks, such as mixing paint to achieve a good match and using spray guns to apply primer coats or final coats to small areas.

Painters should have keen eyesight and a good sense of colour. The completion of high school generally is not required, but is advantageous. Additional instruction is offered at many community colleges and vocational or technical schools. Such programmes enhance one's employment prospects and can speed promotion to the next level.

Some employers sponsor training programmes to help their workers become more productive. Training is available from manufacturers of chemicals, paints, or equipment or from other private sources and may include safety and quality tips, as well as impart knowledge of products, equipment and general business practices. Some automotive painters are sent to technical schools to learn the intricacies of mixing and applying different types of paint.

Voluntary certification by the National Institute for Automotive Service Excellence (ASE) is recognized as the standard of achievement for automotive painters. For certification, painters must pass a written examination and have at least 2 years of experience in the field. High school, trade or vocational school, or community or junior college training in automotive refinishing that meets ASE standards may substitute for up to 1 year of experience. To retain their certification, painters must retake the examination at least every 5 years.

Experienced painting and coating workers with leadership ability may become team leaders or supervisors. Those who acquire practical experience, college, or other formal training may become sales or technical representatives for chemical or paint companies. Eventually, some automotive painters open their own shops.

***Employment:*** Painting and coating workers held about 186,000 jobs in 2004. Lesser skilled coating, painting and spraying machine setters, operators and tenders accounted for about 103,000 jobs, while more skilled transportation equipment painters constituted about 53,000. Another 29,000 jobs were held by painting, coating and decorating workers.

Approximately 70 percent of salaried jobs were found in manufacturing establishments, where the workers applied coatings to items such as fabricated metal products, motor vehicles and related equipment, industrial machines, household and office furniture and plastic, wood and paper products. Outside manufacturing, workers included automotive painters employed by independent automotive repair shops and workers employed by body repair and paint shops operated by retail motor vehicle dealers. About 6 percent of painting and coating workers were self-employed.

***Job Outlook:*** Overall employment of painting and coating workers is expected to grow more slowly than the average for all occupations through the year 2014. Employment growth for highly skilled transportation painters and automotive refinishers is projected to be faster than for painting, coating and decorating workers. In addition to jobs arising from growth, some jobs will become available each year as employers replace experienced operators who transfer to other occupations or leave the labour force.

Despite increasing demand for manufactured goods, employment of coating, painting and spraying machine setters, operators and tenders is expected to decline as part of that demand will be met by products manufactured abroad. Employment will be further decreased by improvements in the automation of paint and coating applications that will raise worker productivity. For example, operators will be able to coat goods more rapidly as they use sophisticated industrial machinery that moves and aims spray guns more efficiently. Legislation has set limits on the emissions of ozone-forming volatile organic compounds and is expected to impede job growth among operators in manufacturing. As manufacturing firms switch to water-based and powder coatings to comply with the law, they will introduce more efficient automation.

Painting, coating and decorating workers should grow more slowly than the average for all occupations. Increasing demand for hand-painted tiles and related specialty products will lead to growth among these workers. Although competition from imports should temper increases in employment, the specialized skills required by workers in this occupation should keep them from seeing as much of an impact of automation on employment.

Since the detailed work of refinishing automobiles in collision repair shops and motor vehicle dealerships does not lend itself to automation, painters employed in these establishments are projected to experience employment growth about as fast as the average for all occupations. As the demand for refinishing continues to grow, slower productivity growth among these workers will lead to employment increases that are more in line with the growing demand for their services.

The number of job openings for painting and coating workers in manufacturing industries may fluctuate from year to year due to cyclical changes in economic conditions. When demand for manufactured goods lessens, production may be suspended or reduced and workers may be laid off or face a shortened workweek. Automotive painters, by contrast, can expect relatively steady work because automobiles damaged in accidents require repair and refinishing regardless of the state of the economy.

***Earnings:*** Median hourly earnings of coating, painting and spraying machine setters, operators and tenders were $12.64 in May 2004. The middle 50 percent earned between $10.16 and $15.78 an hour. The lowest 10 percent earned less than $8.54 and the highest 10 percent earned more than $19.39 an hour.

Median hourly earnings of transportation equipment painters were $16.89 in May 2004. The middle 50 percent earned between $12.85 and $22.74 an hour. The lowest 10 percent earned less than $10.17 and the highest 10 percent earned more than $27.52 an hour. Median hourly earnings of transportation equipment painters were $16.84 in automotive repair and maintenance shops and $24.13 in motor vehicle manufacturing.

Median hourly earnings of painting, coating and decorating workers were $10.95 in May 2004. The middle 50 percent earned between $8.76 and $13.94 an hour. The lowest 10 percent earned less than $7.44 and the highest 10 percent earned more than $18.23 an hour.

Many automotive painters employed by motor vehicle dealers and independent automotive repair shops receive a commission based on the labour cost charged to the customer. Under this method, earnings depend largely on the amount of work a painter does and how fast it is completed. Employers frequently guarantee commissioned painters a minimum weekly salary. Helpers and trainees usually receive an hourly rate until they become sufficiently skilled to work on commission. Trucking companies, bus lines and other organizations that repair and refinish their own vehicles usually pay by the hour.

Many painting and coating machine operators belong to unions, including the International Brotherhood of Painters and Allied Trades, the Sheet Metal Workers International Association and the International Brotherhood of Teamsters. Most union operators work for manufacturers and large motor vehicle dealers.

## Painters and Paperhangers

***Significant Points:*** Employment prospects should be excellent due to the expected job growth, coupled with the large numbers of workers who retire or leave the occupation for other jobs.

Most workers learn informally on the job as helpers, but training experts recommend completion of an apprenticeship programme.

Nearly one-half of all painters and paperhangers are self employed.

***Nature of the Work:*** Paint and wall coverings make surfaces clean, attractive and bright. In addition, paints and other sealers protect exterior surfaces from wear caused by exposure to the weather.

*Painters* apply paint, stain, varnish and other finishes to buildings and other structures. They choose the right paint or finish for the surface to be covered, taking into account durability, ease of handling, method of application and customers' wishes. Painters first prepare the surfaces to be covered, so that the paint will adhere properly. This may require removing the old coat of paint by stripping, sanding, wire brushing, burning, or water and abrasive blasting. Painters also wash walls and trim to remove dirt and grease, fill nail holes and cracks, sandpaper rough spots and brush off dust. On new surfaces, they apply a primer or sealer to prepare the surface for the finish coat. Painters also mix paints and match colours, relying on knowledge of paint composition and colour harmony. In large paint shops or hardware stores, these functions are automated.

There are several ways to apply paint and similar coverings. Painters must be able to choose the right paint applicator for each job, depending on the surface to be covered, the characteristics of the finish and other factors. Some jobs need only a good bristle brush with a soft, tapered edge; others require a dip or fountain pressure roller; still others can best be done using a paint sprayer. Many jobs need several types of applicators. The right tools for each job not only expedite the painter's work but also produce the most attractive surface.

When working on tall buildings, painters erect scaffolding, including "swing stages," scaffolds suspended by ropes, or cables attached to roof hooks. When painting steeples and other conical structures, they use a bosun's chair, a swing-like device.

*Paperhangers* cover walls and ceilings with decorative wall coverings made of paper, vinyl, or fabric. They first prepare the surface to be covered by applying "sizing," which seals the surface and makes the covering adhere better. When redecorating, they may first remove the old covering by soaking, steaming, or applying solvents. When necessary, they patch holes and take care of other imperfections before hanging the new wall covering.

After the surface has been prepared, paperhangers must prepare the paste or other adhesive. Then, they measure the area to be covered, check the covering for flaws, cut the covering into strips of the proper size and closely examine the pattern in order to match it when the strips are hung. Much of this process can now be handled by specialized equipment.

The next step is to brush or roll the adhesive onto the back of the covering, if needed and to then place the strips on the wall or ceiling, making sure the pattern is matched, the strips are hung straight and the edges are butted together to make tight, closed seams. Finally, paperhangers smooth the strips to remove bubbles and wrinkles, trim the top and bottom with a razor knife and wipe off any excess adhesive.

***Working Conditions:*** Most painters and paperhangers work 40 hours a week or less; about one-fourth have variable schedules or work part time. Painters and paperhangers must stand for long periods, often working from scaffolding and ladders. Their jobs also require a considerable amount of climbing and bending. These workers must have stamina, because much of the work is done with their arms raised overhead. Painters often work outdoors but seldom in wet, cold, or inclement weather. Some painting jobs can leave a worker covered with paint.

Painters and paperhangers sometimes work with materials that are hazardous or toxic, such as when they are required to remove lead-based paints. In the most dangerous situations, painters work in a sealed self-contained suit to prevent inhalation of or contact with hazardous materials.

***Training, Other Qualifications and Advancement:*** Painting and paperhanging is learned mostly through on-the-job training and by working as a helper to an experienced painter. However, there are a number of formal and informal training programmes that provide more thorough instruction and a better career foundation. In general, the more formal the training received the more likely the individual will enter the profession at a higher level. Besides apprenticeships, some workers gain skills by attending technical schools that offer training prior to employment. These schools can take about a year to complete. Others receive training through local vocational high schools. Applicants should have good manual dexterity and colour sense. There are limited opportunities for informal training for paperhangers because there are fewer paperhangers and helpers are usually not required.

If available, apprenticeships are usually the best way to enter the profession. They generally provide a mixture of classroom instruction and on-the-job training. Apprenticeships for painters and paperhangers consist of 2 to 4 years of on-the-job training, supplemented by 144 hours of related classroom instruction each year.

Apprentices or helpers generally must be at least 18 years old and in good physical condition. A high school education or its equivalent, with courses in mathematics, usually is required to enter an apprenticeship programme. Apprentices receive instruction in colour harmony, use and care of tools and equipment, surface preparation, application techniques, paint mixing and matching, characteristics of different finishes, blueprint reading, wood finishing and safety.

Whether a painter learns the trade through a formal apprenticeship or informally as a helper, on-the-job instruction covers similar skill areas. Under the direction of experienced workers, trainees carry supplies, erect scaffolds and do simple painting and surface preparation tasks while they learn about paint and painting equipment. As they gain experience, trainees learn to prepare surfaces for painting and paperhanging, to mix paints and to apply paint and wall coverings efficiently and neatly. Near the end of their training, they may learn decorating concepts, colour coordination and cost-estimating techniques. In addition to learning craft skills, painters must become familiar with safety and health regulations so that their work complies with the law.

Painters and paperhangers may advance to supervisory or estimating jobs with painting and decorating contractors. Many establish their own painting and decorating businesses. For those who would like to advance, it is increasingly important to be able to communicate in both English and Spanish in order to relay instructions and safety precautions to workers with limited English skills; Spanish speaking workers make up a large part of the construction workforce in many areas. Painting contractors need good English skills in order to deal with clients and subcontractors.

***Employment:*** Painters and paperhangers held about 486,000 jobs in 2004; most were painters. Around one-third of painters and paperhangers work for painting and wall covering contractors engaged in new construction, repair, restoration, or remodelling work.

In addition, organizations that own or manage large buildings—such as apartment complexes—employ maintenance painters, as do some schools, hospitals, factories and government agencies.

Self-employed independent painting contractors accounted for nearly one-half of all painters and paperhangers, significantly greater than the one in five of construction trades workers in general.

***Job Outlook:*** Job prospects should be excellent because each year thousands of painters retire or leave for jobs in other occupations. There are no strict training requirements for entry into these jobs, so many people with limited skills work as painters or helpers for a short time and then move on to other types of work. Many fewer openings will arise for paperhangers because the number of these jobs is comparatively small.

In addition to the need to replace experienced workers who leave, new jobs will be created. Employment of painters is expected to grow as fast as average for all occupations through the year 2014, reflecting increases in the level of new construction and in the stock of buildings and other structures that require maintenance and renovation.

The relatively short life of exterior paints as well as changing colour trends will stir demand for painters. Painting is labour-intensive and not susceptible to technological changes that might make workers more productive and slow employment growth. Paperhangers should see slower than average employment growth as easy application materials and reduced demand for paperhanging services limits growth.

Jobseekers considering these occupations should expect some periods of unemployment, especially until they gain experience. Many construction projects are of short duration and construction activity is cyclical and seasonal in nature. Remodelling, restoration and maintenance projects, however, often provide many jobs for painters and paperhangers even when new construction activity declines. The most versatile painters and skilled paperhangers generally are best able to keep working steadily during downturns in the economy.

***Earnings:*** In May 2004, median hourly earnings of painters, construction and maintenance, were $14.55. The middle 50 percent earned between $11.59 and $19.04. The lowest 10 percent earned less than $9.47 and the highest 10 percent earned more than $25.11. Median hourly earnings in the industries employing the largest numbers of painters in May 2004 were as follows:

| | |
|---|---|
| Local government | $18.36 |
| Residential building construction | 15.09 |
| Nonresidential building construction | 14.97 |
| Building finishing contractors | 14.44 |
| Employment services | 11.31 |

In May 2004, median earnings for paperhangers were $15.73. The middle 50 percent earned between $12.23 and $20.71. The lowest 10 percent earned less than $9.57 and the highest 10 percent earned more than $26.58.

Earnings for painters may be reduced on occasion because of bad weather and the short-term nature of many construction jobs. Hourly wage rates for apprentices usually start at 40 to 50 percent of the rate for experienced workers and increase periodically.

Some painters and paperhangers are members of the International Brotherhood of Painters and Allied Trades. Some maintenance painters are members of other unions.

## Dancers and Choreographers

***Significant Points:*** Many dancers stop performing by their late thirties, but some remain in the field as choreographers, dance teachers, or artistic directors.

Most dancers begin formal training at an early age—between 5 and 15—and many have their first professional audition by age 17 or 18.

Dancers and choreographers face intense competition; only the most talented find regular work.

***Nature of the Work:*** From ancient times to the present, dancers have expressed ideas, stories and rhythm with their bodies. They use a variety of dance forms that allow free movement and self-expression, including classical ballet, modern dance and culturally specific dance styles. Many dancers combine performance work with teaching or choreography.

Dancers perform in a variety of settings, such as musical productions and may present folk, ethnic, tap, jazz and other popular kinds of dance. They also perform in opera, musical theatre, television, movies, music videos and commercials, in which they also may sing and act. Dancers most often perform as part of a group, although a few top artists perform solo.

Dancers work with choreographers, who create original dances and develop new interpretations of existing dances. Because few dance routines are written down, choreographers instruct performers at rehearsals to achieve the desired effect. In addition, choreographers usually are involved in auditioning performers.

***Working Conditions:*** Dance is strenuous. Many dancers stop performing by their late thirties because of the physical demands on the body. However, some continue to work in the field as choreographers, dance teachers and coaches, or artistic directors. Others move into administrative positions, such as company managers. A few celebrated dancers, however, continue performing even beyond the age of 50.

Daily rehearsals require very long hours. Many dance companies tour for part of the year to supplement a limited performance schedule at home. Dancers who perform in musical productions and other family entertainment spend much of their time on the road; others work in nightclubs or on cruise ships. Most dance performances are in the evening, whereas rehearsals and practice take place during the day. As a result, dancers often work very long and late hours. Generally, dancers and choreographers work in modern and temperature-controlled facilities; however, some studios may be older and less comfortable.

***Training, Other Qualifications and Advancement:*** Training varies with the type of dance and is a continuous part of all dancers' careers. Many dancers and dance instructors believe that dancers should start with a good foundation in classical dance before selecting a particular dance style. Ballet training for women usually begins at 5 to 8 years of age with a private teacher or through an independent ballet school. Serious training traditionally begins between the ages of 10 and 12. Men often begin their ballet training between the ages of 10 and 15. Students who demonstrate potential in their early teens may seek out more intensive and advanced professional training.

At about this time, students should begin to focus their training on a particular style and decide whether to pursue additional training through a dance company's school or a college dance programme. Leading dance school companies often have summer training programmes from which they select candidates for admission to their regular full-time training programmes. Formal training for modern and culturally specific dancers often begins later than training in ballet; however, many folk dance forms are taught to very young children. Many dancers have their first professional auditions by age 17 or 18.

Training is an important component of professional dancers' careers. Dancers normally spend 8 hours a day in class and rehearsal, keeping their bodies in shape and preparing for performances. Their daily training period includes time to warm up and cool down before and after classes and rehearsals.

Because of the strenuous and time-consuming training required, some dancers view formal education as secondary. However, a broad, general education including music, literature, history and the visual arts is helpful in the interpretation of dramatic episodes, ideas and feelings. Dancers sometimes conduct research to learn more about the part they are playing.

Many colleges and universities award bachelor's or master's degrees in dance, typically through departments of dance, theatre, or fine arts. The National Association of Schools of Dance accredits about 60 programmes in dance. Many programmes concentrate on modern dance, but some also offer courses in jazz, culturally specific, ballet, or classical techniques; dance composition, history and criticism; and movement analysis.

A college education is not essential to obtaining employment as a professional dancer; however, many dancers obtain degrees in unrelated fields to prepare themselves for careers after dance. The completion of a college programme in dance and education is essential to qualify to teach dance in college, high school, or elementary school. Colleges and conservatories sometimes require graduate degrees but may accept performance experience. A college background is not necessary, however, for teaching dance or choreography in local recreational programmes. Studio schools prefer teachers to have experience as performers.

Because of the rigorous practice schedules of most dancers, self-discipline, patience, perseverance and a devotion to dance are essential for success in the field. Dancers also must possess good problem-solving skills and an ability to work with people. Good health and physical stamina also are necessary attributes. Above all, dancers must have flexibility, agility, coordination, grace, a sense of rhythm, a feeling for music and a creative ability to express themselves through movement.

Because dancers typically perform as members of an ensemble made up of other dancers, musicians and directors or choreographers, they must be able to function as part of a team. They also should be highly motivated and prepared to face the anxiety of intermittent employment and rejections when auditioning for work. For dancers, advancement takes the form of a growing reputation, more frequent work, bigger and better roles and higher pay. Some dancers may take on added responsibilities, such as by becoming a dance captain in musical theatre or ballet master/ballet mistress in concert dance companies, by leading rehearsals, or by working with less experienced dancers in the absence of the choreographer.

Choreographers typically are experienced dancers with years of practice working in the theatre. Through their performance as dancers, they develop reputations that often lead to opportunities to choreograph productions.

***Employment:*** Professional dancers and choreographers held about 38,000 jobs in 2004. Many others were between engagements, so that the total number of people available for work as dancers over the course of the year was greater. Dancers and choreographers worked in a variety of industries, such as private educational services, which includes dance studios and schools, as well as colleges and universities; food services and drinking establishments; performing arts companies, which includes dance, theatre and opera companies; and amusement and recreation venues, such as casinos and theme parks. Over one-fifth of dancers and choreographers were self-employed.

Most major cities serve as home to major dance companies; however, many smaller communities across the Nation also support home-grown, full-time professional dance companies.

***Job Outlook:*** Dancers and choreographers face intense competition for jobs. Only the most talented find regular employment.

Employment of dancers and choreographers is expected to grow about as fast as the average for all occupations through 2014. The public's continued interest in dance will sustain larger dance companies, but funding from public and private organizations is not expected to keep pace with rising production costs. For many small and midsize organizations, the result will be fewer performances and more limited employment opportunities. Although job openings will arise each year because dancers and choreographers retire or leave the occupation for other reasons, the number of applicants will continue to vastly exceed the number of job openings.

National dance companies likely will continue to provide jobs in this field. Opera companies and dance groups affiliated with colleges and universities and with television and motion pictures also will offer some opportunities. Moreover, the growing popularity of dance for recreational and fitness purposes has resulted in increased opportunities to teach dance. Finally, music video channels will provide opportunities for both dancers and choreographers.

***Earnings:*** Median hourly earnings of dancers were $8.54 in May 2004. The middle 50 percent earned between $6.71 and $15.62. The lowest 10 percent earned less than $5.87 and the highest 10 percent earned more than $21.59. Annual earnings data for dancers were not available, because of the wide variation in the number of hours worked by dancers and the short-term nature of many jobs—which may last for 1 day or 1 week—made it extremely rare for dancers to have guaranteed employment that exceeded 3 to 6 months. Median hourly earnings in the industries employing the largest number of dancers were as follows:

| | |
|---|---|
| Other schools and instruction | $14.94 |
| Performing arts companies | 14.82 |
| Drinking places, alcoholic beverages | 6.78 |
| Other amusement and recreation industries | 7.68 |

Median annual earnings of salaried choreographers were $33,670 in May 2004. The middle 50 percent earned between $21,530 and $48,940. The lowest 10 percent earned less than $14,980 and the highest 10 percent earned more than $68,190. Median annual earnings were $34,090 in "other schools and instruction," a North American Industry Classification System category that includes dance studios and schools.

Dancers who were on tour usually received an additional allowance for room and board, as well as extra compensation for overtime. Earnings from dancing are usually low because employment is part year and irregular. Dancers often supplement their income by working as guest artists with other dance companies, teaching dance, or taking jobs unrelated to the field.

Earnings of dancers at many of the largest companies and in commercial settings are governed by union contracts. Dancers in the major opera ballet, classical ballet and modern dance corps belong to the American Guild of Musical Artists, Inc. of the AFL-CIO; those who appear on live or videotaped television programmes belong to the American Federation of Television and Radio Artists; those who perform in films and on television belong to the Screen Actors Guild; and those in musical theatre are members of the Actors' Equity Association.

The unions and producers sign basic agreements specifying minimum salary rates, hours of work, benefits and other conditions of employment. However, the contract each dancer signs with the producer of the show may be more favourable than the basic agreement.

Most salaried dancers and choreographers covered by union contracts receive some paid sick leave and various health and pension benefits, including extended sick pay and family-leave benefits provided by their unions. Employers contribute toward these benefits. Dancers and choreographers not covered by union contracts usually do not enjoy such benefits.

## Musicians, Singers and Related Workers

***Significant Points:*** Part-time schedules and intermittent unemployment are common; many musicians supplement their income with earnings from other sources.

Aspiring musicians begin studying an instrument or training their voices at an early age.

Competition for jobs is keen; those who can play several instruments and perform a wide range of musical styles should enjoy the best job prospects.

***Nature of the Work:*** Musicians, singers and related workers play musical instruments, sing, compose or arrange music, or conduct groups in instrumental or vocal performances. They may perform solo or as part of a group. Musicians, singers and related workers entertain live audiences in nightclubs, concert halls and theaters featuring opera, musical theatre, or dance. Many of these entertainers play for live audiences; others perform exclusively for recording or production studios. Regardless of the setting, musicians, singers and related workers spend considerable time practicing, alone and with their bands, orchestras, or other musical ensembles.

*Musicians* often gain their reputation or professional standing by exhibiting a high level of professionalism and proficiency in a particular kind of music or performance. However, those who learn several related instruments and who can perform equally well in several musical styles have better employment opportunities. Instrumental musicians, for example, may play in a symphony orchestra, rock group, or jazz combo one night, appear in another ensemble the next and work in a studio band the following day. Some play a variety of string, brass, woodwind, or percussion instruments or electronic synthesizers.

*Singers* interpret music and text, using their knowledge of voice production, melody and harmony. They sing character parts or perform in their own individual style. Singers are often classified according to their voice range—soprano, contralto, tenor, baritone, or bass—or by the type of music they sing, such as opera, rock, popular, folk, rap, or country and western.

*Music directors* conduct, direct, plan and lead instrumental or vocal performances by musical groups, such as orchestras, choirs and glee clubs. *Conductors* lead instrumental music groups, such as symphony orchestras, dance bands, show bands and various popular ensembles. These leaders audition and select musicians, choose the music most appropriate for their talents and abilities and direct rehearsals and performances. Choral directors lead choirs and glee clubs, sometimes working with a band or an orchestra conductor. Directors audition and select singers and lead them at rehearsals and performances to achieve harmony, rhythm, tempo, shading and other desired musical effects.

*Composers* create original music such as symphonies, operas, sonatas, radio and television jingles, film scores and popular songs. They transcribe ideas into musical notation, using harmony, rhythm, melody and tonal structure. Although most composers and songwriters practice their craft on instruments and transcribe the notes with pen and paper, some use computer software to compose and edit their music.

*Arrangers* transcribe and adapt musical compositions to a particular style for orchestras, bands, choral groups, or individuals. Components of music—including tempo, volume and the mix of instruments needed—are arranged to express the composer's message. While some arrangers write directly into a musical composition, others use computer software to make changes.

***Working Conditions:*** Musicians typically perform at night and on weekends. They spend much additional time practicing or in rehearsal. Full-time musicians with long-term employment contracts, such as those with symphony orchestras or television and film production companies, enjoy steady work and less travel. Nightclub, solo, or recital musicians frequently travel to perform in a variety of local settings and may tour nationally or internationally. Because many musicians find only part-time or intermittent work, experiencing unemployment between engagements, they often supplement their income with other types of jobs. The stress of constantly looking for work leads many musicians to accept permanent, full-time jobs in other occupations, while working only part time as musicians.

Most instrumental musicians work closely with a variety of other people, including their colleagues, agents, employers, sponsors and audiences. Although they usually work indoors, some perform outdoors for parades, concerts and festivals. In some nightclubs and restaurants, smoke and odours may be present and lighting and ventilation may be poor.

***Training, Other Qualifications and Advancement:*** Aspiring musicians begin studying an instrument at an early age. They may gain valuable experience playing in a school or community band or an orchestra or with a group of friends. Singers usually start training when their voices mature. Participation in school musicals or choirs often provides good early training and experience.

Musicians need extensive and prolonged training and practice to acquire the necessary skills, knowledge and ability to interpret music at a professional level. Like other artists, musicians and singers continually strive to stretch themselves—exploring different forms of music. Formal training may be obtained through private study with an accomplished musician, in a college or university music programme, or in a music conservatory. For university or conservatory study, an audition generally is necessary. The National Association of Schools of Music accredits more than 600 college-level programmes in music. Courses typically include music theory, music interpretation, composition, conducting and performance in a particular instrument or in voice. Music directors, composers, conductors and arrangers need considerable related work experience or advanced training in these subjects.

Many colleges, universities and music conservatories grant bachelor's or higher degrees in music. A master's or doctoral degree usually is required to teach advanced music courses in colleges and universities; a bachelor's degree may be sufficient to teach basic courses. A degree in music education qualifies graduates for a State certificate to teach music in public elementary or secondary schools. Musicians who do not meet public school music education requirements may teach in private schools and recreation associations or instruct individual students in private sessions.

Musicians must be knowledgeable about a broad range of musical styles but keenly aware of the form that interests them most. Having a broader range of interest, knowledge and training can help expand employment opportunities and musical abilities. Voice training and private instrumental lessons, taken especially when the individual is young, also help develop technique and enhance one's performance.

Young persons considering careers in music should have musical talent, versatility, creativity, poise and a good stage presence. Because quality performance requires constant study and practice, self-discipline is vital. To sustain a career as a musician or singer, performers must achieve a level performing excellence and be counted on to be on their game whenever they perform. Moreover, musicians who play in concerts or in nightclubs and those who tour must have physical stamina to endure frequent travel and an irregular performance schedule. Because musicians and singers always must make their performances look effortless, preparation and practice are important. Musicians and singers also must be prepared to face the anxiety of intermittent employment and of rejection when auditioning for work.

Advancement for musicians usually means becoming better known, finding work more easily and performing for higher earnings. Successful musicians often rely on agents or managers to find them performing engagements, negotiate contracts and develop their careers.

***Employment:*** Musicians, singers and related workers held about 249,000 jobs in 2004. Around 40 percent worked part time; almost half were self-employed. Many found jobs in cities in which entertainment and recording activities are concentrated, such as New York, Los Angeles, Las Vegas, Chicago and Nashville.

Musicians, singers and related workers are employed in a variety of settings. Of those who earn a wage or salary, almost two-thirds were employed by religious organizations and almost one-fourth by performing arts companies such as professional orchestras, small chamber music groups, opera companies, musical theatre companies and ballet troupes. Musicians and singers also perform in nightclubs and restaurants and for weddings and other events. Well-known musicians and groups may perform in concerts, appear on radio and television broadcasts and make recordings and music videos. The Armed Forces also offer careers in their bands and smaller musical groups.

***Job Outlook:*** Competition for jobs for musicians, singers and related workers is expected to be keen. The vast number of persons with the desire to perform will continue to greatly exceed the number of openings. Talent alone is no guarantee of success: many people start out to become musicians or singers but leave the profession because they find the work difficult, the discipline demanding and the long periods of intermittent unemployment unendurable.

Overall employment of musicians, singers and related workers is expected to grow about as fast as the average for all occupations through 2014. Most new wage and salary jobs for musicians will arise in religious organizations. Slower-than-average growth is expected for self-employed musicians, who generally perform in nightclubs, concert tours and other venues. Growth in demand for musicians will generate a number of job opportunities and many openings also will arise from the need to replace those who leave the field each year because they are unable to make a living solely as musicians or for other reasons.

***Earnings:*** Median hourly earnings of musicians and singers were $17.85 in May 2004. The middle 50 percent earned between $9.68 and $30.75. The lowest 10 percent earned less than $6.47 and the highest 10 percent earned more than $53.59. Median hourly earnings were $20.70 in performing arts companies and $12.17 in religious organizations. Annual earnings data for musicians and singers were not available, because of the wide variation in the number of hours worked by musicians and singers and the short-term nature of many jobs, which may last for 1 day or 1 week; it is extremely rare for musicians and singers to have guaranteed employment that exceeds 3 to 6 months.

Median annual earnings of salaried music directors and composers were $34,570 in May 2004. The middle 50 percent earned between $24,040 and $51,770. The lowest 10 percent earned less than $15,960 and the highest 10 percent earned more than $75,380.

Yearly earnings typically reflect the number of gigs a freelance musician or singer played or the number of hours and weeks of salaried contract work, in addition to a performer's professional reputation and setting: performers who can fill large concert halls, arenas, or outdoor stadiums generally command higher pay than those who perform in local clubs. Soloists or headliners usually receive higher earnings than band members or opening acts. The most successful musicians earn performance or recording fees that far exceed the median earnings.

According to the American Federation of Musicians, weekly minimum salaries in major orchestras ranged from about $700 to $2,080 during the 2004–05 performing season. Each orchestra works out a separate contract with its local union, but individual musicians may negotiate higher salaries. Top orchestras have a season ranging from 24 to 52 weeks, with 18 orchestras reporting 52-week contracts. In regional orchestras, minimum salaries are often less because fewer performances are scheduled. Regional orchestra musicians often are paid for their services, without any guarantee of future employment. Community orchestras often have even more limited levels of funding and offer salaries that are much lower for seasons of shorter duration.

Although musicians employed by some symphony orchestras work under master wage agreements, which guarantee a season's work up to 52 weeks, many other musicians face relatively long periods of unemployment between jobs. Even when employed, many musicians and singers work part time in unrelated occupations. Thus, their earnings usually are lower than earnings in many other occupations. Moreover, because they may not work steadily for one employer, some performers cannot qualify for unemployment compensation and few have typical benefits such as sick leave or paid vacations. For these reasons, many musicians give private lessons or take jobs unrelated to music to supplement their earnings as performers.

Many musicians belong to a local of the American Federation of Musicians. Professional singers who perform live often belong to a branch of the American Guild of Musical Artists; those who record for the broadcast industries may belong to the American Federation of Television and Radio Artists.

## Ceramic Art and Design

Ceramic art and design programmes teach people to create art works out of clay and similar materials. Students learn how to hand mold and throw clay on a wheel. They study slips and glaze techniques. They also learn how to operate kilns to fire ceramics. Before recorded history, artists used clay to make pottery and bricks. They learned early to harden clay with fire. Clay - soil whose particles are smaller than five one-thousandths of a millimeter - adheres with special strength because of its density. The oldest form of clay pottery is earthenware. Later forms include stoneware and porcelain. Because of its durability, clay is an important element in earth dams and cement.

Now, clay is appreciated not only for its functional qualities, but for its beauty. A range of objects can be made from clay, from platters to jewellery to abstract sculpture. Potters and ceramicists are uniquely skilled in that they can make both things we use everyday, like plates and bowls and artistic pieces meant for display only.

In addition, there are many different kinds of clay, glaze and firing techniques that can make two objects look very different from one another. What's more, some artists prefer to build all their pieces by hand where others prefer to "throw" them on the potter's wheel. It's easy to see that clay is a fascinating medium!

In ceramics programmes, your course work teaches you basic art principles such as art history, drawing and design. You then concentrate on all the different aspects of ceramic art, from throwing to handbuilding to sculpture. You also learn basic skills such as how to operate a kiln and mix and measure glazes. Many courses are designed to give you ample time in a studio where you create your own style and focus on a particular method of building your pieces.

Many colleges and universities offer ceramics programmes that lead to the bachelor of fine arts (BFA) degree and the master of fine arts (MFA) degree. Community colleges and independent schools of art and design also offer studio training and programmes in ceramics and ceramic design. They may lead to associate of art (AA) degrees. Independent art schools may also grant BFA degrees.

They focus more intensively on studio work while colleges and universities offer more in the way of general requirements in addition to studio work.

It takes four to five years after high school to earn a BFA degree and six to seven years to earn an MFA degree. The MFA is considered a "terminal" degree, meaning that you do not need a doctorate if you desire to teach at the college level. However, a few schools do offer doctorate degrees in ceramics. Keep in mind that graduate study is almost always offered through a larger art and fine arts programme, so be sure to read this programme of study as well."

### *College preparation*

Many programmes require you to submit separate application materials in addition to your general college application. Usually you have to complete preliminary art courses, write a personal statement and demonstrate skill working with clay.

You can prepare for this programme by taking courses in high school that prepare you for college. This typically includes four years of English, three years of math, three years of social studies and two years of science. Some colleges also require two years of a second language.

*Art Appreciation*

*Art History*

*Art*

*Drawing and Painting*

*Pottery*

*Chemistry*

### *Graduate Admissions*

Admission to graduate programmes is competitive. You need a bachelor's degree, good grades, good test scores and a developing ceramic project portfolio.

Additional requirements at some schools include:

- Graduate Record Exam (GRE) General
- Letters of recommendation
- Personal interview

### *Typical Course Work*

This programme typically includes courses in the following subjects:

- Ceramic Sculpture
- Contemporary Ceramic Art and Artists
- Drawing and Sketching
- Firing and Glazing Methods
- Fundamentals of Design

- Handbuilding
- History of Ceramics
- Kiln Operation
- Materials
- Painting
- Throwing on the Wheel

Graduate programmes in ceramics typically require:

- Required courses
- Thesis and portfolio of finished work (master's degree)
- Preliminary exam (doctoral degree)
- Dissertation (doctoral degree)

### *Things to Know*

Most people with degrees in ceramic art and design become independent artists and teachers. Many local arts and craft centres, as well as community colleges, offer ceramics courses to the public. While most people don't associate the hard sciences with ceramics, it helps to have a basic knowledge of chemistry. This is because glazes are made up of minerals and other elements that must be measured and mixed precisely.

Often, ceramic students are employed in the ceramic studio. Students get paid while learning how to load, unload and monitor kilns. They also learn how to mix clay and glazes.

In many cases you have to pay a fee in addition to regular course tuition. The fee covers the cost of art materials, which include clay, glazes and energy used to fire kilns.

Many programmes offer personal studio space to ceramic students. Usually this is for junior- and senior-level students.

Most programmes require that you display your finished pieces in a showing at the school's local gallery. Also, some schools allow you to sell your work in shows that are open to the public.

## Crafts

Crafts programmes teach people about the methods and traditions of folk art. Students learn about aesthetics and designs in handcrafting. They learn to create artistic items using techniques such as wax molding, weaving and metalworking.

Craft arts blend values of decoration and utility. While craft artists use techniques and skills of the fine arts, they place a greater emphasis on making things that are used everyday. The craft arts include ceramics, glassware, baskets, jewellery, metalwork, furniture and textiles.

Although you don't always need formal training to create works of art, going to art school can help you refine your skills and learn how to use them to earn a living. Formal training also allows you to share inspiration with other students who have similar interests and talents. Your course work usually focuses on general art principles, such as design, sketching and art history, while also allowing you to study your particular craft in depth. Often your courses are structured to give you lots of studio time. This allows you to focus on a project or a skill over the length of the course. In addition, many programmes offer business courses in marketing, budgeting and sales.

About 15 colleges and universities offer crafts programmes that lead to the bachelor of fine arts (BFA) degree and the master of fine arts (MFA) degree. Community colleges and independent schools of art and design often provide studio training and degrees in crafts as well. Independent art schools may grant certificates, associate and bachelor's degrees. Some offer graduate degree programmes as well.

An associate's degree typically takes two years after high school. For a bachelor's degree, you need two more years. The master of fine arts degree typically takes two to three years after the bachelor's degree. The MFA is considered a "terminal" degree, meaning that you do not need a doctorate if you desire to teach at the college level. However, a few schools do offer doctorate degrees in crafts. Keep in mind that graduate study is almost always offered through a larger art and fine arts programme, so be sure to read this programme of study as well."

***College Preparation:*** Many programmes require you to submit separate application materials in addition to your general college application. Usually you have to complete preliminary art courses, write a personal statement and demonstrate skill working with in a particular craft.

You can prepare for this programme by taking courses in high school that prepare you for college. This typically includes four years of English, three years of math, three years of social studies and two years of science. Some colleges also require two years of a second language.

*Art Appreciation*

*Art History*

*Art*

*Drawing and Painting*

*Pottery*

*Crafts*

*Marketing*

*Business Math*

***Graduate Admissions***

Admission to graduate programmes is competitive. You need a bachelor's degree, good grades and good test scores.

Additional requirements at some schools include:

- Graduate Record Exam (GRE) General
- Letters of recommendation
- Undergraduate degree or significant course work in art
- Portfolio and personal interview

***Typical Course Work***

This programme typically includes courses in the following subjects:

- Accounting
- Anthropology
- Art History
- Business Management
- Candles and Waxworks
- Ceramics

- Drawing
- Folk Art
- Jewellery
- Painting
- Pottery
- Purchasing
- Sales and Marketing
- Sculpture
- Weaving
- Woodworking

Graduate degrees in crafts typically include:

- Required courses
- Thesis and portfolio of finished work (master's degree)
- Preliminary exam (doctoral degree)
- Dissertation and portfolio of finished work (doctoral degree)

***Things to Know***

Many craft artists learn their art by working as helpers for experienced artists.

In most programmes, you focus on one or two crafts.

Independent art schools may focus more intensively on studio work and career preparation. Colleges and universities typically require certain general courses in addition to studio art requirements.

In many cases you have to pay a fee in addition to regular course tuition. The fee covers the cost of art materials, such as metal, wood and fabric. Most people with an art degree in crafts become both professional artists and teachers. Many provide private instruction or teach at community colleges and local art centres, where classes are offered to the public.

## Dramatic Arts

Programmes in dramatic arts teach people the history and styles of acting in theatre or film performances. Students learn about the common themes that appear in major dramatic works across time. They study different genres of dramatic literature. They also study methods for producing and directing live or filmed theatrical performances.

Do you remember the joy at Halloween of putting on masks, makeup, costumes and assuming the identity of someone (or something!) else? Have you ever seen someone play a role in a movie or television show and have a hard time remembering that s/he has an identity outside of that character? Do you believe it's important for a person to walk in other people's shoes? Do you love performing?

If you answered "yes" to any of these questions, then dramatic arts may be the programme of study for you.

Whether your interest in the dramatic arts began by reading a Shakespeare play in school, acting in a production, helping backstage, or watching a play in a theatre, this programme may be right for you. It provides an of all aspects of the dramatic arts, from dramatic literature and theory to the actual production of plays. This variety gives you the chance to explore the field and decide what aspect most interests you.

A background in the dramatic arts helps prepare you for careers as an actor, director and producer. If you'd prefer to stay offstage, you could also be a theatre historian, costume designer, stage manager, or director of an acting troupe.

As a student, you take courses in classical Greek tragedies, Shakespeare, modern world dramas and avant-garde plays. You study the developments not just in dramatic literature but also in dramatic theory and criticism. You might examine, for example, the changes in the relationship between actors and audience and how the shape and set-up of theaters reflected these changes.

In addition to theoretical courses, you also learn the practical elements of producing a play. You learn the fundamentals of acting, set design, sound and lighting. You also study the principles of directing and producing plays and other theatrical works. Many programmes allow you to specialize. You can concentrate your course work on learning the craft of acting. Or, you can focus on writing plays or directing films.

Many colleges and universities offer programmes in the dramatic arts where you can earn an associate, a bachelor's, a master's, or a doctoral degree. In general, a bachelor's degree takes about four years of full-time study and a master's degree about two years after that. A doctoral degree usually takes about three to four years after a master's degree.

If you want to pursue an associate degree, you typically need about two years. In some cases, you may be able to transfer these credits to a four-year bachelor's degree programme."

### College Preparation

Additional helpful preparation includes active participation in school or community theatre programmes.

Some schools may require you to audition and complete a personal interview as well. These requirements are generally for bachelor of fine arts degrees which tend to emphasize dramatic arts performance and production."

You can prepare for this programme by taking courses in high school that prepare you for college. This typically includes four years of English, three years of math, three years of social studies and two years of science. Some colleges also require two years of a second language.

*Public Speaking*

*Introduction to the Theatre*

*Drama, Acting and Performance*

*Drama, Stagecraft*

*Directing*

*Playwriting*

*History and Literature of the Theatre*

*Film and Videotape*

*Fine and Performing Art, Independent Study*

### Graduate Admissions

Admission to graduate programmes is competitive. You need a bachelor's degree and good grades. You also need to submit letters of recommendation and a personal statement Your bachelor's degree does not necessarily have to be in dramatic arts, although it would be helpful. However, you should take several related courses and participate in related extracurricular activities, where possible

If you want to pursue a doctoral degree, you do need a master's degree in this programme of study or a closely related one.

Additional requirements at many schools include:

- Graduate Record Exam (GRE) General
- Related experience
- Personal interview
- Scholarly writing sample

Programmes that are geared towards performance often require applicants to audition as well."

***Typical Course Work***

In this undergraduate programme, you typically take courses such as the following:

- Acting Theory and Performance
- Comparative Theatre and Drama
- Dialects
- Directing Theory and Production
- Dramatic Art
- Dramatic Theory and Criticism
- Fundamentals of Acting
- Fundamentals of Scene Design
- Lighting Design
- Makeup and Costume
- Modes of Drama
- Period Studies in Theatre
- Rise of Professional Theatre
- Scene Analysis
- Screenwriting and Playwriting
- Second Language(s)

- Stagecraft
- Survey of Dramatic Literature
- Technical Theatre
- Theatre and Society
- Theatre Arts
- Theatre History
- Theatre Workshop
- Trends in Contemporary Theatre
- Voice and Movement for the Stage

Graduate course work tends to vary depending on the programme. However, the general outline of a typical graduate curriculum looks like the following:

- Required courses
- Elective courses
- Comprehensive exams
- Thesis and thesis defense (master's degree only)
- Dissertation and dissertation defense (doctoral degree only)

Depending on your programme, you may also have opportunities for dramatic productions. An extensive production and analysis may count as your thesis in a master's degree programme that places more emphasis on performance than scholarship.

### *Things to Know*

Many schools offer different kinds of bachelor's and master's degrees depending on your desired concentration. Some of these degrees focus more on performance and production. Others combine their teaching of production skills with a broad liberal arts education.

Doctoral programmes, however, are mainly intended for people who want to pursue extensive research or teach at the university level. Acting in or working for various community theaters helps to get your name and talent into the field. Seek out summer and extracurricular acting or production gigs to gain a wider variety of acting experience.

Not all actors, especially beginning actors, can make a living for themselves only from acting. You may consider interning in stagecraft or theatre administration to widen your skills base.

Many private acting academies and conservatories concentrate only on performance. If you're truly committed to performance and performance only, you may consider programmes in these institutions. However, you should also keep in mind that some programmes also provide you with a broad liberal arts foundation which can help make you a more well-rounded person in general.

### *Fiber, Textile and Weaving Arts*

Programmes in fiber, textile and the weaving arts teach people how to create works of art from fabrics and fibres. Students learn how to operate looms and weave fibres into fabrics. They study ways to dye, knit and quilt fabrics.

When you study fiber, textile and weaving, you travel to a time before machines made weaving and knitting faster and easier. Even though mass production is faster, people appreciate work that is unique and shows the artist's personal touch. For that reason, handmade art using fibres and fabrics holds a respected place with artists and their customers.

Although you don't always need formal training to create works of art, going to art school can help you refine your skills and learn how to use them to earn a living. Formal training also allows you to share inspiration with other students who have similar interests and talents.

In fiber, textile and weaving programmes, your course work teaches you basic art principles such as art history, drawing and design. You then concentrate on your specific area of fiber art. This can mean constructing new fibres or coming up with original fabric designs. You can study different techniques for weaving rugs and blankets on a loom. Through your studies, you can even create new paper or wallpaper styles! You also learn basic skills such as how to use a loom, dye different fabrics and textiles and work with different types of wool and cloth. Many courses are designed to give you ample time in a studio where you create your own style and focus on a particular method of creating your pieces. In addition, several programmes offer courses in using computer graphics software as a design tool.

About 40 colleges and universities offer fiber, textile and weaving programmes that lead to the bachelor of fine arts (BFA) degree and the master of fine arts (MFA) degree. Community colleges and independent schools of art and design also offer studio training and programmes in fiber arts. They may lead to associate of art (AA) degrees. In some cases, schools offer certificate programmes. These are usually more technically focused and allow you to gain or update your skills in an area of fiber arts for personal enjoyment.

It takes four to five years after high school to earn a BFA degree and six to seven years to earn an MFA degree. The MFA is considered a "terminal" degree, meaning that you do not need a doctorate if you desire to teach at the college level. However, a few schools do offer doctorate degrees in fiber arts. Keep in mind that graduate study is almost always offered through a larger art and fine arts programme, so be sure to read this programme of study as well."

***College Preparation***

Many programmes require you to submit separate application materials in addition to your general college application. Usually you have to complete preliminary art courses, write a personal statement and submit a portfolio of work.

You can prepare for this programme by taking courses in high school that prepare you for college. This typically includes four years of English, three years of math, three years of social studies and two years of science. Some colleges also require two years of a second language.

*Clothing and Sewing*

*Art Appreciation*

*Art History*

*Art*

*Printmaking and Graphics*

*Textiles*

*Integrated Fine Arts*

*Graduate admissions*

Admission to graduate programmes is competitive. You need a bachelor's degree, good grades and good test scores.

Additional requirements at some schools include:

- Graduate Record Exam (GRE) General
- Undergraduate degree or significant course work in the fiber arts
- Letters of recommendation
- Portfolio review and personal interview

***Typical Course Work***

This programme typically includes courses in the following subjects:

- 2-D and 3-D Design
- Art History
- Basketry
- Batik
- Computer-Aided Design
- Design Principles
- Drawing
- Dyes and Colours
- Fiber Construction
- Fiber Forms
- Fiber Science
- Folk Art
- Leatherworking
- Loom Weaving
- Papermaking
- Philosophy of Art
- Rag Rug Weaving
- Silkscreen Techniques

- Textiles
- Wearable Art
- Yarns, Wools and Knitting

Graduate programmes in fiber arts typically require:

- Required courses
- Thesis and portfolio of finished work (master's degree)
- Preliminary exam (doctoral degree)
- Dissertation (doctoral degree)

***Things to Know***

You can begin developing your portfolio in high school with hobby and project work. As your skills develop, your portfolio improves.

In many cases you have to pay a fee in addition to regular course tuition. The fee covers the cost of art materials, which include dyes, fabrics, wool and other materials.

In some programmes you learn how to build your own loom. Many programmes offer personal studio space to fiber arts students. Usually this is for junior- and senior-level students.

Most BFA and MFA programmes require that you display your finished pieces in a showing at the school's local gallery. Also, some schools allow you to sell your work in shows that are open to the public. Many fiber, textile and weaving artists learn their art by working as helpers for experienced artists.

Independent art schools may focus more intensively on studio work and career preparation. Colleges and universities typically require certain general courses in addition to studio art requirements.

Most people with an art degree in an area of fiber arts become both professional artists and teachers. Many provide private instruction or teach at community colleges and local art centres, where classes are offered to the public.

## Theatre/Television Designer

Theatre/television designers create or select exterior and interior scenes for theatrical or television/film productions.

They then prepare a scale model or drawing and supervise the construction of their sets.

***Work Activities***

Theatre/television designers design and supervise the creation of exterior and interior settings for theatre, television and film productions. Designers read and analyse scripts then make decisions about the shape and size of sets, colour schemes and scenic features.

Designers begin by carrying out detailed research. If they are working on a period drama they need to find details about how people lived in the past. Details may include:

- what accommodation was like
- how people furnished rooms
- what colour schemes were popular at particular times.

They do this by consulting text books, period magazines, visiting museums and art galleries and examining old photographs. If they are collecting modern material they may spend time taking photographs, recording measurements and making rough sketches of everyday objects and buildings.

After the research stage, designers produce scale models and detailed working drawings called 'ground plans' and 'elevations'. These show how sets will look from above and from eye-level. Directors and performers can use these to determine entrances, exits and positions. Television and film directors can also use them to plan camera angles and to decide where to put sound equipment.

While sets are being built, designers find, buy, or hire props, which they use to dress the sets. Scenic artists add all the finishing touches. They paint backcloths, gauzes and floors and create finer details such as paintings, tapestries and wall hangings.

Designers work closely with directors, producers, stage/floor managers, costume designers, lighting designers, craftworkers and technicians.

The work may involve local travel, or more extensive travel in the UK and possibly overseas.

***Personal Qualities and Skills:*** You will need to pay great attention to detail as audiences soon spot any inaccuracies. You need to be able to express your ideas clearly through the drawings and models you produce. You will also need a thorough knowledge of technical and production processes.

***Pay and Opportunities:*** Pay rates for theatre designers vary depending on the media they work in: theatre, television or film. Theatre/television designers earn in the range of £15,000-£18,000 a year, rising to £24,000 - £30,500. Higher earners can make around £40,000 a year.

Designers work a basic 39-hour week. However, early starts, late finishes, evening and weekend work may be required. They may also be required to work intensively for periods, especially in the run-up to a production.

Designers work in theatre, television and film. Many are self-employed, freelance designers. They are usually employed on short contracts and may move from production to production between all three media.

Comparatively few posts in this area of design are available and there is fierce competition for freelance work.

The following information is sourced from government statistics. The government's definition of types of job is slightly different to that used in this programme. For this type of job, the most relevant Government-defined occupation is 'Product, clothing and related designers'.

In 2001 there were 2,600 people working as 'Product, clothing and related designers' in Scotland. 12 in every 10,000 employees working in Scotland were employed as 'Product, clothing and related designers'.

***Entry Routes and Training:*** The most common route into television and theatre design is through an appropriate degree. Suitable degree courses include Theatre Design, Interior Design and Architecture. Alternatively, students may study for an appropriate Higher National Diploma, or a suitable course offered by a theatre school or drama college.

There are also specialist courses at postgraduate level.

Entry to any course in art and design is very competitive.

***Qualifications:*** Usual entry requirements for Art and Design courses are:

- some Standard Grades for National Certificate level
- a suitable National Certificate or 1/3 Highers for Higher National Certificate/Higher National Diploma level
- 3 Highers (A-C), normally including English and Art and Design, plus 2 Standard Grades (1-3), for degree level

However, entry requirements vary between courses and alternative qualifications may be accepted - check prospectuses for details.

A central feature of the selection procedure for admission to any course in Art and Design is the submission of a comprehensive portfolio of work which demonstrates a candidate's potential.

Entry to all courses is very competitive.

***Adult Opportunities:*** Work experience gained as an assistant in a design studio or workshop, or in a design consultancy is valued. Commercial awareness and understanding of theatre and the broadcast industry is an advantage.

Suitable applicants aged 21 or over may do a college or university Access course. No formal qualifications are required to enter an Access course, but you should check individual course details. They lead to relevant degree/HND courses.

Many colleges relax the normal academic entry requirements for applicants with experience in arts, crafts or design.

Some employers may prefer a postgraduate course in a relevant subject.

To enter this work or relevant courses, you need to have a portfolio of work showing your creative ability.

- 22% of people in occupations such as design assistant work part-time.
- 9% have flexible hours.
- 2% of employees work on a temporary basis.

## Theatre Arts and Drama

*College of Liberal Arts*

*Theatre Arts and Drama*

Theatre arts encompasses live performance before an audience by actors, singers and dancers supported by musicians and backstage production technicians and artists. Drama includes the study of theatre history, the forms and structure of dramatic criticism and the theoretical foundations of theatrical art.

- Offered at WSU: Bachelor of arts, minor
- Available at: Pullman

***Facilities:*** The theatre programme is housed in Daggy Hall, which contains two performance spaces: R.R. Jones Theatre and the Wadleigh Theatre. The former has a large, flexible stage capable of both proscenium and thrust arrangements and seats 467; the latter, a small "black box" often used for experimental work, has 148 moveable seats, which permits a wide range of audience-performer relationships. Both facilities are equipped with current electronic lighting and audio boards. (A third theatre on campus, Bryan Auditorium, is also available for productions. It is a traditional proscenium house seating 800.) Classrooms, scene and costume shops, design lab, make-up and dressing rooms and storage space complete the layout.

***Careers in Theatre Arts and Drama:*** Over the past decade, the theatre programme has served as a major source of theatre technicians and artists working professionally in such venues as Empty Space, Intiman, Tacoma Actors Guild and Portland Center Stage. Freelance designers and many drama teachers at Washington high schools and community colleges have trained at WSU. In addition, because of the program's liberal arts approach, WSU graduates are prepared to assume management positions in the business world that call for strong communication and team organization skills and analytical thinking.

Suggested Strengths, Interests and Preparation:

- Some previous theatre experience in high school or community college
- A sincere interest in studying theatre

### *Scholarships and Financial Aid*

The theatre programme offers various scholarships and merit awards for undergraduates. The Visual and Performing Arts Scholarship is awarded to entering freshmen and transfer students based on talent and background. Other endowed service scholarships are presented annually to active theatre majors who exhibit achievement and dedication in theatre production and academics. All students are encouraged to apply for University-wide scholarships and financial aid as well.

## Actors, Producers and Directors

***Significant Points:*** Actors endure long periods of unemployment, intense competition for roles and frequent rejections in auditions.

Formal training through a university or acting conservatory is typical; however, many actors, producers and directors find work on the basis of their experience and talent alone.

Because earnings for actors are erratic, many supplement their incomes by holding jobs in other fields.

***Nature of the Work:*** Actors, producers and directors express ideas and create images in theatre, film, radio, television and other performing arts media. They interpret a writer's script to entertain, inform, or instruct an audience. Although the most famous actors, producers and directors work in film, network television, or theatre in New York or Los Angeles, far more work in local or regional television studios, theaters, or film production companies preparing advertising, public-relations, or independent, small-scale movie productions.

*Actors* perform in stage, radio, television, video, or motion picture productions. They also work in cabarets, nightclubs, theme parks, commercials and "industrial" films produced for training and educational purposes. Most actors struggle to find steady work; only a few ever achieve recognition as stars. Some well-known, experienced performers may be cast in supporting roles. Others work as "extras," with no lines to deliver, or make brief, cameo appearances, speaking only one or two lines. Some actors do voiceover and narration work for advertisements, animated features, books on tape and other electronic media, including computer games. They also teach in high school or university drama departments, acting conservatories, or public programmes.

*Producers* are entrepreneurs, overseeing the business and financial decisions of a motion picture, made-for-television feature, or stage production. They select scripts, approve the development of ideas for the production, arrange financing and determine the size and cost of the endeavour. Producers hire or approve the selection of directors, principal cast members and key production staff members. They also negotiate contracts with artistic and design personnel in accordance with collective bargaining agreements and guarantee payment of salaries, rent and other expenses. Television and radio producers determine which programmes, episodes, or news segments get aired. They may research material, write scripts and oversee the production of individual pieces. Producers in any medium coordinate the activities of writers, directors, managers and agents to ensure that each project stays on schedule and within budget.

*Directors* are responsible for the creative decisions of a production. They interpret scripts, express concepts to set and costume designers, audition and select cast members, conduct rehearsals and direct the work of cast and crew. They approve the design elements of a production, including the sets, costumes, choreography and music. Assistant directors cue the performers and technicians to make entrances or to make light, sound, or set changes.

***Working Conditions:*** Actors, producers and directors work under constant pressure. Many face stress from the continual need to find their next job. To succeed, actors, producers and directors need patience and commitment to their craft. Actors strive to deliver flawless performances, often while working under undesirable and unpleasant conditions. Producers and directors organize rehearsals and meet with writers, designers, financial backers and production technicians. They experience stress not only from these activities, but also from the need to adhere to budgets, union work rules and production schedules.

Acting assignments typically are short term—ranging from a day to a few months—which means that actors frequently experience long periods of unemployment between jobs. The uncertain nature of the work results in unpredictable earnings and intense competition for even the lowest-paid jobs. Often, actors, producers and directors must hold other jobs in order to sustain a living.

When performing, actors typically work long, irregular hours. For example, stage actors may perform one show at night while rehearsing another during the day. They also might travel with a show when it tours the country. Movie actors may work on location, sometimes under adverse weather conditions and may spend considerable time in their trailers or dressing rooms waiting to perform their scenes. Actors who perform in a television series often appear on camera with little preparation time, because scripts tend to be revised frequently or even written moments before taping. Those who appear live or before a studio audience must be able to handle impromptu situations and calmly ad lib, or substitute, lines when necessary.

Evening and weekend work is a regular part of a stage actor's life. On weekends, more than one performance may be held per day. Actors and directors working on movies or television programmes—especially those who shoot on location—may work in the early morning or late evening hours to film night scenes or tape scenes inside public facilities outside of normal business hours.

Actors should be in good physical condition and have the necessary stamina and coordination to move about theatre stages and large movie and television studio lots. They also need to manoeuvre about complex technical sets while staying in character and projecting their voices audibly. Actors must be fit to endure heat from stage or studio lights and the weight of heavy costumes. Producers and directors ensure the safety of actors by conducting extra rehearsals on the set so that the actors can learn the layout of set pieces and props, by allowing time for warmups and stretching exercises to guard against physical and vocal injuries and by providing an adequate number of breaks to prevent heat exhaustion and dehydration.

***Training, Other Qualifications and Advancement:*** Persons who become actors, producers and directors follow many paths. Employers generally look for people with the creative instincts, innate talent and intellectual capacity to perform. Actors should possess a passion for performing and enjoy entertaining others. Most aspiring actors participate in high school and college plays, work in college radio stations, or perform with local community theatre groups. Local and regional theatre experience and work in summer stock, on cruise lines, or in theme parks helps many young actors hone their skills and earn qualifying credits toward membership in one of the actors' unions. Union membership and work experience in smaller communities may lead to work in larger cities, notably New York or Los Angeles. In television and film, actors and directors typically start in smaller television markets or with independent movie production companies and then work their way up to larger media markets and major studio productions. Intense competition, however, can be expected at each level, because ever more applicants will be vying for increasingly fewer numbers of available positions.

Formal dramatic training, either through an acting conservatory or a university programme, generally is necessary, but some people successfully enter the field without it. Most people studying for a bachelor's degree take courses in radio and television broadcasting, communications, film, theatre, drama, or dramatic literature. Many continue their academic training and receive a Master of Fine Arts (MFA) degree. Advanced curricula may include courses in stage speech and movement, directing, playwriting and design, as well as intensive acting workshops. The National Association of Schools of Theatre accredits 135 programmes in theatre arts. A few people go into acting following successful careers in other fields, such as broadcasting or announcing.

Actors, regardless of experience level, may pursue workshop training through acting conservatories or mentoring by a drama coach. Actors also research roles so that they can grasp concepts quickly during rehearsals and understand the story's setting and background. Sometimes actors learn a foreign language or train with a dialect coach to develop an accent to make their characters more realistic.

Actors need talent, creativity and training that will enable them to portray different characters. Because competition for parts is fierce, versatility and a wide range of related performance skills, such as singing, dancing, skating, juggling, or miming are especially useful. Experience in horseback riding, fencing, or stage combat also can lift some actors above the average and get them noticed by producers and directors. Actors must have poise, stage presence, the capability to affect an audience and the ability to follow direction. Modelling experience also may be helpful. Physical appearance, such as possessing the right size, weight, or features, often is a deciding factor in being selected for particular roles.

Many professional actors rely on agents or managers to find work, negotiate contracts and plan their careers. Agents generally earn a percentage of the pay specified in an actor's contract. Other actors rely solely on attending open auditions for parts. Trade publications list the times, dates and locations of these auditions.

To become a movie extra, one usually must be listed by a casting agency, such as Central Casting, a no-fee agency that supplies extras to the major movie studios in Hollywood. Applicants are accepted only when the numbers of persons of a particular type on the list—for example, athletic young women, old men, or small children—falls below the foreseeable need. In recent years, only a very small proportion of applicants have succeeded in being listed.

There are no specific training requirements for producers. They come from many different backgrounds. Talent, experience and business acumen are important determinants of success for producers. Actors, writers, film editors and business managers commonly enter the field. Also, many people who start out as actors move into directing, while some directors might try their hand at acting. Producers often start in a theatrical management office, working for a press agent, managing director, or business manager. Some start in a performing arts union or service organization. Others work behind the scenes with successful directors, serve on boards of directors, or promote their own projects. No formal training exists for producers; however, a growing number of colleges and universities now offer degree programmes in arts management and in managing nonprofits.

As the reputations and box-office draw of actors, producers and directors grow, they might work on bigger budget productions, on network or syndicated broadcasts, or in more prestigious theaters. Actors may advance to lead roles and receive star billing. A few actors move into acting-related jobs, such as drama coaches or directors of stage, television, radio, or motion picture productions. Some teach drama privately or in colleges and universities.

***Employment:*** In 2004, actors, producers and directors held about 157,000 jobs, primarily in motion picture and video, performing arts and broadcast industries. Because many others were between jobs, the total number of actors, producers and directors available for work was higher. Employment in the theatre and other performing arts companies, is cyclical—higher in the fall and spring seasons—and concentrated in New York and other major cities with large commercial houses for musicals and touring productions. Also, many cities support established professional regional theaters that operate on a seasonal or year-round basis. About one-fourth of actors, producers and directors were self-employed.

Actors, producers and directors may find work in summer festivals, on cruise lines and in theme parks. Many smaller, nonprofit professional companies, such as repertory companies, dinner theaters and theaters affiliated with drama schools, acting conservatories and universities, provide employment opportunities for local amateur talent and professional entertainers. Auditions typically are held in New York for many productions across the country and for shows that go on the road.

Employment in motion pictures and in films for television is centred in New York and Hollywood. However, small studios are located throughout the country. Many films are shot on location and may employ local professional and nonprofessional actors. In television, opportunities are concentrated in the network centres of New York and Los Angeles, but cable television services and local television stations around the country also employ many actors, producers and directors.

A growing number of actors and other entertainers appear on the payrolls of firms who do accounting and payroll work. Frequently film production companies will hire actors through casting agencies or contract out their payroll services to accounting firms. Similarly, many actors arrange with a company in this industry to collect their pay from producers or entrepreneurs; make the appropriate deductions for taxes, union dues and benefits payments; and pay them their net earnings for each job. The result of these increasingly more common payroll arrangements is that many actors appear to be working for accounting offices, rather than for the theatrical production companies or studios where they actually perform.

***Job Outlook:*** Employment of actors, producers and directors is expected to grow about as fast as the average for all occupations through 2014. Although a growing number of people will aspire to enter these professions, many will leave the field early because the work—when it is available—is hard, the hours are long and the pay is low. Competition for jobs will be stiff, in part because the large number of highly trained and talented actors auditioning for roles generally exceeds the number of parts that become available. Only performers with the most stamina and talent will find regular employment.

Expanding cable and satellite television operations, increasing production and distribution of major studio and independent films and continued growth and development of interactive media, such as direct-for-Web movies and videos, should increase demand for actors, producers and directors. However, greater emphasis on national, rather than local, entertainment productions may restrict employment opportunities in the broadcasting industry.

Venues for live entertainment, such as Broadway and Off-Broadway theaters, touring productions and repertory theaters in many major metropolitan areas, as well as theme parks and resorts, are expected to offer many job opportunities. However, prospects in these venues are more variable, because they fluctuate with economic conditions.

***Earnings:*** Median hourly earnings of actors were $11.28 in May 2004. The middle 50 percent earned between $7.75 and $30.76. The lowest 10 percent earned less than $6.63 and the highest 10 percent earned more than $56.48. Median annual earnings were $15.20 in performing arts companies and $9.27 in motion picture and video industries. Annual earnings data for actors were not available because of the wide variation in the number of hours worked by actors and the short-term nature of many jobs, which may last for 1 day or 1 week; it is extremely rare for actors to have guaranteed employment that exceeded 3 to 6 months.

Minimum salaries, hours of work and other conditions of employment are covered in collective bargaining agreements between the producers and the unions representing workers. The Actors' Equity Association (Equity) represents stage actors; the Screen Actors Guild (SAG) covers actors in motion pictures, including television, commercials and films; and the American Federation of Television and Radio Artists (AFTRA) represents television and radio studio performers. Some actors who regularly work in several media find it advantageous to join multiple unions, while SAG and AFTRA may share jurisdiction for work in additional areas, such as the production of training or educational films not slated for broadcast, television commercial work and interactive media. While these unions generally determine minimum salaries, any actor or director may negotiate for a salary higher than the minimum.

Under terms of a joint SAG and AFTRA contract covering all unionized workers, motion picture and television actors with speaking parts earned a minimum daily rate of $716 or $2,483 for a 5-day week as of October 1, 2005. Actors also receive contributions to their health and pension plans and additional compensation for reruns and foreign telecasts of the productions in which they appear.

According to Equity, the minimum weekly salary for actors in Broadway productions as of June 30, 2005 was $1,422. Actors in Off-Broadway theaters received minimums ranging from $493 to $857 a week as of October 23, 2005, depending on the seating capacity of the theatre. Regional theaters that operate under an Equity agreement pay actors $531 to $800 per week. For touring productions, actors receive an additional $777 per week for living expenses ($819 per week in higher cost cities). New terms were negotiated under an "experimental touring programme" provision for lower budget musicals that tour to smaller cities or that perform for fewer performances at each stop. In an effort to increase the number of paid workweeks while on tour, actors may be paid less than the full production rate for touring shows in exchange for higher per diems and profit participation.

Some well-known actors—stars—earn well above the minimum; their salaries are many times the figures cited, creating the false impression that all actors are highly paid. For example, of the nearly 100,000 SAG members, only about 50 might be considered stars. The average income that SAG members earn from acting—less than $5,000 a year—is low because employment is sporadic. Therefore, most actors must supplement their incomes by holding jobs in other occupations.

Many actors who work more than a qualifying number of days, or weeks per year or earn over a set minimum pay, are covered by a union health, welfare and pension fund, which includes hospitalization insurance to which employers contribute. Under some employment conditions, Equity and AFTRA members receive paid vacations and sick leave.

Median annual earnings of salaried producers and directors were $52,840 in May 2004. The middle 50 percent earned between $35,550 and $87,980. Median annual earnings were $75,200 in motion picture and video industries and $43,890 in radio and television broadcasting.

Many stage directors belong to the Society of Stage Directors and Choreographers (SSDC) and film and television directors belong to the Directors Guild of America. Earnings of stage directors vary greatly. According to the SSDC, summer theaters offer compensation, including "royalties" (based on the number of performances), usually ranging from $2,500 to $8,000 for a 3- to 4-week run. Directing a production at a dinner theatre generally will pay less than directing one at a summer theatre, but has more potential for generating income from royalties. Regional theaters may hire directors for longer periods, increasing compensation accordingly. The highest-paid directors work on Broadway and commonly earn $50,000 per show. However, they also receive payment in the form of royalties—a negotiated percentage of gross box office receipts—that can exceed their contract fee for long-running box office successes.

Stage producers seldom get a set fee; instead, they get a percentage of a show's earnings or ticket sales.

## Announcers

***Significant Points:*** Competition for announcer jobs will continue to be keen.

Jobs at small stations usually have low pay, but offer the best opportunities for inexperienced announcers.

Related work experience at a campus radio station or as an intern at a commercial station can be helpful in breaking into the occupation.

Employment is projected to decline.

***Nature of the Work:*** Announcers in radio and television perform a variety of tasks on and off the air. They announce station programme information, such as programme schedules and station breaks for commercials, or public service information and they introduce and close programmes. Announcers read prepared scripts or ad lib commentary on the air, as they present news, sports, the weather, time and commercials. If a written script is required, they may do the research and writing. Announcers also interview guests and moderate panels or discussions. Some provide commentary for the audience during sporting events, at parades and on other occasions. Announcers often are well known to radio and television audiences and may make promotional appearances and do remote broadcasts for their stations.

Radio announcers who broadcast music often are called *disc jockeys* (*DJs*). Some DJs specialize in one kind of music, announcing selections as they air them. Most DJs do not select much of the music they play (although they often did so in the past); instead, they follow schedules of commercials, talk and music provided to them by management. While on the air, DJs comment on the music, weather and traffic. They may take requests from listeners, interview guests and manage listener contests.

*Newscasters*, or *anchors*, work at large stations and specialize in news, sports, or weather. *Show hosts* may specialize in a certain area of interest, such as politics, personal finance, sports, or health. They contribute to the preparation of the program's content, interview guests and discuss issues with viewers, listeners, or the studio audience.

Announcers at smaller stations may cover all of these areas and tend to have more off-air duties as well. They may operate the control board, monitor the transmitter, sell commercial time to advertisers, keep a log of the station's daily programming and produce advertisements and other recorded material. Advances in technology make it possible for announcers to do some work previously performed by broadcast technicians. At many music stations, the announcer is simultaneously responsible both for announcing and for operating the control board, which is used to broadcast programming, commercials and public-service announcements according to the station's schedule. Public radio and television announcers are involved in station fundraising efforts.

Changes in technology have led to more remote operation of stations. Several stations in different locations of the same region may be operated from one office. Some stations operate overnight without any staff, playing programming from a satellite feed or using programming that was recorded earlier, including segments from announcers.

*Public address system announcers* provide information to the audience at sporting, performing arts and other events. Some DJs announce and play music at clubs, dances, restaurants and weddings. They generally have their own equipment with which to produce announcements and other material and they rent their services out on a job-by-job basis.

Announcers frequently participate in community activities. Sports announcers, for example, may serve as masters of ceremonies at sports club banquets or may greet customers at openings of sporting goods stores.

***Working Conditions:*** Announcers usually work in well-lighted, air-conditioned, soundproof studios. The broadcast day is long for radio and TV stations—many are on the air 24 hours a day—so announcers can expect to work unusual hours. Many present early-morning shows, when most people are getting ready for work or commuting, while others do late-night programmes. The shifts, however, may not be as varied as in the past because new technology is allowing stations to prerecord programmes and air them at a later time, especially for the overnight hours.

Announcers often work within tight schedules, which can be physically and mentally stressful. For many announcers, the intangible rewards—creative work, many personal contacts and the satisfaction of becoming widely known—far outweigh the disadvantages of irregular and often unpredictable hours, work pressures and disrupted personal lives.

***Training, Other Qualifications and Advancement:*** Entry into this occupation is highly competitive. Formal training in broadcasting from a college, a technical school, or a private broadcasting school is valuable. These programmes prepare students to work with emerging technologies, a skill that is becoming increasingly important. Many announcers have a bachelor's degree in a major such as communications, broadcasting, or journalism. Station officials pay particular attention to taped auditions that show an applicant's delivery and—in television—appearance and style in commercials, news reports and interviews.

Those hired by television stations usually start out as production assistants, researchers, or reporters and are given a chance to move into announcing if they show an aptitude for "on-air" work. A beginner's chance of landing an on-air job is remote. The best chances for an on-air job for inexperienced announcers may be as a substitute for a familiar announcer at a small radio station or on the late-night shift at a larger station. In radio, newcomers usually start out taping interviews and operating equipment.

Announcers usually begin at a station in a small community and, if they are qualified, may move to a better paying job in a large city. They also may advance by hosting a regular programme as a disc jockey, sportscaster, or other specialist. Competition for employment by networks is particularly intense and employers look for college graduates with at least several years of successful announcing experience.

Announcers must have a pleasant and well-controlled voice, good timing, excellent pronunciation and correct grammar. College broadcasting programmes offer courses, such as voice and diction, to help students improve their vocal qualities. Television announcers need a neat, pleasing appearance as well. Knowledge of theatre, sports, music, business, politics and other subjects likely to be covered in broadcasts improves one's chances for success.

Announcers should be capable of using computers, editing equipment and other broadcast-related devices because new advances in technology allow more of these responsibilities to be incorporated into an announcer's work. Announcers also need strong writing skills, because they normally write their own material. In addition, they should be able to ad lib all or part of a show and to work under tight deadlines. The most successful announcers attract a large audience by combining a pleasing personality and voice with an appealing style.

High school and college courses in English, public speaking, drama, foreign languages and computer science are valuable and hobbies such as sports and music are additional assets. Students may gain valuable experience at campus radio or TV facilities and at commercial stations while serving as interns. Paid or unpaid internships provide students with hands-on training and the chance to establish contacts in the industry. Unpaid interns often receive college credit and are allowed to observe and assist station employees. Although the Fair Labour Standards Act limits the amount of work that unpaid interns may perform in a station, unpaid internships are more common than paid internships. Unpaid internships sometimes lead to paid internships, however, which are valuable because interns do work ordinarily performed by regular employees and may even go on the air.

Individuals considering enrolling in a broadcasting school should contact personnel managers of radio and television stations, as well as broadcasting trade organizations, to determine the school's reputation for producing suitably trained candidates.

***Employment:*** Announcers held about 69,000 jobs in 2004. About 57 percent were employed in broadcasting. Another 27 percent were self-employed freelance announcers who sold their services for individual assignments to networks and stations, to advertising agencies and other independent producers, or to sponsors of local events. About 30 percent of all announcers worked part time.

***Job Outlook:*** Competition for jobs as announcers will be keen because the broadcasting field attracts many more jobseekers than there are jobs. Small radio stations are more inclined to hire beginners, but the pay is low. Applicants who have completed internships and those with related work experience usually receive preference for available positions. Because competition for ratings is so intense in major metropolitan areas, large stations will continue to seek announcers who have proven that they can attract and retain a sizable audience. Announcers who are knowledgeable about business, consumer and health news also may have an advantage over others. While subject-matter specialization is more common at large stations and the networks, many small stations also encourage it.

Employment of announcers is projected to decline through 2014 because of the lack of growth in the number of new radio and television stations and the consolidation of existing stations. Some job openings will arise from the need to replace those who transfer to other kinds of work or leave the labour force. In some cases, announcers leave the field because they cannot advance to better paying jobs. Changes in station ownership, format and ratings frequently cause periods of unemployment for many announcers.

Increasing consolidation of radio and television stations, the advent of new technology and growth of alternative media sources, such as cable television and satellite radio, will contribute to the expected decline in employment of announcers. Consolidation among broadcasting companies may lead to an increased use of syndicated programming and programmes originating outside a station's viewing or listening area. Digital technology is increasing the productivity of announcers, reducing the time required to edit material or perform other off-air technical and production work.

***Earnings:*** Salaries in broadcasting vary widely, but generally are relatively low, except for announcers who work for large stations in major markets or for networks. Earnings are higher in television than in radio and higher in commercial broadcasting than in public broadcasting.

Median hourly earnings of wage and salary radio and television announcers in May 2004 were $10.64. The middle 50 percent earned between $7.43 and $16.81. The lowest 10 percent earned less than $6.16 and the highest 10 percent earned more than $27.61. Median hourly earnings of radio and television announcers were $10.49 in the radio and television broadcasting industry.

Median hourly earnings of wage and salary public address and other system announcers in May 2004 were $10.56. The middle 50 percent earned between $7.72 and $16.24. The lowest 10 percent earned less than $6.33 and the highest 10 percent earned more than $23.90.

### *News Analysts, Reporters and Correspondents*

***Significant Points:*** Competition will be keen for jobs at large metropolitan and national newspapers, broadcast stations and magazines; most entry-level openings arise at small broadcast stations and publications.

Most employers prefer individuals with a bachelor's degree in journalism or mass communications and experience gained at school newspapers or broadcasting stations or through internships with news organizations.

Jobs often involve irregular hours, night and weekend work and pressure to meet deadlines.

Slower than average employment growth is expected.

***Nature of the Work:*** News analysts, reporters and correspondents gather information, prepare stories and make broadcasts that inform us about local, State, national and international events; present points of view on current issues; and report on the actions of public officials, corporate executives, interest groups and others who exercise power.

*News analysts*—also called *newscasters* or *news anchors*—examine, interpret and broadcast news received from various sources. News anchors present news stories and introduce videotaped news or live transmissions from on-the-scene reporters. Newscasters at large stations and networks usually specialize in a particular type of news, such as sports or weather. *Weathercasters*, also called weather reporters, report current and forecasted weather conditions. They gather information from national satellite weather services, wire services and local and regional weather bureaus. Some weathercasters are trained meteorologists and can develop their own weather forecasts. *Sportscasters* select, write and deliver sports news. This may include interviews with sports personalities and coverage of games and other sporting events. *News correspondents* report on news occurring in the large U.S. and foreign cities where they are stationed.

In covering a story, *reporters* investigate leads and news tips, look at documents, observe events at the scene and interview people. Reporters take notes and also may take photographs or shoot videos. At their office, they organize the material, determine the focus or emphasis, write their stories and edit accompanying video material. Many reporters enter information or write stories using laptop computers and electronically submit the material to their offices from remote locations. In some cases, *newswriters* write a story from information collected and submitted by reporters. Radio and television reporters often compose stories and report "live" from the scene. At times, they later tape an introduction to or commentary on their story in the studio. Some journalists also interpret the news or offer opinions to readers, viewers, or listeners. In this role, they are called *commentators* or *columnists.*

General-assignment reporters write about newsworthy occurrences—such as accidents, political rallies, visits of celebrities, or business closings—as assigned. Large newspapers and radio and television stations assign reporters to gather news about specific topics, such as crime or education. Some reporters specialize in fields such as health, politics, foreign affairs, sports, theatre, consumer affairs, social events, science, business, or religion. Investigative reporters cover stories that may take many days or weeks of information gathering. Some publications use teams of reporters instead of assigning each reporter one specific topic, allowing reporters to cover a greater variety of stories. News teams may include reporters, editors, graphic artists and photographers working together to complete a story. Reporters on small publications cover all aspects of the news. They take photographs, write headlines, lay out pages, edit wire-service stories and write editorials. Some also solicit advertisements, sell subscriptions and perform general office work.

***Working Conditions:*** The work of news analysts, reporters and correspondents is usually hectic. They are under great pressure to meet deadlines. Broadcasts sometimes are aired with little or no time for preparation. Some news analysts, reporters and correspondents work in comfortable, private offices; others work in large rooms filled with the sound of keyboards and computer printers, as well as the voices of other reporters. Curious onlookers, police, or other emergency workers can distract those reporting from the scene for radio and television. Covering wars, political uprisings, fires, floods and similar events is often dangerous.

Working hours vary. Reporters on morning papers often work from late afternoon until midnight. Radio and television reporters usually are assigned to a day or evening shift. Magazine reporters usually work during the day.

Reporters sometimes have to change their work hours to meet a deadline or to follow late-breaking developments. Their work demands long hours, irregular schedules and some travel. Because many stations and networks are on the air 24 hours a day, newscasters can expect to work unusual hours.

***Training, Other Qualifications and Advancement:*** Most employers prefer individuals with a bachelor's degree in journalism or mass communications, but some hire graduates with other majors. They look for experience at school newspapers or broadcasting stations and internships with news organizations. Large-city newspapers and stations also may prefer candidates with a degree in a subject-matter specialty such as economics, political science, or business. Some large newspapers and broadcasters may hire only experienced reporters.

More than 1,200 institutions offer programmes in communications, journalism and related programmes. In 2004, 104 of these were accredited by the Accrediting Council on Education in Journalism and Mass Communications. About three-fourths of the courses in a typical curriculum are in liberal arts; the remaining courses are in journalism. Examples of journalism courses are introductory mass media, basic reporting and copy editing, history of journalism and press law and ethics. Students planning a career in broadcasting take courses in radio and television news and production. Those planning newspaper or magazine careers usually specialize in news-editorial journalism. To create stories for online media, they need to learn to use computer software to combine online story text with audio and video elements and graphics.

Some schools also offer a master's or Ph.D. degree in journalism. Some graduate programmes are intended primarily as preparation for news careers, while others prepare journalism teachers, researchers and theorists and advertising and public relations workers. A graduate degree may help those looking to advance.

High school courses in English, journalism and social studies provide a good foundation for college programmes. Useful college liberal arts courses include English with an emphasis on writing, sociology, political science, economics, history and psychology. Courses in computer science, business and speech are useful as well. Fluency in a foreign language is necessary in some jobs. Reporters typically need more than good word-processing skills.

Computer graphics and desktop-publishing skills also are useful. Computer-assisted reporting involves the use of computers to analyze data in search of a story. This technique and the interpretation of the results require computer skills and familiarity with databases. Knowledge of news photography also is valuable for entry-level positions, which sometimes combine the responsibilities of a reporter with those of a camera operator or photographer.

Employers report that practical experience is the most important part of education and training. Upon graduation many students already have gained much practical experience through part-time or summer jobs or through internships with news organizations. Most newspapers, magazines and broadcast news organizations offer reporting and editing internships. Work on high school and college newspapers, at broadcasting stations, or on community papers or U.S. Armed Forces publications also provides practical training. In addition, journalism scholarships, fellowships and assistantships awarded to college journalism students by universities, newspapers, foundations and professional organizations are helpful. Experience as a stringer or freelancer—a part-time reporter who is paid only for stories printed—is advantageous.

Reporters should be dedicated to providing accurate and impartial news. Accuracy is important, both to serve the public and because untrue or libelous statements can lead to lawsuits. A nose for news, persistence, initiative, poise, resourcefulness, a good memory and physical stamina are important, as is the emotional stability to deal with pressing deadlines, irregular hours and dangerous assignments. Broadcast reporters and news analysts must be comfortable on camera. All reporters must be at ease in unfamiliar places and with a variety of people. Positions involving on-air work require a pleasant voice and appearance.

Most reporters start at small publications or broadcast stations as general assignment reporters or copy editors. They are usually assigned to cover court proceedings and civic and club meetings, summarize speeches and write obituaries. With experience, they report more difficult assignments or specialize in a particular field. Large publications and stations hire few recent graduates; as a rule, they require new reporters to have several years of experience.

Some news analysts and reporters can advance by moving to larger newspapers or stations. A few experienced reporters become columnists, correspondents, writers, announcers, or public relations specialists. Others become editors in print journalism or programme managers in broadcast journalism, who supervise reporters. Some eventually become broadcasting or publishing industry managers.

***Employment:*** News analysts, reporters and correspondents held about 64,000 jobs in 2004. About 61 percent worked for newspaper, periodical, book and directory publishers. Another 25 percent worked in radio and television broadcasting. About 7 percent of news analysts, reporters and correspondents were self-employed.

***Job Outlook:*** Competition will continue to be keen for jobs on large metropolitan and national newspapers, broadcast stations and networks and magazines. Most job opportunities will be with small-town and suburban newspapers and radio and television stations. Talented writers who can handle highly specialized scientific or technical subjects have an advantage. Also, newspapers increasingly are hiring stringers and freelancers.

Journalism graduates have the background for work in closely related fields such as advertising and public relations and many take jobs in these fields. Other graduates accept sales, managerial, or other nonmedia positions.

Employment of news analysts, reporters and correspondents is expected to grow more slowly than average for all occupations through the year 2014. Many factors will contribute to the limited job growth in this occupation. Consolidation and convergence should continue in the publishing and broadcasting industries. As a result, companies will be better able to allocate their news analysts, reporters and correspondents to cover news stories. Constantly improving technology also is allowing workers to do their jobs more efficiently, another factor that will limit the number of workers needed to cover a story or certain type of news. However, the continued demand for news will create some job opportunities. For example, some job growth likely will occur in newer media areas, such as online newspapers and magazines. Job openings also will result from the need to replace workers who leave their occupations permanently; some news analysts, reporters and correspondents find the work too stressful and hectic or do not like the lifestyle and transfer to other occupations.

The number of job openings in the newspaper and broadcasting industries—in which news analysts, reporters and correspondents are employed—is sensitive to economic ups and downs because these industries depend on advertising revenue.

***Earnings:*** Salaries for news analysts, reporters and correspondents vary widely. Median annual earnings of reporters and correspondents were $31,320 in May 2004. The middle 50 percent earned between $22,900 and $47,860. The lowest 10 percent earned less than $18,470 and the highest 10 percent earned more than $68,250. Median annual earnings of reporters and correspondents were $30,070 in newspaper, periodical, book and directory publishers and $34,050 in radio and television broadcasting.

Median annual earnings of broadcast news analysts were $36,980 in May 2004. The middle 50 percent earned between $25,560 and $68,440. The lowest 10 percent earned less than $19,040 and the highest 10 percent earned more than $122,800. Median annual earnings of broadcast news analysts were $37,840 in radio and television broadcasting.

### *Writers and Editors*

***Significant Points:*** Most jobs in this occupation require a college degree in communications, journalism, or English, although a degree in a technical subject may be useful for technical-writing positions.

The outlook for most writing and editing jobs is expected to be competitive because many people are attracted to the occupation.

Online publications and services are growing in number and sophistication, spurring the demand for writers and editors, especially those with Web experience.

***Nature of the Work:*** Communicating through the written word, writers and editors generally fall into one of three categories. *Writers and authors* develop original fiction and nonfiction for books, magazines, trade journals, online publications, company newsletters, radio and television broadcasts, motion pictures and advertisements. *Editors* examine proposals and select material for publication or broadcast. They review and revise a writer's work for publication or dissemination. *Technical writers* develop technical materials, such as equipment manuals, appendixes, or operating and maintenance instructions. They also may assist in layout work.

Most writers and editors have at least a basic familiarity with technology, regularly using personal computers, desktop or electronic publishing systems, scanners and other electronic communications equipment. Many writers prepare material directly for the Internet. For example, they may write for electronic newspapers or magazines, create short fiction or poetry, or produce technical documentation that is available only online. Also, they may write text for Web sites. These writers should be knowledgeable about graphic design, page layout and multimedia software. In addition, they should be familiar with interactive technologies of the Web so that they can blend text, graphics and sound together.

Writers—especially of nonfiction—are expected to establish their credibility with editors and readers through strong research and the use of appropriate sources and citations. Sustaining high ethical standards and meeting publication deadlines are essential.

*Creative writers, poets and lyricists,* including novelists, playwrights and screenwriters, create original works—such as prose, poems, plays and song lyrics—for publication or performance. Some works may be commissioned by a sponsor;

others may be written for hire (on the basis of the completion of a draft or an outline).

Nonfiction writers either propose a topic or are assigned one, often by an editor or publisher. They gather information about the topic through personal observation, library and Internet research and interviews. Writers then select the material they want to use, organize it and use the written word to express ideas and convey information. Writers also revise or rewrite sections, searching for the best organization or the right phrasing. *Copy writers* prepare advertising copy for use by publication or broadcast media or to promote the sale of goods and services. *Newsletter writers* produce information for distribution to association memberships, corporate employees, organizational clients, or the public.

Freelance writers sell their work to publishers, publication enterprises, manufacturing firms, public relations departments, or advertising agencies. Sometimes, they contract with publishers to write a book or an article. Others may be hired to complete specific assignments, such as writing about a new product or technique.

Bloggers write for the Internet. Most bloggers write personal reflections on a subject of close personal or professional interest. Some blogs take the form of a personal diary; others read like reports from the field—first-hand, subjective accounts of an event or an activity. Most blogs are written for recreational reasons with little expectation of earning a fee; however, some blogs promote a business or support a cause and may generate interest or income through other activities.

*Editors* review, rewrite and edit the work of writers. They may also do original writing. An editor's responsibilities vary with the employer and type and level of editorial position held. Editorial duties may include planning the content of books, technical journals, trade magazines and other general-interest publications. Editors also decide what material will appeal to readers, review and edit drafts of books and articles, offer comments to improve the work and suggest possible titles. In addition, they may oversee the production of the publications. In the book-publishing industry, an editor's primary responsibility is to review proposals for books and decide whether to buy the publication rights from the author.

Major newspapers and newsmagazines usually employ several types of editors. The *executive editor* oversees *assistant editors,* who have responsibility for particular subjects, such as local news, international news, feature stories, or sports. Executive editors generally have the final say about what stories are published and how they are covered. The *managing editor* usually is responsible for the daily operation of the news department. *Assignment editors* determine which reporters will cover a given story. *Copy editors* mostly review and edit a reporter's copy for accuracy, content, grammar and style.

In smaller organizations, such as small daily or weekly newspapers or the membership or publications departments of nonprofit or similar organizations, a single editor may do everything or share responsibility with only a few other people. Executive and managing editors typically hire writers, reporters and other employees. They also plan budgets and negotiate contracts with freelance writers, sometimes called "stringers" in the news industry. In broadcasting companies, programme *directors* have similar responsibilities.

Editors and programme directors often have assistants, many of whom hold entry-level jobs. These assistants, such as copy editors and *production assistants*, review copy for errors in grammar, punctuation and spelling and check the copy for readability, style and agreement with editorial policy. They suggest revisions, such as changing words and rearranging sentences, to improve clarity or accuracy. They also carry out research for writers and verify facts, dates and statistics. Production assistants arrange page layouts of articles, photographs and advertising; compose headlines; and prepare copy for printing. *Publication assistants* who work for publishing houses may read and evaluate manuscripts submitted by freelance writers, proofread printers' galleys and answer letters about published material. Production assistants on small newspapers or in radio stations compile articles available from wire services or the Internet, answer phones and make photocopies.

*Technical writers* put technical information into easily understandable language. They prepare operating and maintenance manuals, catalogues, parts lists, assembly instructions, sales promotion materials and project proposals. Many technical writers work with engineers on technical subject matters to prepare written interpretations of engineering and design specifications and other information for a general readership. Technical writers also may serve as part of a team conducting usability studies to help improve the design of a product that still is in the prototype stage. They plan and edit technical materials and oversee the preparation of illustrations, photographs, diagrams and charts.

*Science and medical writers* prepare a range of formal documents presenting detailed information on the physical or medical sciences. They convey research findings for scientific or medical professions and organize information for advertising or public relations needs. Many writers work with researchers on technical subjects to prepare written interpretations of data and other information for a general readership.

***Working Conditions:*** Some writers and editors work in comfortable, private offices; others work in noisy rooms filled with the sound of keyboards and computer printers, as well as the voices of other writers tracking down information over the telephone. The search for information sometimes requires that writers travel to diverse workplaces, such as factories, offices, or laboratories, but many find their material through telephone interviews, the library and the Internet.

Advances in electronic communications have changed the work environment for many writers. Laptop computers and wireless communications technologies allow growing numbers of writers to work from home and even on the road. The ability to e-mail, transmit and download stories, research, or editorial review materials using the Internet allows writers and editors greater flexibility in where and how they complete assignments.

Some writers keep regular office hours, either to maintain contact with sources and editors or to establish a writing routine, but most writers set their own hours. Many writers, especially freelance writers, are paid per assignment; therefore, they work any number of hours necessary to meet a deadline. As a result, writers must be willing to work evenings, nights, or weekends to produce a piece acceptable to an editor or client by the publication deadline. Those who prepare morning or weekend publications and broadcasts also may regularly work nights and weekends.

While many freelance writers enjoy running their own businesses and the advantages of working flexible hours, most routinely face the pressures of juggling multiple projects with competing demands and the continual need to find new work in order to earn a living. Deadline pressures and long, erratic work hours—often part of the daily routine in these jobs—may cause stress, fatigue, or burnout; use of computers for extended periods may cause some individuals to experience back pain, eyestrain, or fatigue.

***Training, Other Qualifications and Advancement:*** A college degree generally is required for a position as a writer or editor. Although some employers look for a broad liberal arts background, most prefer to hire people with degrees in communications, journalism, or English. For those who specialize in a particular area, such as fashion, business, or law, additional background in the chosen field is expected. Knowledge of a second language is helpful for some positions.

Increasingly, technical writing requires a degree in, or some knowledge about, a specialized field—for example, engineering, business, or one of the sciences. In many cases, people with good writing skills can acquire specialized knowledge on the job. Some transfer from jobs as technicians, scientists, or engineers. Others begin as research assistants or as trainees in a technical information department, develop technical communication skills and then assume writing duties.

Writers and editors must be able to express ideas clearly and logically and should love to write. Creativity, curiosity, a broad range of knowledge, self-motivation and perseverance also are valuable. Writers and editors must demonstrate good judgment and a strong sense of ethics in deciding what material to publish. Editors also need tact and the ability to guide and encourage others in their work.

For some jobs, the ability to concentrate amid confusion and to work under pressure is essential. Familiarity with electronic publishing, graphics and video production equipment increasingly is needed. Use of electronic and wireless communications equipment to send e-mail, transmit work and review copy often is necessary. Online newspapers and magazines require knowledge of computer software used to combine online text with graphics, audio, video and animation.

High school and college newspapers, literary magazines, community newspapers and radio and television stations all provide valuable, but sometimes unpaid, practical writing experience. Many magazines, newspapers and broadcast stations have internships for students. Interns write short pieces, conduct research and interviews and learn about the publishing or broadcasting business.

In small firms, beginning writers and editors hired as assistants may actually begin writing or editing material right away. Opportunities for advancement can be limited, however. Many writers look for work on a short-term, project-by-project basis. Many small or not-for-profit organizations either do not have enough regular work or cannot afford to employ writers on a full-time basis. However, they routinely contract out work to freelance writers.

In larger businesses, jobs usually are more formally structured. Beginners generally do research, fact checking, or copy editing. Advancement to full-scale writing or editing assignments may occur more slowly for newer writers and editors in larger organizations than for employees of smaller companies. Advancement often is more predictable, though, coming with the assignment of more important articles.

Advancement for freelancers often means working on larger, more complex projects for more money. Building a reputation and establishing a track record for meeting deadlines also makes it easier to get future assignments, as does instituting long-term freelance relationships with the same publications.

The growing popularity of blogs could allow some writers to get their work read; a few well-written blogs may garner some recognition for the author and may lead to a few paid pieces in other print or electronic publications. However, most bloggers do not earn much money writing their blogs.

***Employment:*** Writers and editors held about 320,000 jobs in 2004. More than one-third were self-employed. Writers and authors held about 142,000 jobs; editors, about 127,000 jobs; and technical writers, about 50,000 jobs. About one-half of the salaried jobs for writers and editors were in the information sector, which includes newspaper, periodical, book and directory publishers; radio and television broadcasting; software publishers; motion picture and sound-recording industries; Internet service providers, Web search portals and data-processing services; and Internet publishing and broadcasting. Substantial numbers also worked in advertising and related services, computer systems design and related services and public and private educational services. Other salaried writers and editors worked in computer and electronic product manufacturing; government agencies; religious organizations; and business, professional, labour, political and similar organizations.

Jobs with major book publishers, magazines, broadcasting companies, advertising agencies and public relations firms are concentrated in New York, Chicago, Los Angeles, Boston, Philadelphia and San Francisco; however, many writers work elsewhere and travel regularly to meet with personnel at the headquarters. Jobs with newspapers, business and professional journals and technical and trade magazines are more widely dispersed throughout the country.

Thousands of other individuals work as freelance writers, earning some income from their articles, books and, less commonly, television and movie scripts. Most support themselves with income derived from other sources.

***Job Outlook:*** Employment of writers and editors is expected to grow about as fast as the average for all occupations through the year 2014. The outlook for most writing and editing jobs is expected to be competitive because many people with writing or journalism training are attracted to the occupation.

Employment of salaried writers and editors for newspapers, periodicals, book publishers and nonprofit organizations is expected to increase as demand grows for these publications. Magazines and other periodicals increasingly are developing market niches, appealing to readers with special interests. Businesses and organizations are developing newsletters and websites and more companies are experimenting with publishing materials directly on the Internet.

Online publications and services are growing in number and sophistication, spurring the demand for writers and editors, especially those with Web experience. Advertising and public relations agencies, which also are growing, should be another source of new jobs.

Opportunities should be best for technical writers and those with training in a specialized field. Demand for technical writers and writers with expertise in areas such as law, medicine, or economics is expected to increase because of the continuing expansion of scientific and technical information and the need to communicate it to others. Legal, scientific and technological developments and discoveries generate demand for people to interpret technical information for a more general audience. Rapid growth and change in the high-technology and electronics industries result in a greater need for people to write users' guides, instruction manuals and training materials. This work requires people who not only are technically skilled as writers, but also are familiar with the subject area.

In addition to job openings created by employment growth, some openings will arise as experienced workers retire, transfer to other occupations, or leave the labour force. Replacement needs are relatively high in this occupation; many freelancers leave because they cannot earn enough money.

***Earnings:*** Median annual earnings for salaried writers and authors were $44,350 in May 2004. The middle 50 percent earned between $31,720 and $62,930. The lowest 10 percent earned less than $23,330 and the highest 10 percent earned more than $91,260. Median annual earnings were $54,410 in advertising and related services and $37,010 in newspaper, periodical, book and directory publishers.

Median annual earnings for salaried editors were $43,890 in May 2004. The middle 50 percent earned between $33,130 and $58,850. The lowest 10 percent earned less than $25,780 and the highest 10 percent earned more than $80,020. Median annual earnings of those working for newspaper, periodical, book and directory publishers were $43,620.

Median annual earnings for salaried technical writers were $53,490 in May 2004. The middle 50 percent earned between $41,440 and $68,980. The lowest 10 percent earned less than $32,490 and the highest 10 percent earned more than $86,780. Median annual earnings in computer systems design and related services were $54,710.

According to the Society for Technical Communication, the median annual salary for entry level technical writers was $42,500 in 2004. The median annual salary for midlevel nonsupervisory technical writers was $51,500 and for senior nonsupervisory technical writers, $66,000.

### *Interpreters and Translators*

***Significant Points:*** 15 percent of these workers are self-employed.

Work is often sporadic and many interpreters and translators work part time.

Although training requirements can vary, most interpreters and translators have a bachelor's degree.

Job outlook varies by specialty and language combination.

***Nature of the Work:*** Interpreters and translators enable the cross-cultural communication necessary in today's society by converting one language into another. However, these language specialists do more than simply translate words—they relay concepts and ideas between languages.

They must thoroughly understand the subject matter in which they work so that they are able to convert information from one language, known as the source language, into another, the target language. In addition, they must remain sensitive to the cultures associated with their languages of expertise. Interpreters and translators are often discussed together because they share some common traits. For example, both need a special ability, known as language combination. This enables them to be fluent in at least two languages—a native, or active, language and a secondary, or passive, language; a small number of interpreters and translators are fluent in two or more passive languages. Their active language is the one that they know best and into which they interpret or translate and their passive language is one of which they have nearly perfect knowledge.

Although some people do both, interpretation and translation are different professions. Each requires a distinct set of skills and aptitudes and most people are better suited for one or the other. While interpreters often work into and from both languages, translators generally work only into their active language.

*Interpreters* convert one spoken language into another—or, in the case of sign-language interpreters, between spoken communication and sign language. This requires interpreters to pay attention carefully, understand what is communicated in both languages and express thoughts and ideas clearly. Strong research and analytical skills, mental dexterity and an exceptional memory also are important.

The first part of an interpreter's work begins before arriving at the jobsite. The interpreter must become familiar with the subject matter that the speakers will discuss, a task that may involve research to create a list of common words and phrases associated with the topic. Next, the interpreter usually travels to the location where his or her services are needed. Physical presence may not be required for some work, such as telephone interpretation. But it is usually important that the interpreter see the communicators in order to hear and observe the person speaking and to relay the message to the other party.

There are two types of interpretation: simultaneous and consecutive. Simultaneous interpretation requires interpreters to listen and speak (or sign) at the same time. In simultaneous interpretation, the interpreter begins to convey a sentence being spoken while the speaker is still talking. Ideally, simultaneous interpreters should be so familiar with a subject that they are able to anticipate the end of the speaker's sentence. Because they need a high degree of concentration, simultaneous interpreters work in pairs, with each interpreting for 20- to 30-minute segments. This type of interpretation is required at international conferences and is sometimes used in the courts.

In contrast to simultaneous interpretation's immediacy, consecutive interpretation begins only after the speaker has verbalized a group of words or sentences. Consecutive interpreters often take notes while listening to the speakers, so they must develop some type of note-taking or shorthand system. This form of interpretation is used most often for person-to-person communication, during which the interpreter sits near both parties.

*Translators* convert written materials from one language into another. They must have excellent writing and analytical ability. And because the documents that they translate must be as flawless as possible, they also need good editing skills.

Translators' assignments may vary in length, writing style and subject matter. When they first receive text to convert into another language, translators usually read it in its entirety to get an idea of the subject. Next, they identify and look up any unfamiliar words. Multiple additional readings are usually needed before translators begin to actually write and finalize the translation.

Translators also might do additional research on the subject matter if they are unclear about anything in the text. They consult with the text's originator or issuing agency to clarify unclear or unfamiliar ideas, words, or acronyms.

Translating involves more than replacing a word with its equivalent in another language; sentences and ideas must be manipulated to flow with the same coherence as those in the source document so that the translation reads as though it originated in the target language. Translators also must bear in mind any cultural references that may need to be explained to the intended audience, such as colloquialisms, slang and other expressions that do not translate literally. Some subjects may be more difficult than others to translate because words or passages may have multiple meanings that make several translations possible. Not surprisingly, translated work often goes through multiple revisions before final text is submitted.

The way in which translators do their jobs has changed with advancements in technology. Today, nearly all translation work is done on a computer and most assignments are received and submitted electronically. This enables translators to work from almost anywhere and a large percentage of them work from home. The Internet provides advanced research capabilities and valuable language resources, such as specialized dictionaries and glossaries. In some cases, use of machine-assisted translation—including memory tools that provide comparisons of previous translations with current work—helps save time and reduce repetition.

The services of interpreters and translators are needed in a number of subject areas. While these workers may not completely specialize in a particular field or industry, many do focus on one area of expertise. Some of the most common areas are described below; however, interpreters and translators also may work in a variety of other areas, including business, social services, or entertainment.

*Conference interpreters* work at conferences that involve non-English-speaking attendees. This work includes international business and diplomacy, although conference interpreters also may interpret for any organization that works with foreign language speakers. Employers prefer high-level interpreters who have the ability to translate from at least two passive languages into one active (native) language—for example, the ability to interpret from Spanish and French into English. For some positions, such as those with the United Nations, this qualification is mandatory.

Much of the interpreting performed at conferences is simultaneous; however, at some meetings with a small number of attendees, consecutive interpreting also may be used. Usually, interpreters sit in soundproof booths, listening to the speakers through headphones and interpreting into a microphone what is said. The interpreted speech is then relayed to the listener through headsets. When interpreting is needed for only one or two people, the interpreter generally sits behind or next to the attendee and whispers a translation of the proceedings.

*Guide or escort interpreters* accompany either U.S. visitors abroad or foreign visitors in the United States to ensure that they are able to communicate during their stay. These specialists interpret on a variety of subjects, both on an informal basis and on a professional level. Most of their interpretation is consecutive and work is generally shared by two interpreters when the assignment requires more than an 8-hour day. Frequent travel, often for days or weeks at a time, is common, an aspect of the job that some find particularly appealing.

*Judiciary interpreters and translators* help people appearing in court who are unable or unwilling to communicate in English. These workers must remain detached from the content of their work and not alter or modify the meaning or tone of what is said. Legal translators must be thoroughly familiar with the language and functions of the U.S. judicial system, as well as other countries' legal systems. Court interpreters work in a variety of legal settings, such as attorney-client meetings, preliminary hearings, depositions, trials and arraignments. Success as a court interpreter requires an understanding of both legal terminology and colloquial language. In addition to interpreting what is said, court interpreters also may be required to translate written documents and read them aloud, also known as sight translation.

*Literary translators* adapt written literature from one language into another. They may translate any number of documents, including journal articles, books, poetry and short stories. Literary translation is related to creative writing; literary translators must create a new text in the target language that reproduces the content and style of the original. Whenever possible, literary translators work closely with authors in order to best capture their intended meanings and literary characteristics.

This type of work often is done as a sideline by university professors; however, opportunities exist for well-established literary translators. As is the case with writers, finding a publisher and maintaining a network of contacts in the publishing industry is a critical part of the job. Most aspiring literary translators begin by submitting a short sample of their work, in the hope that it will be printed and give them recognition. For example, after receiving permission from the author, they might submit to a publishing house a previously unpublished short work, such as a poem or essay.

*Localization translators* constitute a relatively recent and rapidly expanding specialty. Localization involves the complete adaptation of a product for use in a different language and culture. At its earlier stages, this work dealt primarily with software localization, but the specialty has expanded to include the adaptation of Internet sites and products in manufacturing and other business sectors.

Translators working in localization need a solid grasp of the languages to be translated, a thorough understanding of technical concepts and vocabulary and a high degree of knowledge about the intended target audience or users of the product. The goal of these specialists is for the product to appear as if it were originally manufactured in the country where it will be sold and supported. Because software often is involved, it is not uncommon for people who work in this area of translation to have a strong background in computer science or computer-related work experience.

Providing language services to health care patients with limited English proficiency is the realm of *medical interpreters and translators*. Medical interpreters help patients to communicate with doctors, nurses and other medical staff. Translators working in this specialty primarily convert patient materials and informational brochures, issued by hospitals and medical facilities, into the desired language. Medical interpreters need a strong grasp of medical and colloquial terminology in both languages, along with cultural sensitivity regarding how the patient receives the information. They must remain detached but aware of the patient's feelings and pain.

*Sign language interpreters* facilitate communication between people who are deaf or hard of hearing and people who can hear. Sign language interpreters must be fluent in English and in American Sign Language (ASL), which combines signing, finger spelling and specific body language. ASL has its own grammatical rules, sentence structure, idioms, historical contexts and cultural nuances. Sign language interpreting, like foreign language interpreting, involves more than simply replacing a word of spoken English with a sign representing that word.

Most sign language interpreters either interpret, aiding communication between English and ASL, or transliterate, facilitating communication between English and contact signing—a form of signing that uses a more English language-based word order. Some interpreters specialize in oral interpreting for deaf or hard of hearing persons who lip-read instead of sign. Other specialties include tactile signing, which is interpreting for persons who are blind as well as deaf by making manual signs into a person's hands; cued speech; and signing exact English.

Self-employed and freelance interpreters and translators need general business skills to successfully manage their finances and careers. They must set prices for their work, bill customers, keep financial records and market their services to attract new business and build their client base.

***Working Conditions:*** Working environments of interpreters and translators vary. Interpreters work in a variety of settings, such as hospitals, courtrooms and conference centres. They are required to travel to the site—whether it is in a neighbouring town or on the other side of the world—where their services are needed. Interpreters who work over the telephone generally work on call, often in call centres in urban areas and keep to a standard 5-day, 40-hour workweek. Interpreters for deaf students in schools usually work in a school setting for 9 months out of the year. Translators usually work alone and they must frequently perform under pressure of deadlines and tight schedules. Many translators choose to work at home; however, technology allows translators to work from virtually anywhere.

Because many interpreters and translators freelance, their schedules are often erratic, with extensive periods of no work interspersed with others requiring long, irregular hours. For those who freelance, a significant amount of time must be dedicated to looking for jobs. In addition, freelancers must manage their own finances and payment for their services may not always be prompt. Freelancing, however, offers variety and flexibility and allows many workers to choose which jobs to accept or decline.

The number of work-related accidents in these occupations is relatively low. The work can be stressful and exhausting and translation can be lonesome or dull. However, interpreters and translators may use their irregular schedules to pursue other interests, such as travelling, dabbling in a hobby, or working a second job. Many interpreters and translators enjoy what they do and value the ability to control their schedules and workloads.

***Training, Other Qualifications and Advancement:*** The educational backgrounds of interpreters and translators vary. Knowing a language in addition to a native language is essential. Although it is not necessary to have been raised bilingual to succeed, many interpreters and translators grew up speaking two languages.

In high school, students can prepare for these careers by taking a broad range of courses that include English writing and comprehension, foreign languages and basic computer proficiency. Other helpful pursuits include spending time abroad, engaging in comparable forms of direct contact with foreign cultures and reading extensively on a variety of subjects in English and at least one other language.

Beyond high school, there are many educational options. Although a bachelor's degree is often required, interpreters and translators note that it is acceptable to major in something other than a language. However, specialized training in how to do the work is generally required. A number of formal programmes in interpreting and translation are available at colleges nationwide and through nonuniversity training programmes, conferences and courses. Many people who work as conference interpreters or in more technical areas—such as localization, engineering, or finance—have master's degrees, while those working in the community as court or medical interpreters or translators are more likely to complete job-specific training programmes.

There is currently no universal form of certification required of all interpreters and translators in the United States, but there are a variety of different tests that workers can voluntarily take to demonstrate proficiency. The American Translators Association provides accreditation in more than 24 language combinations for its members; other options include a certification programme offered by The Translators and Interpreters Guild. Many interpreters are not certified. Federal courts have certification for Spanish, Navajo and Haitian Creole interpreters and many State and municipal courts offer their own forms of certification. The National Association of Judiciary Interpreters and Translators also offers certification for court interpreting.

The U.S. Department of State has a three-test series for interpreters, including simple consecutive interpreting (for escort work), simultaneous interpreting (for court or seminar work) and conference-level interpreting (for international conferences). These tests are not referred to directly as certification, but successful completion often indicates that a person has an adequate level of skill to work in the field.

The National Association of the Deaf and the Registry of Interpreters for the Deaf (RID) jointly offer certification for general sign interpreters. In addition, RID offers specialty tests in legal interpreting, speech reading and deaf-to-deaf interpreting—which includes interpreting between deaf speakers with different native languages and from ASL to tactile signing.

Experience is an essential part of a successful career in either interpreting or translation. In fact, many agencies or companies use only the services of people who have worked in the field for 3 to 5 years or who have a degree in translation studies or both.

A good way for translators to learn firsthand about the profession is to start out working in-house for a company; however, such jobs are not very numerous. Persons seeking to enter interpreter or translator jobs should begin by getting experience whatever way they can—even if it means doing informal or unpaid work. All translation can be used as examples for potential clients, even translation done as practice. Mentoring relationships and internships are other ways to build skills and confidence. Escort interpreting may offer an opportunity for inexperienced candidates to work alongside a more seasoned interpreter. Interpreters might also find it easier to break into areas with particularly high demand for language services, such as court or medical interpretation. Once interpreters and translators have gained sufficient experience, they may then move up to more difficult or prestigious assignments, may seek certification, may be given editorial responsibility, or may eventually manage or start their own translation agency.

***Employment:*** Interpreters and translators held about 31,000 jobs in 2004. However, the actual number of interpreters and translators is probably significantly higher because many work in the occupation only sporadically. Interpreters and translators are employed in a variety of industries, reflecting the diversity of employment options in the field. About 9,900 worked in public and private educational institutions, such as schools, colleges and universities. About 4,100 worked in health care, many of which worked for hospitals. Another 3,400 worked in other areas of government, such as Federal, State and local courts. Other employers of interpreters and translators include publishing companies, telephone companies, airlines and interpreting and translating agencies.

About 4,600 interpreters and translators are self-employed. To find work, these interpreters and translators may submit resumes to many different employment agencies and then wait to be contacted when an agency matches their skills with a job. After establishing a few regular clients, interpreters and translators may receive enough work from a few clients to stay busy and they often hear of subsequent jobs by word of mouth or through referrals from existing clients. Many who freelance in the occupation work only part time, relying on other sources of income to supplement earnings from interpreting or translation.

***Job Outlook:*** Employment of interpreters and translators is projected to increase faster than the average for all occupations over the 2004-14 period, reflecting strong growth in the industries employing interpreters and translators. Higher demand for interpreters and translators in recent years has resulted directly from the broadening of international ties and the increase in the number of foreign language speakers in the United States. Both of these trends are expected to continue, contributing to relatively rapid growth in the number of jobs for interpreters and translators. Demand will remain strong for translators of the languages referred to as "PFIGS"—Portuguese, French, Italian, German and Spanish—and the principal Asian languages—Chinese, Japanese and Korean. In addition, current events and changing political environments, often difficult to foresee, will increase the need for persons who can work with other languages. For example, homeland security needs are expected to drive increasing demand for interpreters and translators of Middle Eastern and North African languages, primarily in Federal Government agencies.

Technology has made the work of interpreters and translators easier. However, technology is not likely to have a negative impact on employment of interpreters and translators because such innovations are incapable of producing work comparable with work produced by these professionals.

Urban areas, especially those in California and New York and Washington DC, provide the largest numbers of employment possibilities, especially for interpreters; however, as the immigrant population spreads into more rural areas, jobs in smaller communities will become more widely available.

Job prospects for interpreters and translators vary by specialty. In particular, there should be strong demand for specialists in localization, driven by imports and exports, the expansion of the Internet and demand in other technical areas, such as medicine or law. Rapid employment growth among interpreters and translators in health services industries will be fuelled by the implementation of relatively recent guidelines regarding compliance with Title VI of the Civil Rights Act, which require all health care providers receiving Federal aid to provide language services to non-English speakers. Similarly, the Americans with Disabilities Act and other laws, such as the Rehabilitation Act, mandate that, in certain situations, an interpreter must be available for people who are deaf or hard of hearing. Given the shortage of interpreters and translators meeting the desired skill level of employers, interpreters for the deaf will continue to have favourable employment prospects. On the other hand, job growth is expected to be limited for both conference interpreters and literary translators.

***Earnings:*** Salaried interpreters and translators had median hourly earnings of $16.28 in May 2004. The middle 50 percent earned between $12.40 and $21.09. The lowest 10 percent earned less than $9.67 and the highest 10 percent earned more than $27.45.

Earnings depend on language, subject matter, skill, experience, education, certification and type of employer and salaries of interpreters and translators can vary widely. Interpreters and translators with language skills for which there is a greater demand, or for which there are relatively few people with the skills, often have higher earnings. Interpreters and translators with specialized expertise, such as those working in software localization, also generally command higher rates. Individuals classified as language specialists for the Federal Government earned an average of $71,625 annually in 2005. Limited information suggests that some highly skilled interpreters and translators—for example, high-level conference interpreters—working full time can earn more than $100,000 annually.

For those who are not salaried, earnings may fluctuate, depending on the availability of work. Furthermore, freelancers do not have any employer-paid benefits. Freelance interpreters usually earn an hourly rate, whereas translators who freelance typically earn a rate per word or per hour.

## Arts, Entertainment and Recreation

***Significant Points:*** The industry is characterized by a large number of seasonal and part-time jobs and relatively young workers.

About 40 percent of all workers have no formal education beyond high school.

Rising incomes, more leisure time and growing awareness of the health benefits of physical fitness will increase the demand for arts, entertainment and recreation services.

Earnings are relatively low.

***Nature of the Industry:*** As leisure time and personal incomes have grown across the Nation, so has the arts, entertainment and recreation industry. This industry includes about 115,000 establishments, ranging from art museums to fitness centres. Practically any activity that occupies a person's leisure time, excluding the viewing of motion pictures and video rentals, is part of the arts, entertainment and recreation industry. The diverse range of activities offered by this industry can be categorized into three broad groups-live performances or events; historical, cultural, or educational exhibits; and recreation or leisure-time activities.

Live performances or events. This segment of the industry includes professional sports, as well as establishments providing sports facilities and services to amateurs. Commercial sports clubs operate professional and amateur athletic clubs and promote athletic events. All kinds of popular sports can be found in these establishments, including baseball, basketball, boxing, football, ice hockey, soccer, wrestling and even auto racing. Professional and amateur companies involved in sports promotion also are part of this industry segment, as are sports establishments in which gambling is allowed, such as dog and horse racetracks and jai alai courts.

A variety of businesses and groups involved in live theatrical and musical performances are included in this segment. Theatrical production companies, for example, coordinate all aspects of producing a play or theatre event, including employing actors and actresses and costume designers and contracting with lighting and stage crews who handle the technical aspects of productions. Agents and managers, who represent actors and entertainers and assist them in finding jobs or engagements, are also included. Booking agencies line up performance engagements for theatrical groups and entertainers.

Performers of live musical entertainment include popular music artists, dance bands, disc jockeys, orchestras, jazz musicians and rock-and-roll bands. Orchestras range from major professional orchestras with million dollar budgets to community orchestras, which often have part-time schedules. The performing arts segment also includes dance companies, which produce all types of live theatrical dances. The majority of these dance troupes perform ballet, folk dance, or modern dance.

Historical, cultural, or educational exhibits. Privately owned museums, zoos, botanical gardens, nature parks and historical sites make up this segment of the industry; publicly owned facilities are included in sections on Federal, State, or local government elsewhere in the Career Guide. Each institution in this segment preserves and exhibits objects, sites and natural wonders with historical, cultural, or educational value.

Recreation or leisure activities. A variety of establishments provide amusement for a growing number of customers. Some of these businesses provide video game, pinball and gaming machines for the public at amusement parks, arcades and casinos. Casinos and other gaming establishments offering off-track betting are a rapidly growing part of this industry segment. This segment also includes amusement and theme parks, which range in size from local carnivals to multiacre parks. These establishments may have mechanical rides, shows and refreshment stands. Other recreation and leisure-time services include golf courses, skating rinks, ski lifts, marinas, day camps, gocart tracks, riding stables, waterslides and establishments offering rental sporting goods.

This segment of the industry also includes physical fitness facilities that feature exercise and weight loss programmes, gyms, health clubs and day spas. These establishments also frequently offer aerobics, dance, yoga and other exercise classes. Other recreation and leisure-time businesses include bowling centres that rent lanes and equipment for tenpin, duckpin, or candlepin bowling.

These facilities may be open to the public or available on a membership basis. Sports and recreation clubs that are open only to members and their guests include some golf courses, country clubs and yacht, tennis, racquetball, hunting and fishing and gun clubs. Public golf courses and marinas, unlike private clubs, offer facilities to the general public on a fee-per-use basis.

Technology is a major part of producing arts, entertainment and recreation activities; for example, lighting and sound are vital for concerts and themed events and elaborate sets often are required for plays. However, most of this work is contracted to firms outside of the arts, entertainment and recreation industry.

***Working Conditions:*** Jobs in arts, entertainment and recreation are more likely to be part time than those in other industries. In fact, the average nonsupervisory worker in the arts, entertainment and recreation industry worked 25.7 hours a week in 2004, as compared to an average of 33.7 hours for all private industry. Musical groups and artists were likely to work the fewest hours due to the large number of performers competing for a limited number of engagements, which may require a great amount of travel. The majority of performers are unable to support themselves in this profession alone and are forced to supplement their income through other jobs.

Many types of arts, entertainment and recreation establishments dramatically increase employment during the summer and either scale back employment during the winter or close down completely. Workers may be required to work nights, weekends and holidays because that is when most establishments are busiest. Some jobs require extensive travel. Music and dance troupes, for example, frequently tour or travel to major metropolitan areas across the country, in hopes of attracting large audiences.

Many people in this industry work outdoors, whereas others may work in hot, crowded, or noisy conditions. Some jobs, such as those at fitness facilities or in amusement parks, involve some manual labour and, thus, require physical strength and stamina. Also, athletes, dancers and many other performers must be in particularly good physical condition. Many jobs include customer service responsibilities, so employees must be able to work well with the public.

In 2003, cases of work-related illness and injury averaged 5.9 for every 100 full-time workers, higher than the average of 5.0 for the entire private sector. Risks of injury are high in some jobs, especially those of athletes. Although most injuries are minor, including sprains and muscle pulls, they may prevent an employee from working for a period.

***Employment:*** The arts, entertainment and recreation industry provided about 1.8 million wage-and-salary jobs in 2004. About 58 percent of these jobs were in the industry segment other amusement and recreation industries-which includes golf courses, membership sports and recreation clubs and physical fitness facilities.

***Employment in Arts, Entertainment and Recreation by Industry Segment, 2004 (Employment in Thousands)***

| *Industry segment* | *Employment* |
|---|---|
| Arts, entertainment and recreation, total | 1,833 |
| Other amusement and recreation industries | 1,060 |
| Gambling industries | 154 |
| Amusement parks and arcades | 137 |
| Spectator sports | 120 |
| Museums, historical sites and other institutions | 117 |
| Performing arts companies | 115 |
| Promoters of performing arts, sports and similar events | 73 |
| Independent artists, writers and performers | 42 |

Agents and managers for artists, athletes, entertainers and other public figures.

Although most establishments in the arts, entertainment and recreation industry are small, 42 percent of all jobs were in establishments that employ more than 100 workers.

The arts, entertainment and recreation industry is characterized by a large number of seasonal and part-time jobs and by workers who are younger than the average for all industries. About 46 percent of all workers are under 35. Many businesses in the industry increase hiring during the summer, often employing high school-age and college-age workers. Most establishments in the arts, entertainment and recreation industry contract out lighting, sound, set-building and exhibit-building work to firms not included in this industry.

***Occupations in the Industry***

About 59 percent of wage-and-salary workers in the industry are employed in service occupations. Amusement and recreation attendants-the largest occupation in the arts, entertainment and recreation industry-perform a variety of duties depending on where they are employed. Common duties include setting up games, handing out sports equipment, providing caddy services for golfers, collecting money and operating amusement park rides.

Fitness trainers and aerobics instructors lead or coach groups or individuals in exercise activities and in the fundamentals of sports.

Recreation workers organize and promote activities, such as arts and crafts, sports, games, music, drama, social recreation, camping and hobbies. They generally are employed by schools; theme parks and other tourist attractions; or health, sports and other recreational clubs. Recreation workers schedule organized events to structure leisure time.

Gaming services workers assist in the operation of games, such as keno, bingo and gaming table games. They may calculate and pay off the amount of winnings, or collect players' money or chips.

Tour and travel guides escort individuals or groups on sightseeing tours or through places of interest, such as industrial establishments, public buildings and art galleries. They may also plan, organize and conduct long-distance cruises, tours and expeditions for individuals or groups.

Animal care and service workers feed, water, bathe, exercise, or otherwise care for animals in zoos, circuses, aquariums, or other settings. They may train animals for riding or performance.

Other service workers include waiters and waitresses, who serve food in entertainment establishments; fast food and counter workers and cooks and food preparation workers, who may serve or prepare food for patrons; and bartenders, who mix and serve drinks in arts, entertainment and recreation establishments.

Building grounds, cleaning and maintenance occupations include building cleaning workers, who clean up after shows or sporting events and are responsible for the daily cleaning and upkeep of facilities. Landscaping and groundskeeping workers care for athletic fields and golf courses. These workers maintain artificial and natural turf fields, mark boundaries and paint team logos. They also mow, water and fertilize natural athletic fields and vacuum and disinfect synthetic fields. Establishments in this industry also employ workers in protective service occupations. Security guards patrol the property and guard against theft, vandalism and illegal entry. At sporting events, guards maintain order and direct patrons to various facilities. Gaming surveillance officers and gaming investigators observe casino operations to detect cheating, theft, or other irregular activities by patrons or employees.

Professional and related occupations account for 11 percent of all jobs in this industry. Some of the most well-known members of these occupations, athletes and sports competitors, perform in any of a variety of sports. Professional athletes compete in events for compensation, either through salaries or prize money. Organizations such as the Women's National Basketball Association (WNBA) and the National Football League (NFL) sanction events for professionals. Few athletes are able to make it to the professional level, where high salaries are common. In some professional sports, minor leagues offer lower salaries with a chance to develop skills through competition before advancing to major league play.

Coaches and scouts train athletes to perform at their highest level. Often, they are experienced athletes who have retired and are able to provide insight from their own experiences to players. Although some umpires, referees and other sports officials work full time, the majority usually work part time and often have other full-time jobs. For example, many professional sport referees and umpires also officiate at amateur games.

Musicians and singers may play musical instruments, sing, compose, arrange music, or conduct groups in instrumental or vocal performances. The specific skills and responsibilities of musicians vary widely by type of instrument, size of ensemble and style of music. For example, musicians can play jazz, classical, or popular music, either alone or in groups ranging from small rock bands to large symphony orchestras.

Actors entertain and communicate with people through their interpretation of dramatic and other roles. They can belong to a variety of performing groups, ranging from those appearing in community and local dinner theaters to those playing in full-scale Broadway productions. Dancers express ideas, stories, rhythm and sound with their bodies through different types of dance, including ballet, modern dance, tap, folk and jazz. Dancers usually perform in a troupe, although some perform solo. Many become teachers when their performing careers end. Choreographers create and teach dance and they may be called upon to direct and stage presentations. Producers and directors select and interpret plays or scripts and give directions to actors and dancers. They conduct rehearsals, audition cast members and approve choreography. They also arrange financing, hire production staff members and negotiate contracts with personnel.

Archivists, curators and museum technicians play an important role in preparing museums for display. Archivists appraise, edit and direct safekeeping of permanent records and historically valuable documents. They may also participate in research activities based on archival materials. Curators administer a museum's affairs and conduct research programmes. Museum technicians and conservators prepare specimens, such as fossils, skeletal parts, lace and textiles, for museum collection and exhibits. They may also take part in restoring documents or installing and arranging materials for exhibit.

Audio and video equipment technicians set up and operate audio and video equipment, including microphones, sound speakers, video screens, projectors, video monitors, recording equipment, connecting wires and cables, sound and mixing boards and related electronic equipment for theme parks, concerts and sports events. They may also set up and operate associated spotlights and other custom lighting systems.

About 8 percent of all jobs in this industry are in sales and related occupations. The largest of these, cashiers, often use a cash register to receive money and give change to customers. In casinos, gaming change persons and booth cashiers exchange coins and tokens for patrons' money. Counter and rental clerks check out rental equipment to customers, receive orders for service and handle cash transactions.

Another 9 percent of jobs in this industry are in office and administrative support occupations. Receptionists and information clerks, one of the larger occupations in this category, answer questions and provide general information to patrons. Other large occupations in this group include general office clerks and secretaries and administrative assistants. Gaming cage workers conduct financial transactions for patrons in gaming establishments. For example, they may accept a patron's credit application and verify credit references to provide check-cashing authorizations or to establish house credit accounts. Also, they may reconcile daily summaries of transactions to balance books or sell gambling chips, tokens, or tickets to patrons. At a patron's request, gaming cage workers may convert gaming chips, tokens, or tickets to currency.

Management, business and financial occupations make up 6 percent of employment in this industry. Managerial duties in the performing arts include marketing, business management, event booking, fundraising and public outreach. Agents and business managers of artists, performers and athletes represent their clients to prospective employers and may handle contract negotiations and other business matters. Recreation supervisors and park superintendents oversee personnel, budgets, grounds and facility maintenance and land and wildlife resources. Some common administrative jobs in sports are tournament director, health club manager and sports programme director.

Installation, maintenance and repair occupations make up 4 percent of this industry's employment. General maintenance and repair workers are the largest occupation in this group.

***Employment of Wage and Salary Workers in Arts, Entertainment and Recreation by Occupation, 2004 and Projected Change, 2004-14 (Employment in Thousands)***

| *Occupation* | *Employment, 2004* | | *Percent change, 2004-14* |
|---|---|---|---|
| | *Number* | *Percent* | |
| Total, all occupations | 1,833 | 100.0 | 25.1 |
| Management, business and financial occupations | 101 | 5.5 | 28.1 |
| Top executives | 39 | 2.1 | 27.2 |
| Agents and business managers of artists, performers and athletes | 7 | 0.4 | 20.0 |
| Professional and related occupations | 199 | 10.9 | 28.4 |
| Archivists | 2 | 0.1 | 16.3 |
| Curators | 5 | 0.2 | 18.7 |
| Museum technicians and conservators | 4 | 0.2 | 23.4 |
| Artists and related workers | 7 | 0.4 | 37.8 |
| Set and exhibit designers | 3 | 0.2 | 11.9 |
| Actors | 14 | 0.8 | 9.2 |
| Producers and directors | 7 | 0.4 | 24.4 |
| Athletes, coaches, umpires, and related workers | 39 | 2.2 | 29.8 |
| Dancers and choreographers | 9 | 0.5 | 24.7 |
| Musicians, singers and related workers | 34 | 1.9 | 33.6 |
| Service occupations | 1,088 | 59.3 | 25.7 |
| Security guards and gaming surveillance officers | 42 | 2.3 | 6.7 |
| Lifeguards, ski patrol and other recreational protective service workers | 33 | 1.8 | 30.1 |
| Supervisors, food preparation and serving workers | 24 | 1.3 | 24.8 |
| Cooks and food preparation workers | 68 | 3.7 | 26.2 |
| Bartenders | 40 | 2.2 | 19.0 |
| Fast food and counter workers | 57 | 3.1 | 30.9 |
| Waiters and waitresses | 93 | 5.1 | 16.4 |
| Dining room and cafeteria attendants and bartender helpers | 18 | 1.0 | 20.5 |
| Dishwashers | 19 | 1.0 | 19.4 |
| Building cleaning workers | 58 | 3.1 | 30.5 |

*Contd...*

| *Occupation* | *Employment, 2004* | | *Percent change, 2004-14* |
|---|---|---|---|
| | *Number* | *Percent* | |
| Landscaping and groundskeeping workers | 115 | 6.3 | 24.5 |
| Gaming supervisors | 6 | 0.4 | 42.8 |
| Animal care and service workers | 14 | 0.8 | 39.8 |
| Gaming services workers | 36 | 2.0 | 28.4 |
| Ushers, lobby attendants and ticket takers | 37 | 2.0 | 18.1 |
| Amusement and recreation attendants | 155 | 8.5 | 30.0 |
| Tour and travel guides | 16 | 0.9 | 24.8 |
| Child care workers | 31 | 1.7 | 27.3 |
| Recreation and fitness workers | 137 | 7.5 | 28.5 |
| Sales and related occupations | 145 | 7.9 | 23.9 |
| Cashiers | 65 | 3.5 | 18.8 |
| Counter and rental clerks | 23 | 1.2 | 35.5 |
| Office and administrative support occupations | 172 | 9.4 | 16.8 |
| Gaming cage workers | 8 | 0.5 | 25.2 |
| Receptionists and information clerks | 39 | 2.1 | 22.6 |
| Secretaries and administrative assistants | 28 | 1.5 | 12.5 |

***Note:*** May not add to totals due to omission of occupations with small employment.

### *Training and Advancement*

About 40 percent of all workers in the arts, entertainment and recreation industry have no formal education beyond high school. In the case of performing artists or athletes, talent and years of training are more important than education. However, upper-level management jobs usually require a college degree.

Most service jobs require little or no previous training or education beyond high school. Many companies hire young, unskilled workers, such as students, to perform low-paying seasonal jobs. Employers look for people with the interpersonal skills necessary to work with the public.

In physical fitness facilities, fitness trainer and aerobic instructor positions usually are filled by persons who develop an avid interest in fitness and then become certified to teach. Certification from a professional organization may require knowledge of cardiopulmonary resuscitation (CPR); an associate degree or experience as an instructor at a health club; and successful completion of written and oral exams covering a variety of areas, including anatomy, nutrition and fitness testing. Sometimes, fitness workers become health club managers or owners. To advance to a management position, a degree in physical education, sports medicine, or exercise physiology is useful.

In the arts, employment in professional and related occupations usually requires a great deal of talent. There are many highly talented performers, creating intense competition for every opening. Performers such as musicians, dancers and actors often study their professions most of their lives, taking private lessons and spending hours practicing. Usually, performers have completed some college or related study. Musicians, dancers and actors often go on to become teachers after completing the necessary requirements for at least a bachelor's degree. Musicians who complete a graduate degree in music sometimes move on to a career as a conductor. Dancers sometimes become choreographers and actors can advance into producer and director jobs.

Almost all arts administrators have completed 4 years of college and the majority possess a master's or a doctoral degree. Experience in marketing and business is helpful because promoting events is a large part of the job.

Entry-level supervisory or professional jobs in recreation sometimes require completion of a 2-year associate degree in parks and recreation at a junior college. Completing a 4-year bachelor's degree in this field is necessary for high-level supervisory positions. Students can specialize in such areas as aquatics, therapeutic recreation, aging and leisure and environmental studies. Those who obtain graduate degrees in the field and have years of experience may obtain administrative or university teaching positions. The National Recreation and Parks Association (NRPA) certifies individuals who meet eligibility requirements for professional and technical jobs.

Certified park and recreation professionals must pass an exam; earn a bachelor's degree with a major in recreation, park resources, or leisure services from a programme accredited by the NRPA or by the American Association for Leisure and Recreation; or earn a bachelor's degree and have at least 5 years of relevant full-time work experience, depending on the major field of study.

***Outlook:*** Wage and salary jobs in arts, entertainment and recreation are projected to grow about 25 percent over the 2004-14 period, compared with 14 percent for all industries combined. Rising incomes, leisure time and awareness of the health benefits of physical fitness will increase the demand for arts, entertainment and recreation services.

Employment opportunities should be available in a wide range of settings, including golf courses, parks and outdoor recreational facilities and amusement parks. Employment in fitness centres and similar establishments also will grow substantially, driven by several factors. Aging baby boomers are concerned with staying healthy, physically fit and independent and have become the largest demographic group of health club members.

The reduction of physical education programmes in schools, combined with parents' growing concern about child obesity, has rapidly increased child health club membership. Membership among young adults has also grown steadily, driven by concern about physical fitness and funded by rising incomes. The proliferation of group exercise classes and the focus on overall wellness in health clubs should also increase the demand for workers in this industry.

Strong employment growth is expected in the gaming industry, spurred by the increase in casinos on American Indian reservations and the introduction of slot machines at racetracks. Many States are looking to relax gambling regulations so that they can increase State revenues from gaming establishment taxes.

In addition to these increases, employment in the performing arts will grow steadily, along with demand for entertainment from a growing population. However, the supply of workers in performing arts also will expand because of the appeal of these jobs, ensuring continued intense competition.

The arts, entertainment and recreation industry has relied heavily on workers under the age of 25 to fill seasonal and unskilled positions. About one-fourth of all jobs in this industry are held by workers under age 25, compared to 14 percent in all industries combined. Opportunities should be available for young, seasonal, part-time and unskilled workers. In addition, the industry is expected to hire a growing number of workers in other age groups.

***Earnings:*** Earnings in arts, entertainment and recreation generally are low, reflecting the large number of part-time and seasonal jobs. Nonsupervisory workers in arts, entertainment and recreation averaged $313 a week in 2004, compared with $529 throughout private industry.

Earnings vary according to occupation and segment of the industry. For example, some professional athletes earn millions, but competition for these positions is intense and most athletes are unable to reach even the minor leagues. Many service workers make the minimum wage or a little more. Actors often go long periods with little or no income from acting, so they are forced to work at second jobs. Earnings in selected occupations in arts, entertainment and recreation appear in table.

***Median Hourly Earnings of the Largest Occupations in Arts, Entertainment and Recreation***

| *Occupation* | *Performing arts, spectator sports and related* | *Museums, historical sites and similar institutions* | *Amusement, gambling and recreation industries* | *All Industries* |
|---|---|---|---|---|
| Fitness trainers and aerobics instructors | $9.89 | — | $13.78 | $12.25 |
| Security guards | 9.85 | 10.16 | 9.64 | 9.77 |
| Receptionists and information clerks | 9.80 | 8.93 | 8.26 | 10.50 |
| Landscaping and groundskeeping workers | 8.96 | 10.41 | 9.13 | 9.82 |
| Janitors and cleaners, except maids and housekeeping cleaners | 8.57 | 9.24 | 8.31 | 9.04 |

*Contd...*

| *Occupation* | *Performing arts, spectator sports and related* | *Museums, historical sites and similar institutions* | *Amusement, gambling and recreation industries* | *All Industries* |
|---|---|---|---|---|
| Cashiers | 8.56 | 8.04 | 7.86 | 7.81 |
| Amusement and recreation attendants | 8.07 | 10.11 | 7.69 | 7.42 |
| Ushers, lobby attendants and ticket takers | 7.61 | 7.72 | 7.67 | 7.30 |
| Amusement and recreation attendants | 7.20 | 7.78 | 7.20 | 7.47 |
| Waiters and waitresses | 6.90 | 8.24 | 7.69 | 6.75 |

Because many amusement and theme parks dramatically increase employment during vacation periods, employment for a number of jobs in the industry is seasonal. Theme parks, for example, frequently hire young workers, often students, for summer employment. Also, many sports are not played all year, so athletes and people in the service jobs associated with those sports often are seasonally employed.

Employers in some segments of this industry offer benefits that are not available in other industries. For example, benefits for workers in some theme parks include free passes to the park, transportation to and from work, housing, scholarships and discounts on park merchandise.

Although unions are not common in most segments of this industry, they are important in professional sports and the performing arts. Many professional athletes, actors and performers are members of unions. Consequently, earnings of athletes and performers are often determined by union contracts that specify minimum salary rates and working conditions.

## Motion Picture and Video Industries

***Significant Points:*** Keen competition is expected for the more glamorous jobs-writers, actors, producers and directors-but better job prospects are expected for multimedia artists and animators, film and video editors and others skilled in digital filming and computer generated imaging.

Although many films are shot on location, employment is centred in several major cities, particularly New York and Los Angeles.

Many workers have formal training, but experience, talent, creativity and professionalism are the factors that are most important in getting many jobs in this industry.

***Nature of the Industry***

The U.S. motion picture industry produces much of the world's feature films and many of its recorded television programmes. The industry is dominated by several large studios, based mostly in Hollywood. However, with the increasing popularity and worldwide availability of cable television, digital video recorders, computer graphics and editing software and the Internet, many small and medium-sized independent filmmaking companies have sprung up to fill the growing demand.

In addition to producing feature films and filmed television programmes, the industry produces made-for-television movies, music videos and commercials. Establishments engaged primarily in operating motion picture theaters and exhibiting motion pictures or videos at film festivals also are included in this industry. Other establishments provide postproduction services to the motion picture industry, such as editing, film and tape transfers, titling and subtitling, credits, closed captioning, computer-produced graphics and animation and special effects.

Some motion picture and video companies produce films for limited, or specialized, audiences. Among these films are documentaries, which use film clips and interviews to chronicle actual events with real people and educational films ranging from "do-it-yourself" projects to exercise films. In addition, the industry produces business, industrial and government films that promote an organization's image, provide information on its activities or products, or aid in fundraising or worker training. Some of these films are short enough to release to the public through the Internet; many offer an excellent training ground for beginning filmmakers.

Making a movie can be a difficult, yet rewarding, experience. However, it is also a very risky one. Although thousands of movies are produced each year, only a small number of them account for most box office receipts. Indeed, most films do not make a full return on their investment from domestic box office revenues, so filmmakers rely on profits from other markets, such as broadcast and cable television, videocassette and DVD sales and rentals and foreign distribution. In fact, major film companies are receiving a growing portion of their revenue from abroad. These cost pressures have reduced the number of film production companies to the current seven major studios, who produce most of the filmed television programmes as well as the movies released nationally.

Smaller and independent filmmakers often find it difficult to finance new productions and pay for a film's distribution, because they must compete with large motion picture production companies for talent and available movie screens. However, digital technology is lowering production costs for some small-budget films, enabling more independents to succeed in getting their films released nationally.

Although studios and other production companies are responsible for financing, producing, publicizing and distributing a film or programme, the actual making of the film often is done by hundreds of small businesses and independent contractors hired by the studios on an as-needed basis. These companies provide a wide range of services, such as equipment rental, lighting, special effects, set construction and costume design, as well as much of the creative and technical talent that go into producing a film. The industry also contracts with a large number of workers in other industries that supply support services to the crews while they are filming, such as truck drivers, caterers, electricians and makeup artists. Many of these workers, particularly those in Los Angeles, depend on the motion picture industry for their livelihood.

Most motion pictures are still made on film. However, digital technology and computer-generated imaging are rapidly making inroads and are expected to transform the industry. Making changes to a picture is much easier with digital techniques. Backgrounds can be inserted after the actors perform on a sound stage, or locations can be digitally modified to reflect the script. Even actors can be created digitally.

Independent filmmakers will continue to benefit from this technology, as reduced costs improve their ability to compete with the major studios.

Digital technology also makes it possible to distribute movies to theaters through the use of satellites or fiber-optic cable, although relatively few theaters are capable of receiving them in that manner right now. In the future, however, more theaters will be capable of receiving films digitally and the costly process of producing and distributing bulky films will be sharply reduced.

***Working Conditions:*** Most individuals in this industry work in clean, comfortable surroundings. Filming, or "shooting," outside the studio or "on location," however, may require working in adverse weather and under unpleasant and sometimes dangerous conditions. Actors, producers, directors, cinematographers and camera operators also need stamina to withstand the heat of studio and stage lights, long and irregular hours and travel.

Directors and producers often work under stress as they try to meet schedules, stay within budget and resolve personnel and production problems. Actors, producers, directors, cinematographers and camera operators face the anxiety of rejection and intermittent employment. Writers and editors must deal with criticism and demands to restructure and rewrite their work many times until the producer and director are finally satisfied. All writers must be able to withstand such criticism and disappointment; freelance writers are under the added pressure of always looking for new jobs. In spite of these difficulties, many people find that the glamour and excitement of filmmaking more than compensate for the frequently demanding and uncertain nature of careers in motion pictures.

***Employment:*** In 2004, there were about 368,000 wage and salary jobs in the motion picture and video industries. Most of the workers were in motion picture and video production. They are involved in casting, acting, directing, editing, film processing and motion picture and videotape reproduction. Although seven major studios produce most of the motion pictures released in the United States, many small companies are used as contractors throughout the process. Most motion picture and video establishments employ fewer than 5 workers.

Many additional individuals work in the motion picture and video industries on a freelance, contract, or part-time basis, but accurate statistics on their numbers are not available. Numerous people in the film industry are self-employed, selling their services to anyone who needs them and often working on productions for many different companies during the year. Competition for these jobs is intense and many people are unable to earn a living solely from freelance work.

Employment in the production of motion pictures and other films for television is centred in Los Angeles and New York City. Studios also are located in Chicago; Orlando; Irving, Texas; and Wilmington, North Carolina. In addition, many films are shot on location throughout the United States and abroad.

***Employment of Wage and Salary Workers in Motion Picture and Video Industries by Occupation, 2004 and Projected Change, 2004-14. (Employment in Ihousands)***

| *Occupation* | *Employment, 2004* | | *Percent change, 2004-14* |
|---|---|---|---|
| | *Number* | *Percent* | |
| All occupations | 368 | 100.0 | 17.1 |
| Management, business and financial occupations | 27 | 7.4 | 24.2 |
| General and operations managers | 9 | 2.6 | 17.6 |
| Operations specialties managers | 4 | 1.0 | 27.1 |
| Accountants and auditors | 2 | 0.6 | 26.3 |
| Professional and related occupations | 148 | 40.3 | 26.7 |
| Computer specialists | 6 | 1.7 | 38.1 |
| Multimedia artists and animators | 7 | 2.0 | 39.5 |
| Graphic designers | 2 | 0.6 | 26.7 |
| Actors | 30 | 8.0 | 19.1 |
| Producers and directors | 13 | 3.6 | 26.5 |
| Entertainers and performers, sports and related workers, all other | 43 | 11.8 | 27.3 |
| Audio and video equipment technicians | 8 | 2.2 | 27.7 |
| Sound engineering technicians | 4 | 1.0 | 28.2 |

*Contd...*

| *Occupation* | *Employment, 2004* | | *Percent change, 2004-14* |
|---|---|---|---|
| | *Number* | *Percent* | |
| Camera operators, television, video and motion picture | 7 | 1.9 | 26.4 |
| Film and video editors | 10 | 2.7 | 27.3 |
| Service occupations | 107 | 29.2 | 8.5 |
| First-line supervisors/managers of food preparation and serving workers | 3 | 0.8 | 5.2 |
| Combined food preparation and serving workers, including fast food | 7 | 1.8 | 4.7 |
| Counter attendants, cafeteria, food concession and coffee shop | 33 | 8.9 | 23.0 |
| Janitors and cleaners, except maids and housekeeping cleaners | 4 | 1.2 | 9.7 |
| First-line supervisors/managers of personal service workers | 4 | 1.2 | 4.4 |
| Motion picture projectionists | 9 | 2.5 | -16.4 |
| Ushers, lobby attendants and ticket takers | 42 | 11.3 | 4.2 |
| Sales and related occupations | 36 | 9.9 | 2.3 |
| First-line supervisors/managers of retail sales workers | 3 | 0.8 | -2.7 |
| Cashiers, except gaming | 22 | 6.1 | -5.7 |
| Office and administrative support occupations | 34 | 9.1 | 13.6 |
| Bookkeeping, accounting and auditing clerks | 4 | 1.2 | 12.7 |
| Customer service representatives | 4 | 1.1 | 29.3 |
| Shipping, receiving and traffic clerks | 3 | 0.7 | 15.2 |
| Executive secretaries and administrative assistants | 5 | 1.3 | 19.3 |
| Office clerks, general | 5 | 1.3 | 10.0 |
| Production occupations | 5 | 1.2 | 7.1 |
| Transportation and material moving occupations | 8 | 2.1 | 16.5 |
| Labourers and freight, stock and material movers, hand | 6 | 1.6 | 14.6 |

***Note:*** May not add to totals due to omission of occupations with small employment

***Occupations in the Industry:*** The length of the credits at the end of most feature films and television programmes gives an idea of the variety of workers involved in producing and distributing films. The motion picture industry employs workers in every major occupational group. Professionals and related workers account for about 4 in 10 salaried jobs in the industry. Approximately 3 in 10 salaried workers hold jobs in service occupations.

Jobs in the industry can be broadly classified according to the three phases of filmmaking: Preproduction, production and postproduction. Preproduction is the planning phase, which includes budgeting, casting, finding the right location, set and costume design and construction and scheduling. Production is the actual making of the film. The number of people involved in the production phase can vary from a few, for a documentary film, to hundreds, for a feature film. It is during this phase that the actual filming is done. Postproduction activities take place in editing rooms and recording studios, where the film is shaped into its final form.

Some individuals work in all three phases. Producers, for example, are involved in every phase, from beginning to end. These workers look for ideas that they believe can be turned into lucrative film projects or television shows. They may see many films, read hundreds of manuscripts and maintain numerous contacts with literary agents and publishers. Producers are also responsible for all of the financial aspects of a film, including finding financing for its production. The producer works closely with the director on the selection of the script, the principal members of the cast and the filming locations, because these decisions greatly affect the cost of a film. Once financing is obtained, the producer works out a detailed budget and sees to it that the production costs stay within that budget. In a large production, the producer also works closely with production managers, who are in charge of crews, travel, casting and equipment. For television shows, much of this process requires especially tight recording deadlines.

Directors interpret the script and develop its thematic and visual images for the film. They also are involved in every stage of production. They may supervise hundreds of people, from screenwriters to costume, lighting and set designers. Directors are in charge of all technical and artistic aspects of the film or television show. They conduct auditions and rehearsals and approve the location, scenery, costumes, choreography and music. In short, they direct the entire cast and crew during shooting. Assistant directors (or first and second assistants) help them with such details as handling the transportation of equipment, arranging for food and accommodations and hiring performers who appear in the film, but have no lines. Some directors assume multiple roles, such as director-producer or writer-producer-director. Successful directors must know how to hire the right people and create effective teams.

Preproduction occupations. Before a film or a television programme moves into the production phase, it begins with an idea. Anyone can pitch an idea to a studio executive or an independent producer, but usually an agent representing an actor, writer, or director will have the best opportunity-the best access-to someone who can green light a project.

Once a project is approved, whether developed from an original idea or taken from an existing literary work, screenwriters will be brought in to turn that idea into a screenplay or a script for a television pilot (a sample episode of a proposed television series). Screenwriters work closely with producers and directors. Sometimes they prepare a treatment, a synopsis of the story and how a few scenes will play out, but no dialogue. Before filming or taping can begin, screenwriters will prepare a "shooting script," which has instructions pertaining to shots, camera angles and lighting. Frequently, screenwriters make changes to reflect the directors' and producers' ideas and desires. The work, therefore, requires not only creativity, but also an ability to collaborate with others and to write and rewrite many versions of a script under pressure. Although the work of feature film screenwriters generally ends when shooting begins, writing for a television series usually continues throughout the television season with a new script required for every episode.

Art directors design the physical environment of the film or television set to create the mood called for by the script.

Television art directors may design elaborate sets for use in situation comedies or commercials. They supervise many different people, including illustrators, scenic designers, model makers, carpenters, painters, electricians, labourers, set decorators, costume designers and makeup and hairstyling artists. These positions can provide an entry into the motion picture industry. Many start in such jobs in live theatre productions and then move back and forth between the stage, film and television.

Production occupations. Actors entertain and communicate with the audience through their interpretation of dramatic or comedic roles. Only a small number achieve recognition in motion pictures or television. Many are cast in supporting roles or as walk-ons. Some start as background performers with no lines to deliver. Also called "extras," these are the people in the background-crowds on the street, workers in offices, or dancers at a ball. Others perform stunts, such as driving cars in chase scenes or falling from high places. Although a few actors find parts in feature films straight out of drama school, most support themselves by working for many years outside of the industry. Most acting jobs are found through an agent, who finds auditions that may lead to acting assignments.

Cinematographers, camera operators and gaffers work together to capture the scenes in the script on film. Cinematographers compose the film shots to reflect the mood the director wishes to create. They do not usually operate the camera; instead, they plan and coordinate the actual filming. Camera operators handle all camera movements and perform the actual shooting. Assistant camera operators check the equipment, load and position cameras, run the film to a lab or darkroom and take care of the equipment. Commercial camera operators specialize in shooting commercials.

This experience translates easily into filming documentaries or working on smaller budget independent films. Gaffers, or lighting technicians, set up the different kinds of lighting needed for filming. They work for the director of photography, who plans all lighting needs. Sound engineering technicians, film recordists and boom operators record dialogue, sounds, music and special effects during the filming. Sound engineering technicians are the "ears" of the film, supervising all sound generated during filming. They select microphones and the level of sound from mixers and synthesizers to assure the best sound quality. Recordists help to set up the equipment and are in charge of the individual tape recorders. Boom operators handle long booms with microphones that are moved from one area of the set to another. One person often performs many of these functions because more filming is done on location and the equipment has become compact, lighter and simpler to operate.

Multimedia artists and animators create the movie "magic." Through their imagination, creativity and skill, they can create anything required by the script, from talking animals to flaming office buildings and earthquakes. Many begin as stage technicians or scenic designers. They not only need a good imagination, but also must be part carpenter, plumber, electrician and electronics expert. These workers must be familiar with many ways of achieving a desired special effect, because each job requires different skills.

Computer skills have become very important in this field. Some areas of television and film production, including animation and visual effects, now rely heavily on computer technology. Although there was a time when elaborate computer animation was restricted to blockbuster movies, much of the three-dimensional work being generated today occurs in small to midsized companies. Some specialists create "synthespians"-realistic digital humans-which appear mainly in science fiction productions. These digital images are often used when a stunt or scene is too dangerous for an actor.

Many individuals get their start in the industry by running errands, moving things on the set, controlling traffic and helping with props. Production assistants and grips (stagehands) are often used in this way.

***Postproduction Occupations:*** One of the most important tasks in filmmaking and television production is editing. After a film is shot and processed, film and video editors study footage, select the best shots and assemble them in the most effective way. Their goal is to create dramatic continuity and the right pace for the desired mood. Editors first organize the footage and then structure the sequence of the film by splicing and resplicing the best shots. They must have a good eye and understand the subject of the film and the director's intentions. The ability to work with digital media also is becoming increasingly important. Strong computer skills are mandatory for most jobs. However, few industry wide standards exist, so companies often look for people with skills in the hardware or software they are currently using.

Assistant editors or dubbing editors select the soundtrack and special sound effects to produce the final combination of sight and sound as it appears on the screen. Editing room assistants help with splicing, patching, rewinding, coding and storing film. Some television networks have film librarians, who are responsible for organizing, filing, cataloging and selecting footage for the film editors. There is no one way of entering the occupation of editor; but experience as a film librarian, camera operator, sound editor, or assistant editor-plus talent and perseverance-usually help.

Sound effects editors or audio recording engineers perform one of the final jobs in postproduction: Adding prerecorded and live sound effects and background music by manipulating various elements of music, dialogue and background sound to fit the picture. Their work is becoming increasingly computer driven as electronic equipment replaces conventional tape-recording devices. The best way to gain experience in sound editing is through work in radio stations, with music groups, in music videos, or by adding audio to Internet sites.

Even before the film or television show starts production, marketing personnel develop the marketing strategy for the release. They estimate the demand for the film or show and the audience to whom it will appeal, develop an advertising plan and decide where and when to release the work. They also may follow the filming or review film looking for images to use in movie trailers and advertising. Advertising workers, or "unit publicists," write press releases and short biographies of actors and directors for newspapers and magazines. They may also set up interviews or television appearances for the stars or director to promote a film or television series. Sales representatives sell the finished product. Many production companies hire staff to distribute, lease and sell their films and made-for-television programmes to theatre owners and television networks. The best way to enter sales is to start by selling advertising time for television stations.

Large film and television studios are headed by a chief executive officer (CEO), who is responsible to a board of directors and stockholders. Various managers, such as financial managers and business managers, as well as accountants and lawyers, report to the CEO. Small film companies and those in business and educational film production cannot afford to have so many different people managing only one aspect of the business. As a result, they usually are headed by an owner-producer, who originates, develops, produces and distributes films with just a small staff and some freelance workers. These companies offer good training opportunities to beginners, exposing them to many phases of film and television production.

### *Training and Advancement*

Formal training can be a great asset to workers in filmmaking and television production, but experience, talent, creativity and professionalism usually are the most important factors in getting a job. Many entry-level workers start out by working on documentary, business, educational, industrial, or government films or in the music video industry. This kind of experience can lead to more advanced jobs.

Actors usually are required to have formal dramatic training or acting experience. Training can be obtained in acting conservatories, university programmes, theatre-sponsored training programmes and independent dramatic arts schools. The National Association of Schools of Theatre accredits 135 colleges and universities that offer bachelor's or higher degrees in dramatic and theatre arts. However, many reputable studio programmes offer training on a course-by-course basis or that do not lead to a formal degree. Many professional actors who are between acting jobs obtain additional advanced training through private sessions with an acting coach or by participating in a master class to focus on a particular challenge or to broaden their skills.

Training in singing, dancing, or stage combat, or experience in modelling, stand up comedy, or acting in commercials is especially useful and helps an actor stand out among the many resumes being considered. But actual performance credits, even those for performing in local and regional theatre productions, can be the most useful in getting into an audition. Many actors begin their career by performing in smaller markets and commercials and working as extras. Most professional actors rely on agents or managers to find auditions for them.

There are no specific training requirements for producers and directors. Talent, experience and business acumen are very important. An ability to deal with many different kinds of people while under stress also is essential. Producers and directors come from varied backgrounds. Many start as assistant directors; others gain industry experience first as actors, writers, film editors, or business managers. Formal training in directing and producing is available at some colleges and universities. Individuals interested in production management who have a bachelor's degree or 2 years of on-the-set experience in motion picture or television production may qualify for the Assistant Directors Training Programme offered jointly by the Directors Guild of America and the Alliance of Motion Picture and Television Producers. Training is given in New York City and Los Angeles. To enrol in this highly competitive programme, individuals must take a written exam and go through a series of assessments.

Although many screenwriters have college degrees, talent and creativity are even more important determinants of success in the industry. Screenwriters need to develop creative-writing skills, a mastery of film language and a basic understanding of filmmaking. Self-motivation, perseverance and an ability to take criticism also are valuable. Feature-film writers usually have many years of experience and work on a freelance basis. Many start as copywriters in advertising agencies and as writers for educational film companies, government audiovisual departments, or in-house corporate film divisions. These jobs not only serve as a good training ground for beginners, but also have greater job security than freelancing has.

Cinematographers, camera operators and sound engineers usually have either a college or technical school education, or they go through a formal training programme. Computer skills are required for many editing, special-effects and cinematography positions. In addition to colleges and technical schools, many independent centres offer training programmes on various aspects of filmmaking, such as screenwriting, film editing, directing and acting. For example, the American Film Institute offers training in directing, production, cinematography, screenwriting and production design.

The educational background of managers and top executives varies widely, depending on their responsibilities. Most managers have a bachelor's degree in liberal arts or business administration. Their majors often are related to the departments they direct. For example, a degree in accounting or finance, or in business administration with an emphasis on accounting or finance, is suitable academic preparation for financial managers.

For top-level positions in marketing, promotions, or general or human resources management, employers prefer individuals with an undergraduate degree in a field related to the department in which they will work, such as degrees in marketing, advertising, or business administration. Experience in retail and print advertising also is helpful. A high school diploma and retail or telephone sales experience are beneficial for sales jobs.

Promotion opportunities for many jobs are extremely limited because of the narrow scope of the duties and skills of the occupations. Thousands of jobs are also temporary, intermittent, part time, or on a contract basis, making advancement difficult. Individual initiative is very important for advancement in the motion picture industry.

Screenwriters usually have had writing experience as freelance writers or editors or in other employment settings.

As they build a reputation in their career, demand for their screenplays or teleplays increases and their earnings grow. Some become directors or producers. Film and video editors often begin as camera operators or editing room assistants, cinematographers usually start as assistant camera operators and sound recordists often start as boom operators and gradually progress to become sound engineers. Computer courses in digital sound and electronic mixing often are important for upward mobility.

General managers may advance to top executive positions, such as executive or administrative vice president, either in their own firm or to similar positions in a larger firm. Top-level managers may advance to chief operating officer and chief executive officer. Financial, marketing and other managers may be promoted to top management positions or may transfer to closely related positions in other industries. Some may start their own businesses.

***Outlook:*** Wage and salary employment in the motion picture and video industries is projected to grow 17 percent between 2004 and 2014, which is faster than the 14 percent growth projected for wage and salary employment in all industries combined. Job growth will result from the explosive growth of demand for programming needed to fill an increasing number of cable and satellite television channels, both in the United States and abroad.

Also, more films will be needed to meet in-home demand for videos, DVDs and films over the Internet. Responding to an increasingly fragmented audience will create many opportunities to develop films. The international market for U.S.-made films is expected to continue growing as more countries and foreign individuals acquire the ability to view our films. As the industry registers employment growth, many more job openings will arise through people leaving the industry, mainly for more stable employment.

There is concern in the motion picture industry over the number of films that are being made abroad. Tax breaks offered chiefly by English-speaking countries, especially Canada, have induced U.S. filmmakers to increasingly move the production of films abroad. Production of many lower budget films, such as made-for-television movies and commercials has been moved abroad to reduce production costs.

In addition, more feature films are being made abroad, but mostly for artistic reasons. When film production leaves, it takes away large numbers of jobs that are filled at the site of the filming-most of the noncritical supporting actors and behind-the-scenes workers, caterers, drivers and production assistants. To address this issue, several cities and States have initiated tax breaks and other incentives to encourage filmmakers to make movies in their locales. Also, the U.S. Congress has considered legislation that offers tax incentives for filmmakers to stay in the United States.

The motion picture industry is also concerned about piracy of its work, which can occur in several ways. For example, as the power and speed of the Internet grows, more movies are being downloaded directly into homes, causing declines in theatre attendance and losses in revenue from ticket sales. The industry has launched an anti-piracy initiative in order to combat this trend, which potentially could have an adverse affect on employment. Digital transmission of motion pictures from studios directly to movie houses for exhibition will be able to prevent some piracy problems, but it also has high start up costs-expensive digital projectors and costs to install transmission and distribution technology and security software.

Opportunities will be better in some occupations than in others. Computer specialists, multimedia artists and animators, film and video editors and others skilled in digital filming, editing and computer-generated imaging should have the best job prospects. There also will be opportunities for broadcast and sound engineering technicians and other specialists, such as gaffers and set construction workers. In contrast, keen competition can be expected for the more glamorous high-paying jobs in the industry-writers, actors, producers and directors-as many more people seek a lesser number of these jobs. Small or independent filmmakers may provide the best job prospects because they are likely to grow more quickly as digital technology cuts production costs.

***Median Hourly Earnings of the Largest Occupations in Motion Picture and Video Industries***

| *Occupation* | *Motion picture and video industries* | *All industries* |
|---|---|---|
| General and operations managers | $44.49 | $37.22 |
| Producers and directors | 36.16 | 25.40 |
| Film and video editors | 21.50 | 20.96 |
| Entertainers and performers, sports and related workers, all other | 17.44 | 16.73 |
| Audio and video equipment technicians | 16.19 | 15.66 |
| Actors | 9.27 | 11.28 |
| Motion picture projectionists | 8.05 | 8.32 |
| Cashiers | 7.14 | 7.81 |
| Ushers, lobby attendants and ticket takers | 6.77 | 7.30 |
| Counter attendants, cafeteria, food concession and coffee shop | 6.67 | 7.53 |

***Earnings:*** Earnings of workers in the motion picture and video industries vary, depending on education and experience, type of work, union affiliation and duration of employment. In 2004, median weekly earnings of wage and salary workers in the motion picture and video industries were $592, compared with $529 for wage and salary workers in all industries combined.

On the basis of a union contract negotiated in July 2003, motion picture and television actors who are members of the Screen Actors Guild earn a minimum daily rate of $716, or $2,483 for a 5-day week. They also receive additional compensation for reruns. Annual earnings for many actors are low, however, because employment is intermittent. Many actors supplement their incomes from acting with earnings from other jobs outside the industry. Some established actors get salaries well above the minimums and earnings of the few top stars are astronomical.

Salaries for directors vary widely. Producers seldom have a set salary; they get a percentage of a show's earnings or ticket sales. Earnings in selected occupations in the motion picture and video industries appear in table. Unions are very important in this industry.

Virtually all film production companies and television networks sign contracts with union locals that require the employment of workers according to union contracts. Nonunion workers may be hired because of a special talent, to fill a specific need, or for a short period. Although union membership is not mandated, nonunion workers risk eligibility for future work assignments. Actors who appear in filmed entertainment-including television, commercials and movies-belong to the Screen Actors Guild (SAG), while those in broadcast television generally belong to the American Federation of Television and Radio Artists (AFTRA). SAG and AFTRA, however, share jurisdiction over several types of film work, including industrial/ educational film work not for broadcast, interactive media (computer games) and freelance television commercial work. Actors from either union may qualify for this work; and many actors belong to more than one union.

Film and television directors are members of the Directors Guild of America. Art directors, cartoonists, editors, costumers, scenic artists, set designers, camera operators, sound technicians, projectionists and shipping, booking and other distribution employees belong to the International Alliance of Theatrical Stage Employees, Moving Picture Technicians, Artists and Allied Crafts (I.A.T.S.E.) or the United Scenic Artists Association.

## Dance

In India, dance is an age-old tradition. This vast sub-continent has given birth to varied forms of dancing, each shaped by the influences of a particular period and environment. Indian dance is an extremely intricate art requiring skill, hard work and discipline. All Indian dances portray some expression of life and almost every dance posture has a specific meaning. Dance themes are derived from mythology, folklore, legends and classical literature.

Indian dance is said to have originated from 'Natya Shastra', which is a detailed script written on all aspects of Indian dance. The author of 'Natya Shastra' was 'Bharata Muni' who wrote it some time in the 2nd century B.C.

The two main divisions of dance are classical and folk forms. There are dance forms typical to certain parts of the country and these dance forms are based on ancient dance discipline. The various classical forms are Bharatnatyam of Tamil Nadu, Kuchupudi of Andhra Pradesh, Odissi of Orissa, Kathak, Kathakali and Manipuri. The uniqueness of Indian classical dances is that they are all devotional in content. Of all these dance forms, Bharat Natyam is believed to be the oldest and the purest Indian classical dance.

Training in Dance should start as early as age six or less, much before the official professional training. Besides an in born talent, the basic requirement for a full time Professional training is matriculation or 10 + 2. Some institutes at the time of admission even give preference to students having a talent. Careers in this field can be that of a performer, teacher and choreographer.

***Eligibility & Course Areas***

To be in this field one needs to have an inborn talent, training and guidance can only sharpen these talents.

***Educational:*** To take up a course in this subject the basic requirement is 10+2. However, for post graduate level courses graduation in the subject is compulsory. Courses offered in this area are certificate courses, bachelor courses, diploma courses and post graduate level courses. Duration of various courses: Certificate course is of one year, Bachelor courses is of three years, Diploma and Post Graduate level courses is of two years.

Training in this field is available at a number of schools and institutes all over India. The Kathak Kendra in Delhi, the Kalakshetra in Chennai, Bharatiya Kala Kendra in Delhi are some of the prominent institutes conducting courses in Dance.

Course areas include history and evolution of dance and dance forms, the characteristic features of the dance form one specialises in, covering all aspects of dance as a performing art.

***Personal Attributes:*** Main attributes are talent, versatility, sense of rhythm, dedication, grace, an expressive facial and body language, an ability to interpret roles, attractive appearance, stage presence, creativity, physical stamina etc.

### *Job Prospects & Career Options*

Job prospects: They can find employment in

- Kala Kendras
- Academies
- TV channels
- Dance troupes
- There are also many opportunities for self-employment in the form of holding private classes or starting an institution.

***Career Options:*** Career options available in this areas are that of a performer, teacher and choreographer.

***Teaching:*** To be in this field one needs an aptitude to teach, initiative and patience. They must also have thorough knowledge of practical and theoretical aspects of dance. They should have a perfect sense of rhythm and some proficiency in music.

Dancers who take up teaching as a profession can find opportunities in schools, colleges, universities, dance institutes and even open schools of their own.

***Choreography:*** The choreographer designs and composes dance sequences and coordinates the stage settings, music, costumes and supervises rehearsals. Choreographer must have creative or imaginative powers and an ability to interpret music and compose dance routines for solo as well as group performances. They must be able to work along with a team. Prospects in this field are expanding with more and more stage and TV shows.

Choreographers can find employment in troupes performing stage shows, TV shows and in films.

***Performing:*** To be a performing artist one must have attractive appearance, facial expression, an ability to interpret roles and stage presence. Performers have to spare time everyday for practicing. They must also have to keep in touch with the interest of the general public. They must travel a lot and give performances to be popular. Besides professional training; dedication, talent and the right contacts can only help a performer to become well established.

Performing artists can form their own troupes or even work with other troupes. They also have the option of starting schools and devote time for teaching.

### *Dancer*

***Job description and activities:*** Dancers use movement, gesture and body language to portray a character, situation or abstract concept to an audience, usually to the accompaniment of music. This normally involves interpreting the work of a choreographer, although may sometimes require improvisation.

Dancers work in a variety of genres: from classical ballet and West End musicals, to contemporary dance and disco. A dancer's role may involve education or therapy, as well as performance.

Dancing is a competitive and physically demanding career, which often involves periods of unemployment and underemployment. Many dancers combine part-time jobs in performing, administration and teaching.

***Typical Work Activities:*** Although performing is the most obvious activity, it usually occupies a comparatively small proportion of a dancer's time. Many dancers follow portfolio careers, combining performance with teaching, choreography, development work or administrative work in a dance company.

Work activities will differ from dancer to dancer, depending on the contract, but usually include varying combinations of the following:

- preparing for and attending auditions and casting sessions;
- preparing for performances, by rehearsing and exercising;
- performing to a live audience;
- studying and creating choreography;
- discussing and interpreting choreography with colleagues and choreographers;
- learning and using other skills, such as singing and acting - many roles, for example in musical theatre, require a combination of performance skills;

- looking after costumes and equipment;
- taking care of the health and safety of others, which requires knowledge and observation of physiology and anatomy, as well as safe use of premises and equipment;
- teaching dance, either privately or in the public sector;
- working in dance development and promotion, encouraging and enabling people, especially children, to become involved in dance and to understand and appreciate it;
- running workshops in the community, eg with disabled groups;
- undertaking administrative, promotional or stage management work, particularly in a small company or if setting up your own company;
- liaising with arts and dance organisations, theatres and other venues regarding funding and contracts.

Self-promotion is also a significant feature of the work, be it through sending out your CV and/or publicity photographs, delivering presentations, or attending auditions and meetings.

### *Salary and Conditions*

- Equity, the trade union for artists and The Independent Theatre Council have negotiated a minimum salary of £324 per week for dancers (salary data collected Jan 06). Membership of Equity also includes other sickness and insurance benefits. Non-Equity work normally pays below this, but many dancers are prepared to accept such contracts in order to gain experience and contacts. Others may work voluntarily to gain contacts.
- An experienced dancer may earn £400-£450 per week. This can rise to £600 per week for a West End show (salary data collected Jan 06).
- Hours are normally unsocial, as most performances are in the evening. Many shows run for six days each week.
- Dancers are required to practise daily, even when not performing.
- Rehearsals may take place in purpose-built studios or in rooms, which could be cold, draughty or dirty.

- Competition for jobs is high and many contracts are short-term. Dancers tend to be self-employed and often employ an accountant to prepare tax returns.
- A greater number of women are involved in dance at all levels, which makes the profession less competitive for men. Some companies specialise in Asian and African dance. Others aim to involve people with physical disabilities.
- A dancer's career can be short, rarely lasting beyond the age of 40. Injuries, especially to the feet, back and legs, can have an impact on the length of a performance career. Physical fitness is therefore crucial.
- A career in dance can be stressful because of the instability of employment and the frequent necessity to put yourself forward to be judged by audiences, employers and other people who control funding for the arts.
- Travel is usually associated with a dancer's career. This may involve touring the UK or overseas, or it may be necessary to relocate to find work, eg to a large city.
- Opportunities for employment abroad are frequently available.

***Entry Requirements***

It is unlikely that a graduate in a subject other than dance and with little involvement in dance would be able to enter a dancing career, even in an administrative capacity. That said, entry without a degree, HND, or foundation degree in dance is sometimes possible.

Vocational degrees and courses which specifically train performers are usually based at specialist colleges or vocational schools with 'dance' or 'performing arts' in the title. The content of university dance courses is usually more geared towards the academic and theoretical areas of dance, rather than performance. There are three distinct career areas in dance with three different entry routes:

- Classical—most classically trained performers will have attended ballet classes from childhood. Formal training usually begins aged 11 at a ballet school, such as The Royal Ballet School.

- West End—the best route into musicals is through stage schools, some of which start at age 11, such as the Sylvia Young Theatre School. These offer courses in musical theatre where singing and acting are also taught.
- Contemporary—there are a number of specialised colleges offering degrees in contemporary dance, such as the London Contemporary Dance School and the Laban Centre for Movement and Dance. A number of universities offer contemporary dance as part of a dance degree, such as at Guildford and Coventry.

Once qualified, it is possible to move from one type of dance to another. However, most performers will train in one style and stay working within it.

A postgraduate or vocational course, while not essential, could be helpful in furthering your career once you have gained a few years' experience in the dance industry. Details of courses are available from the Council for Dance Education & Training (CDET) or from the Prospects Postgraduate Directory.

Potential candidates will need to show evidence of the following:

- a thorough knowledge of dance and its related issues;
- confidence and self-belief, physical fitness, stamina and perseverance;
- the skills to perform in a team, not just as an individual;
- an ability to make contacts and promote current work.

Although it is illegal to discriminate against candidates on age grounds, in practice age may continue to be used in selection criteria by some employers and those entering dance later in their career will need to show dedication and put in a lot of work. Many performers in the contemporary dance field may have come to the training later on, possibly from a music or movement background. For more information on equality and diversity in the job market and how to handle discrimination, see the AGCAS publication, A Level Playing Field.

### *Training*

Training continues throughout a dancer's career, with even the most famous dancers attending daily classes. Out-of-work dancers still need to continue to attend open classes in order to maintain and develop skills.

In order to increase your employability, you may wish to gain further training and qualifications, particularly in other types of dance.

Many dancers undertake training to move into teaching. There are two types of qualifications to consider:

- To teach in the private sector, such as leisure centres and private dance schools, you need a qualification recognised by the British Dance Council or the Council for Dance Education & Training (CDET).
- Graduates wishing to teach in state schools must hold qualified teacher status (QTS), usually through taking a BA with QTS or a Postgraduate Certificate in Education (PGCE). Brighton, De Montfort, Exeter, Liverpool John Moores and Middlesex Universities offer a PGCE in Dance, as does the Royal Academy of Dance. PGCEs in physical education normally also include dance. See the GTTR (Graduate Teacher Training Registry) for details of courses. You could also try out-of-hours teaching in primary schools.

Some dancers choose to go into further or higher education lecturing. It is possible to teach in colleges without a degree in dance but you would need to take an appropriate qualification while working. Vocational schools usually run their own CDET accredited dance teacher courses. A postgraduate degree related to dance would be required or preferred for lecturing in higher education.

Some dancers decide to gain or formalise dance-related skills by taking further training in dance performance, or by obtaining a qualification in an area related to performance, such as community theatre work, choreography, scenography, notation, or arts administration. Details are available from the CDET and from dance schools such as the Laban Centre for

Movement and Danceand the Royal Academy of Dance. Dance UK is a good source of information on training opportunities and networking events in the independent sector.

Some dancers also do further training to work in complementary therapies or to take fitness classes such as yoga, pilates and the Alexander Technique. These open up opportunities for self-employment. Another option is to become a personal trainer. It can also be useful to gain IT skills, not only for temporary work but also for work in dance administration and development.

### *Career Development*

There is no clearly defined career path for a dancer. Career development normally involves moving out of performance or combining another aspect of dance with performance.

Many dancers move into teaching, either in the private or the public sector. Many qualified dance teachers run their own courses and some large chains of health and fitness clubs offer franchises to run classes. The Council for Dance Education & Training (CDET) lists accredited teaching qualifications on its website. Contracts are sometimes available to teach in leisure facilities, hotels or on cruise ships. Some dancers open their own dance schools or buy existing schools. Advice can be sought from one of the four Arts Councils (Arts Council England, Arts Council of Northern Ireland, Arts Council of Wales and the Scottish Arts Council (SAC)).

Dancers often move into choreography or work as dance notators. Others move into dance administration or work for dance development organisations, such as a national dance agency, Dance UK or the Foundation for Community Dance.

Experienced dancers sometimes move into writing dance articles or reviewing performances in the press. This is normally part-time, freelance work and tends to be part of a portfolio career alongside teaching or choreography. Short courses in dance writing are offered at festivals, or you could consider an MA in a related subject like journalism.

You might also consider moving into community dance. This could involve running workshops for young people, those with disabilities, or those hoping to pursue a career in dance. It may draw on non-traditional disciplines such as hip hop or streetdance. Some companies employ education officers for this type of work, which often involves an understanding of different cultures. The Foundation for Community Dance can offer advice to these practitioners.

Some dancers go on to become dance therapists, which requires taking an MA in Dance Therapy. Dance therapists help people address their problems through dance and movement.

A large number of dancers leave the profession entirely, although they often use the skills and attributes acquired as a dancer in a new career. Determination, confidence, personal presentation and fitness are all transferable to other jobs.

## Film Making

Film is probably the broadest and most varied creative opportunity in mass media. Films, a blend of creativity and technicality are an important media, not only for entertainment and information, but also for communication. Films, the most international medium, has developed into a universal art form that transcends cultural differences. Film making include feature films, documentaries, newsreels, promotional films, TV commercials, music videos etc.

The craft of filmmaking is a teamwork which needs close coordination of various skilled individuals. It involves acting, directing, producing, script writing, cinematography, sound recording, visual mixing, editing and so on. A film maker like the captain of a ship has to look at all these aspects of film making. He has to start at the very bottom and work his way up. *i.e.* beginning with raising capital for the film to its distribution, screening as well as all the stages of its crafting.

The field of film making which is highly competitive is one that has a lot of scope for employment opportunities especially, India which releases a large number of films every year. If one has artistic and technical skills and at the same time ability to express ideas, this is the right field for you. Even for acting and directing, which are basically creative fields that require inherent talent, training helps to hone the skills. In areas like cinematography, sound engineering and editing, professional training is essential. There are several universities institutions that offer training in these areas. The pioneering institute in this line is the Film and Television Institute of India (FTII), Pune.

### *Remuneration*

Earnings of workers in the motion picture production and distribution industry vary, depending on education and experience, type of work, union affiliation and duration of employment. Salaries for directors vary widely. Producers seldom get a set salary; instead, they get a percentage of a show's earnings or ticket sales.

### *Eligibility & Course Areas*

Educational Qualification: For technical courses basic eligibility is 10+2. For other courses it is graduation. There will be aptitude tests and interviews to assess the candidates talents. Duration of courses depends on the course one opts for and the institution chosen. There are Diploma, Post Diploma and even Certificate courses in each area of specialisation. Specialisation areas include production, direction, editing, cinematography, film processing, animation, acting, sound engineering, make up, photography and so on.

Personal Attributes: Artistic flair, ability to work cooperatively, sense of responsibility, ability to work under pressure, great physical stamina, strong visual sense, good communication skills and for production and direction; leadership qualities, ability to bring out talent in others, creative instincts as well as managerial and administrative abilities are essential.

### *Job Prospects & Career Options*

***Job Prospects:*** Candidates can find employment with Film Studios, Production Companies, Advertising Agencies, Government Department, which make films or start their own venture as producer, director, editors, cameramen, soundmen, lighting crews, assistants and so on.

***Career Options:*** Careers in films can be those related to the actual production of the film and those related to the film field such as a Film critic, Film archivist, Film curator, Film distributor etc.

***Production:*** Production involves too many responsibilities, sheer hardwork and anxiety after the release whether the hard work put in was worth it. Usually the production team is the first to arrive on the sets and the last to leave.

***Producer:*** He is the overall in charge of a film. Producer is responsible right from raising finance up to marketing the film. He is the decision making authority in all matters, plans and manages the technical and artistic resources. It is he who decides the story, obtain legal permission, hires the director, actors, decides the crew and the location etc. Production Manager and Production Assistants help the Producer in his job. The producer's role is sometimes combined with that of directing.

Post graduates in Mass Communication or diploma holders from the Film and Television Institutes can enter as professionals. But it is not a must. Personally he should have good communication skills, patience and stamina. He should also have a through knowledge and experience in the film industry and entrepreneurial ability to succeed.

***Production Manager:*** The production manager shoulders the delegated responsibility for the overall organisation of the film. He is responsible for the technical pre-planning of productions and for coordinating the crew, cast and scenery within a prescribed budget.

***Production Assistant:*** He acts as the coordinator while the producer or director is doing his artistic thing. It is the production assistant who actually make everything happen as planned. He handles all the administrative work, such as booking hotels and flights for the crew, arranging shooting schedules etc. and he is also responsible for keeping records of film sequences, scripts, call sheets and daily reports.

***Direction—Director:*** He is responsible for the management of all the creative aspects that go into the making of a film. These are the people who make the unreal real--who turn the pages of a script into reality on the screen. The director is in complete charge of the studio or location floor and controls the film artistically. He decides the camera angle and directs the work of the cast and crew, costumes, choreography and music, conduct rehearsals etc.

***Assistant Director:*** They ensure all the timely arrangement of things that are required for the shoot. There can be one or more assistant directors, depending upon the film budget.

***Editing, Acting & Animation: Editor:*** The work of an editor requires great skill, it is he who puts the film in correct sequential order. He views processed film and video with production personnel to analyse, evaluate and select scenes and to determine which scenes need to be improved or re-shot. He synchronizes the sound track and adds special effects wherever necessary. Degree in film direction and editing or professional experience is required.

***Screenplay Writer:*** Screen play writer rewrites the original story, on which the film is based, in a format suitable for the screen. A graduate or postgraduate degree in literature with proficiency in creative writing can become a screen play writer.

***Actor:*** An actor should have an ability to emote well and become the character he represents in the film. They are the ones who come in direct contact with the masses and the most appreciated. Actors need a great deal of patience and commitment because most productions require long rehearsal schedules and retakes. Acting is a highly competitive profession and lot of talent, mettle as well as luck is needed to make it to the top and create a place for themselves in the field. A screen presence and a good physical appearance are additional attributes to be successful in the field. Even though formal training is not a necessity, a graduate/post graduate degree in acting will help to sharpen skills and give exposure.

***Animator:*** Animation films are created by filming sequences of drawings or computer graphics and processing them at high speed so that they appear to be moving. Animation graphics are used in action films to stimulate real events.

Animators use their drawing skills to create moving images and effects for feature films, TV commercials and short features. Drawing skills are crucial for all animators and technical and computer training are integrated into the professional training. Personally, they must be artistically inclined, imaginative, skilful and practical, able to generate new ideas and put those ideas into sketches.

One can work as an animator for Cartoons, feature-length movies, TV commercials or motion graphics, multimedia or as a game designer. Proficiency in graphic software's or a graduate or postgraduate degree in Fine arts, Applies Arts, Graphic Design, Animation Design, Visual Communication Design etc. is helpful in getting into this field. The basic qualification for training in this field is 10+2/ equivalent.

***Light and Sound:*** Cinematographer: He is responsible for composing each scene to be shot, decides lighting and camera angles as per directors requirement. He leads the camera/ lighting team and is involved in the planning and execution of a shoot from the pre-production stage. Job requires high technical knowledge and experience in the field. In big units lighting technician may work out the lighting plan for each shot.

***Cameraman:*** The cameraman handles the camera and the camera assistants collaborate with him. The Cameraman operates the camera according to the instructions of the Cinematographer. Good technical ability and knowledge of cameras and lenses is essential.

***Lighting Technician/Operator:*** Lighting is used to change the mood of a scene or to indicate practical aspects such as day or night. Lighting technician arranges all the lighting effects. They determine light needed during each shot.

***Soundmen:*** Responsible for all sounds or effects that accompany visual images (Sound Mixing). The work includes recording, dubbing and mixing of music, dialogues and other sound effects. The Sound Mixer or Sound Engineer puts together the various elements of the sound track and edits it to give it a final shape. The Sound Recordist works under the Sound Mixer and ensures proper recording. Degree or diploma in

Audiography or Electronics is required. For admission to these courses a Science background at plus two level is preferred.

### *Film Related Careers*

***Film Critic:*** A critic needs to be well read, have adequate knowledge and experience in his respective field. Only persons having good knowledge about the particular subject/art can authoritatively write about the subject. He has to interview filmmakers and actors, covers local developments in the film business and attend film festivals from time to time. Reading significant histories and biographies, understanding critical theory of film and becoming familiar with the history of film arts are keys to success as a critic.

***Film Archivist:*** Archivists are involved with the collection, arrangement and provision and preservation of archives. Archives include official documents, photographs, maps, audiovisual material and any other information-bearing media that contains valuable historical information of individuals, companies, government departments and other organisations. An archivist can be a Film Archivist, Reference Archivist, Photographic Archivist, Appraisal Archivist, Manuscript Librarian etc. A graduate or postgraduate degree in one of more of the areas like history, art history, anthropology, archaeology, Latin, English literature, public administration, politics, law or economics or a postgraduate degree in Library and Information Studies; Museum, Gallery and Archives Management and Information Management is essential to get into this field. Archivists need to have good communication skills, analytical and research skills, an eye for detail, problem-solving skills and organisational ability, Knowledge of different databases and, Archivists need to be patient, accurate, thorough and able to make good judgements about what information to keep. They should work in a well organised and methodical manner, be able to keep information private and work well under pressure.

## Music

Music is one of the most profound human achievements. It is a universal sound which can create emotions and express feelings. Music also soothes the mind. There is rarely anybody who is not touched by music in some way at some time in their lives.

Talent, genuine interest, sincerity and willingness to work hard can guarantee a big success in the field of music. Having an inborn talent to sing is a wonderful gift. But making a career out of this talent, demands regular devoted practice. Joining an institution and getting trained is one of the first steps towards making a career in Music but the main emphasis should be real dedication and commitment.

A person considering a career in music should have a genuine love for music, a musical sense, which means a sense of time and rhythm, besides versatility, creative ability and also stage confidence. At the same time one needs to have publicity- contacts with the right people, money for training and for making demo cassettes for commercialization.

Just as there is a wide variety of forms in music like classical, folk, jazz, pop, fusion etc. there are also a variety of opportunities in this field. Besides becoming a performer (vocal or instrumental) or a teacher, one can be a composer/song writer, music publisher, music journalist, Disc Jockeys/ Video Jockeys, Music Therapist, Artist manager/PR and so on in the Music Industry.

Today the advent of satellite television, the growing popularity of the music channels and corporate sponsorship of musical events, has all made music big business. Although fame and money in this field depends a lot on luck and getting a good break, but once you are established there is ample scope for making good money in this field.

### *Eligibility & Course Areas*

***Educational:*** There is no specific qualification required to enter into this field. However, to take up a course in this subject the basic requirement is 10+2. Courses offered in this area are certificate courses, bachelor courses, diploma courses and post graduate level courses. Duration of various courses: Certificate course is of one year, Bachelor courses is of three years, Diploma and Post Graduate level courses is of two years.

Training in this field is imparted by many schools and institutions. Most prominent among them is Kalakshetra in Chennai and The Bharatiya Kala Kendra in Delhi.

Course areas include music theory, music interpretation, history of music, composing, voice instruction etc.

***Personal Attributes:*** Among the attributes, one that top the list is a good voice. Other attributes include inherent talent, dedication, determination and hard work, creativity and adaptability, team work, accept criticism in the right spirit, self confidence, ambition etc.

### *Job Prospects & Career Options*

Talented and qualified persons can find numerous employment opportunities in this field with the advent of satellite television, music channels etc. Various employers in this area are:

- Television channels like Doordarshan
- AIR and private FM channel stations
- Music channels
- Government departments of culture and public relations
- Production houses
- Music troupes
- Music research organisations as a musicologist
- Music companies
- Educational Institutions, Kala kendras etc.
- Hospitals as music therapist
- Newspapers and magazines as music critic or correspondents
- There are also many opportunities for self-employment in the form of holding private classes at home or opening a music school or producing and directing independent programmes.

***Career Options:*** Today with music getting into the league of big business, there are a list of careers one can choose from in the Music Industry. Besides becoming a performer (vocal or instrumental) or a teacher, one can be a composer/song writer, music publisher, music journalist, Disc Jockeys/ Video Jockeys, Music Therapist, Artist manager/PR and so on in the Music Industry.

***Music Composers / Songwriters:*** Those with a flair in writing and an inborn talent in music can take up the career as a music composer. A composer creates and writes music, may combine it with lyrics to give a new song. Musicians in this field create music or lyrics alone or create both together. Composers are required to write music creatively based on their knowledge of sound, understanding of various musical styles and taste of the audience to which it has to be presented. A song writer or lyricist must understand the theme, mood and audience, the music into which one is putting words. There are a separate category known as Jingle writers who specialize in writing music for radio and television commercials.

Composers/ song writers can create music for film, television/ radio jingles, folk songs and for albums. Musicians who are interested in this area are often required to know about the business aspect of song writing such as copyrights, networking, publishing, contracts, performing rights etc.

Music composers often work with advertising firms, production houses, recording companies, music publishing firms, film, television, radio etc. Jingle writers can get in through contacts in ad firms and production houses, contacts with directors / producers help to get in film/ television companies.

***Singers / Performers:*** Performing artists may work alone or in a group with or without musical instrument. One could be a classical or pop artiste or an instrumental musician. Performance careers differ widely and depend a great deal upon the instrument played and the performance medium. A high standard of musical and technical skill is required and expected from performers in all areas. They can undertake challenging performance in concert halls, small or large ensembles, in studios as recording artists and live shows in lounge settings, pubs, night clubs, etc. They can also work for film industry as playback singers.

***Producers:*** Producers brings together the various elements of recording and works to present them as an artistic whole.

They book the studio, hire musicians and engineers, oversee the production of the recorded music and control the recording budget. They have the final say on the development of their material. To be a successful producer technical knowledge and tact is a potent combination. Sometimes ex artists/ sound engineers enter this field.

***Artist/Music Management:*** This is considered as one of the emerging options. Artist management is the planning, organising and negotiating of an artists career. They work in the business area of music and deals with the tough, unpleasant stuff behind the scenes. The work involves meeting with radio and television producers and getting air time for their artist, negotiating with recording companies and programme sponsors etc. Perseverance and knowledge of music and media industries are vital. Experience and training in Music as well as a business background helps to be successful in the field.

They can work for a particular artist or band as well as in a artist management firm, performing organisation, Touring music group etc.

***Music Journalist:*** They review performances and recordings, conduct interviews with performers for various publications and write music reviews. They give news and updates on new releases and performers. Some may work as music critic also. This is one of the option available in music field for freelancing. They can also work for newspapers, magazines and websites.

To take up this career one must have keen interest and knowledge in music, flair for writing and good command of language.

***Music Educator/Teacher:*** Teachers can open music schools and also conduct private classes. Music teaching is often in demand at schools, colleges, universities and institutional setups. Their main job is to instil an interest and enthusiasm for music among the students.

Main attributes required for them is classical music qualification, initiative and patience. They must have a thorough knowledge of music to impart training to their students.

***Music Therapist:*** Music therapist are a unique breed of musician-counsellors, with specialised training in the use of rhythm and melody to improve psychological and emotional well being. Emotional stability and insight are essential for competent therapists. They must have the ability to explore, interpret and develop the creative use of sound.

Music therapists provide therapeutic programmes to people of all age group with psychiatric disorders, mental retardation and developmental disabilities, speech and hearing impairments, physical disabilities and neurological impairments. A career in music therapy offers challenge, opportunity and distinctive rewards to those interested in working with people of all ages with various disabilities. Music therapists are employed in psychiatric hospitals, community mental health agencies, rehabilitation centres, nursing homes, residences for the mentally disabled etc. They can also do private practice.

***Musicologist:*** With good knowledge of music, an aptitude for research and excellent communication skills, one can work as musicologist in research institutes.

Video Jockeys (VJs) & Disc Jockeys (DJs): With the advent of various music channel video jockeying is becoming an exciting career option for the music mad generation. Their job include introducing a music video, conducting interviews with artists and music personalities.

No specific educational background is required for VJs/DJs except some personal attributes. However, background in mass communication, visual communication or the performing arts comes in handy.

Main attributes required to work in this visual medium are excellent presentation skills, clear voice, presence of mind, in depth knowledge about various styles of music, musicians and albums, communication skills, confidence, ability to take split-second decisions, good body language and dress sense.

Music Librarian: Colleges and public libraries offer opportunities for trained music specialists with knowledge of library and research techniques. Some opportunities for music librarians also exist in radio, television and motion pictures.

In addition to any music qualification they need to have bachelors degree in library and information science.

## Music Teaching

If you are interested and enthusiastic about music then maybe you have what it takes to become a good music teacher. Teaching is a demanding role at the best of times. All schools teachers must be good communicators, organisers and managers. They must relate well to people and have the ability to exercise a considerable degree of understanding and patience.

We all remember a good teacher.

A Music teacher needs to have a love and understanding of their subject. They need to be versatile in all aspects of music and to be able to encourage their pupils to achieve their true potential.

There are a number of routes into music teaching. In Scotland the most popular is the four year B.Ed (Hons) which is the equivalent of the BA (Hons) Music with Qualified Teacher Status. Completing students on these courses can take up positions as either Secondary school teachers or as music specialists within primary schools.

All music teacher training courses provide a good mix of practical class experience with the study of professional subjects related to the teaching of music such as psychology, philosophy and sociology. Musical studies will feature highly too.

The best courses will offer wide ranging and diverse approaches to music making in the varied processes, forms and techniques of invention. Some offer opportunities to study other aspects of music such as music therapy, jazz, world music, electro-acoustic music and the integrated arts

Students will be able to enhance their performing skills in voice, piano or other instruments using various practical activities and ensembles. Listening and analysis skills are also important. Music will usually be studied in its social and historical context as well.

Music teaching students will spend some of their time in schools on teaching experience. There will be visits to primary schools as well as to secondary schools, but the majority of time will be spent in secondary schools

To become a music teacher you will need at least 5 GOSEs, 2 of which must be at advanced level. You must have passes in English Literature and English Language at any level, as well as Music.

A minimum of Grade 5 piano (ABRSM) is normally expected and a minimum of Grade 7 (ABRSM) is desirable for first study performance This can be in either an instrument or voice.

B.Ed (Hons) Music graduates are able to teach throughout Britain and subject to the regulations of the member states, within the European Community. Many graduates opt to teach abroad as far afield as New Zealand. Although the main career prospect will be teaching some may go in to other related professions or even go on to study at postgraduate level.

***Musician***

***Job Description and Activities:*** An instrumental performer, singer or composer in the classical music field performs or composes music for the enjoyment of an audience. This can be recorded in a studio or performed live, either as a soloist or in a group of musicians.

It may involve working as a salaried member of a group or could be in the form of freelance work for several organisations. Musicians usually specialise in a particular type of music and are often employed on a sessional basis by orchestras. This occupational profile is concerned only with the professional performance of classical music.

***Typical Work Activities:*** General tasks may include:

- performing in concerts and participating in recording sessions;
- delivering educational work in schools, businesses and the wider community;
- practising regularly and networking.

Orchestral players' tasks specifically include:

- maintaining and setting up/tuning the instrument and arranging for its transportation, if large;

- preparing for rehearsals, rehearsing with the orchestra and responding to the conductor's directions;
- maintaining a diary either through a diary service or a personal diary.

Solo/chamber performers' tasks specifically include:

- organising concerts, with or without the help of an agent, including researching and writing programme notes;
- arranging rehearsals with an accompanist or ensemble;
- re-evaluating performances and thinking about the music, style, composer, repertoire, audience and venue whilst working towards an appropriate version of your performance;
- learning new pieces of music to extend your repertoire;
- handling the administration of business activities, such as organising publicity, negotiating fees, liaising with agents and managing diary services (if working freelance).

Singers' tasks specifically include:

- warming up daily and preparing for rehearsals;
- understanding the text and how to pronounce it in different languages;
- memorising music and sometimes also stage directions.

It is likely that the musician will also teach or work in arts administration or another related area of the business to support their career as a performer or composer.

### *Salary and Conditions*

- In orchestras, range of typical starting salaries: £21,000 - 26,000 for full-time rank and file with a reasonably sized orchestra outside London. Section leader pay (starting salary outside London) is between £27,000 and 35,000 (salary data collected Aug. 06 and supplied by the Musicians' Union).
- For musicians, earning power depends on musical ability, reputation and mobility. Some soloists earn high salaries but they are relatively few in number. Extra payments can be made for overtime, concert fees, recordings,

porterage of large instruments and travel. The Incorporated Society of Musicians (ISM) publishes recommended pay rates for freelancers on its website.

- Royalties may be paid for some time after the actual work has been completed if the relevant piece or performance has been registered with the Performing Right Society (PRS) and/or the Mechanical Copyright Protection Society.
- Part-time work is almost standard for musicians and working hours are not nine to five. Concerts take place in evenings, at weekends and bank holidays. Where orchestras concentrate mainly on recording, the hours of work are more regular and generally take place in the daytime.
- Self-employment is common and many musicians are employed on a sessional basis by orchestras and other ensembles. Solo work can be irregular whether as part of an agency or not. Freelance work is insecure and is dependent upon the musician maintaining a high standard of performance, being dependable and able to establish good working relationships.
- Opportunities for employment in orchestras exist in big cities and cultural centres, though there are limited numbers of full-time orchestras and limited numbers of posts in each orchestra.
- The dress code is relaxed for rehearsals but tends to be prescribed and sometimes very formal for performances.
- Performance can be a stressful experience for some musicians and physical injuries of a repetitive strain nature are an occupational hazard (backache and neckache in particular).
- Touring in the UK and abroad can also be a regular part of the work, which can involve prolonged absence from home or extensive daily commuting.

### *Entry Requirements*

Professional performers and composers often have a degree or qualification in music, but people with degrees in other subjects and non-graduates can also become musicians if their playing, singing or composing ability is of a sufficiently high standard.

Entry for orchestras and opera houses is through an audition followed commonly by a trial period where the musician is paid on a sessional basis for several concerts. This is not the same as a probationary period and it cannot be assumed that a permanent contract will necessarily follow. Several musicians may be on trial at any one time and trial periods can last for any length of time, sometimes even years.

A degree in music will give you the opportunity to develop your performance skills whilst at university or conservatoire, although some university music degree courses may concentrate more on the academic side of music than the practical playing side. Courses run by conservatoires may be more appropriate for a performance or composition career.

Postgraduate courses in performance can help you to develop performance skills and build a network of contacts in the music field. Other qualifications, such as those awarded by The Associated Board of the Royal Schools of Music (ABRSM) or Trinity Guildhall will also be considered.

Networking and personal references are extremely important ways of obtaining work in the music field. Musical directors will be looking for people who have gained considerable experience, playing or singing in a variety of orchestras, ensembles and choirs or as soloists. Potential candidates will also need to show evidence of the following:

- a wide repertoire of music;
- a willingness and ability to tackle new pieces with enthusiasm and accuracy;
- teamworking ability, whether working as a performance musician, as a member of an orchestra, singer or soloist;
- attention to detail;
- accurate sight-reading, particularly if you have limited rehearsal time.

Take any reasonable opportunity that arises to gain experience, such as performing with amateur orchestras and entering festival competitions, to build your confidence and professional network and extend your repertoire. Seek advice from musicians who are already working in your area and ask for introductions.

Even if you hope to be an orchestral performer, try to take up opportunities for solo performances as these will help you prepare for auditions. It is also worth investigating playing positions with smaller ensembles and/or overseas in order to gain relevant experience.

It is advisable to write speculatively to the orchestral manager by name with a CV and introductory letter to obtain freelance work (details of contacts are in the British and International Music Yearbook). Orchestras keep lists of people whom they contact for freelance work as required. Some audition for players to go on these lists. Unsuccessful applicants for permanent posts will often be given the opportunity of freelance work in this way.

Speculative approaches can reap benefits in certain areas of work, so it is worthwhile making yourself known to likely orchestras, choral societies etc. By performing without pay to gain experience, you can establish a track record and proof of your ability.

Entry to full-time posts is very competitive and it is likely to be necessary, at least initially, to build a musical career incorporating performance work in a number of different settings and groups, teaching and arranging music.

Many people start their careers by gaining experience on a freelance basis whilst teaching music either through private lessons or by teaching small groups through a school peripatetic music service.

From 1 October 2006 it is illegal to discriminate against candidates on age grounds but, in practice, age may continue to be used in selection criteria by some employers.

### *Training*

Continuous improvement is a fundamental part of the job and of the art of the performer. Each musician is responsible for their own work and performance. If a performer is working in an orchestra or opera house and their standard is not maintained, they could be required to audition once again, which could have a detrimental effect on future employment.

Further instrumental training is not usually provided by orchestras, but further singing training is provided by opera houses. Many musicians continue to pay for their own lessons to further develop their musical skills. In an opera company, additional training can include stage-craft and movement classes and learning other specialised skills, such as fencing and dancing.

Language skills are essential for singers, bearing in mind that music is written in all major languages and that performing music is very much an international career. The most useful languages for performance purposes would be French, German, Italian, Russian, Spanish and Latin.

Some training might be provided to develop the extra skills needed for related activities, *e.g.* training in running musical skills workshops for community education projects and schools.

Given that most musicians are likely to be working freelance at some stage in their career, gaining skills in running your own business would be very beneficial, covering areas such as financial management and marketing.

### *Career Development*

An orchestral player would normally enter the orchestra at the rank-and-file level and would then hope to move through the numbered posts to sub-principal, principal and section principal over a number of years. Principals and section leaders of an orchestra may have additional duties such as organising a section of the orchestra (if appropriate), editing the music if necessary and discussing options with conductors.

There is not a great deal of movement within the profession, so bottlenecks do occur and progression can be slow. Movement to another orchestra may be the only way to advance in this situation.

It is common for full-time salaried musicians to earn extra money by teaching, coaching and through freelance music work, including recordings. At the same time, orchestral players would also frequently combine with other people to form specialist quartets and ensembles, playing varied repertoires.

Throughout their career an orchestral player or opera singer can move from place to place and often country to country, therefore a firm grasp of European languages may help in the long run, particularly for a singer who can confidently handle a repertoire in several languages.

Solo performers may start their career within an orchestra or amateur choir and then progress to become a soloist, but very often they start their career from day one as a solo performer with a mixture of freelance solo work and teaching. As a performer's reputation builds, they will receive more work. Only truly exceptional performers would expect to achieve a career as a soloist.

Freelancers will develop better networks as their career develops, but bookings will always depend on maintaining a high standard of performance and on their availability. Some freelance musicians may have agents if their career warrants it, but the majority will make their own arrangements and perhaps make use of a diary service.

Many performers starting out in the profession enter national and international music competitions. This can increase chances of future work, particularly if successful in the competition and can also reap financial rewards. Local music festivals are worth entering.

Once they have a reputation as a reliable freelancer, some accomplished musicians add conducting to their repertoire. Conducting utilises organisational and communication skills when setting up rehearsals and explaining to players how to interpret the score clearly.

## Animation Film Design

*Want to Become An Animator?*

*Good Money!*

Animation is the art of conceiving an action by drawing inanimate objects or characters, which are made suitable for filming. It has lately become so high paying a profession that it will soon be matching the pay packets of software professionals. Television channels are increasingly relying on animation techniques to reduce ho-hum viewing.

### *Job Opportunity*

If you have an itch to draw, you can take up this career. Students who have completed higher secondary school and are versatile in drawing, you can enrol in the Visual Communication and Design course. Any graduate in fine arts or any arts student with an aptitude for drawing would do well by joining production houses or studios as a trainee.

Television production houses are increasingly relying on taking in graduates in fine arts or animators who have qualified in 3D Studio Max. Or you can find an opening in some animation companies like Millitoon, Crest Multimedia, Ram Mohan Biographics etc. You can also find openings in advertising agencies as Visualisers.

### *How to Start?*

Do a course in 2D Studio Max. You must be familiar with the various modes of drawing methods available in the software. If you are a non-graduate in fine arts, you can do a one-year course in Visual Design. If you have a certificate in drawing and painting, you can join as a clean up artist Or you can become professionally qualified by joining a course in Animation Film Design offered by the National Institute of Design, Ahmedabad. There is no other institution in India teaching Animation Film Design.

### *Want a Career Sports?*

The acceptability of sports and physical education as a career has gone up several times with the entry of prominent corporate bodies as sponsors of sports and events during the last decade. Some of them have also come forward to extend training facilities to sports persons. This shows the enormous potential that lies ahead for sportsmen.

Active sport careers are short. A few manage to find some work connected with their sport as managers, coaches or by promoting products. The majority have to look elsewhere for employment unless they are already employed with some organization by virtue of their sports prowess.

***Career in Sports:*** For a career in sports and physical education, you should have a keen interest in sports and games, a high level of physical fitness, mental and physical stamina, a competitive spirit, leadership qualities, organizing ability, resilience and will power to cope with injuries and setbacks, self-confidence, self-discipline, mental toughness, dedication and perseverance. Even hobbies such as sports, the performing arts and photography, if pursued with professional training, can be a worthwhile career.

***Job Opportunity:*** Some distinct career streams in sports and physical education may be as professional players or participants, or in teaching or coaching. You can find jobs in schools and colleges as Physical education teachers. As a physical education teacher, you should have the ability to instill in the young the importance of good health and fitness habits. Through the medium of sports, you have to teach children the meaning of leadership, aggression and competition.

***Sports Journalism:*** You can, as a player, engage yourself in writing or reporting sports events. Sports journalism can be taken up by those having a knowledge of various sports events and having a flair for writing.

Sports Physiotherapy can be a specialization for a medically trained person or by a physiotherapist. You can be a sports nutritionist. A nutritionist who has trained to help sports persons according to the requirements of their life styles is called a sports nutritionist.

***Training in Sports and Games:*** The Sports Authority of India (SAI) organizes National Sports Talent Contest for identifying sports talent and providing adequate training in sports and games.

Sports persons in schools / colleges / universities who have secured first/second/ third positions in individual events or winners / runners-up positions in team events in international/ national and state level competitions held during a calendar year may apply for scholarships.

## Theatre Director

### *Job Description and Activities*

A theatre director has artistic control over a performance, coordinating all the stylistic and conceptual aspects of a theatrical presentation. Directors are responsible for interpreting and delivering a text and enabling a production team and cast to work imaginatively under their artistic vision.

A director can be involved in writing initiatives, educational or workshop activities and script development or dramaturgy. Artistic directors may programme their venues and can be responsible for financial and staff management.

Employment can be on a freelance basis or fixed-term contract. A director may work closely with one particular theatre or company, but work can still be irregular.

### *Typical Work Activities*

Theatres are headed by a general manager. Larger theatres may also have an artistic director, who selects the plays to be produced in the theatre each season (and the director for each) and is responsible for managing the company and its finances. In the case of a small performing company, usually in fringe theatre, it is the director who fulfils these roles.

Many directors will begin their working life as assistant directors, undertaking activities such as rehearsing certain scenes away from the main rehearsal and giving feedback to actors once the production is under way.

Associate directors are employed by a particular theatre company full-time. They work closely with the artistic director, direct some of the productions and may assist with programming the season.

Typical activities include:

- breaking down a script and analysing and exploring the content;
- translating and interpreting text;
- auditioning for productions, hiring designers, musicians, etc.;

- conducting rehearsals;
- managing time and organising people and space;
- communicating and liaising with all parties involved, including actors, the creative team, technicians and producers;
- programming and budgeting;
- adapting a script and, if the play is to be newly written, working with the writer or collaborating with playwrights;
- working with writers through workshops or script development schemes;
- working with the designer to conceive the overall look and feel of the production;
- liaising with choreographers, musical directors and fight directors for certain productions.

### *Salary and Conditions*

- Theatre director salaries depend on the length and type of contract undertaken (eg, freelance, repertory, touring). Contact The Independent Theatre Council or the Theatrical Management Association (TMA) for current union agreed rates and advice. Writer-directors are advised to contact The Writers Guild of Great Britain for guidelines on commission rates.
- Salaries are often negotiated and variations in salary may be considerable.
- Low salaries may be supplemented by freelance work, running creative workshops, or script consultancy. Working as a theatre director can be a precarious way to earn a living.
- Some directors are volunteers or work for their own companies. In a large theatre, an assistant director may support the work of the director. For small-budget studio performance runs, or for fringe productions, a director may work alone.
- Working hours involve regular weekend and evening work. Many directors work more hours than they have been contracted for with no time off in lieu. Breaks can often

turn into impromptu meetings. Rehearsal schedules are three to five weeks. Building-based directors tend to have more regular working patterns and conditions.

- Theatre venues can vary enormously. The working environment can be dark, gloomy and hot.
- Theatre work can be unionised - directors can belong to Equity, the Directors Guild of Great Britain or the Broadcasting Entertainment Cinematographic and Theatre Union (BECTU).
- Most directors are employed as freelancers on contract for each production from the planning/rehearsal period through to the first night. Fixed-term contracts tend to last between one and three years or, in the case of artistic directors, three to five years.
- There are many more male directors than female, but this is less noticeable in the regions. The gender balance at the top has improved.
- Friendships and social life are largely within the theatre. Maintaining good working relationships is essential.
- The work can be highly stressful and frustrating, but it is also incredibly rewarding.
- Travel is common and can involve overseas work. If working with a touring company, it is unlikely that the director will be on the road for the full tour, although they may visit certain venues.

***Entry Requirements***

Although this area of work is open to all graduates, a degree in the following subjects may improve your chances:

- English;
- drama/theatre studies;
- music;
- creative/performing arts;
- languages;
- humanities-based subjects involving thought, reflection and interpretation, *e.g.* philosophy, history, psychology.

Entry is also open to all Diplomates, but the following HND/foundation degree subjects may improve your chances:

- creative/performing arts;
- drama/theatre studies;
- music;
- arts in the community.

Entry without a degree or HND/foundation degree is possible, eg through reputation and experience as an actor, writer, assistant director or stage manager.

Postgraduate courses are not essential for those with a relevant degree or HND/foundation degree, or those who have a certain amount of practical experience. Graduates from non-relevant disciplines may choose to do postgraduate study, but should ensure the course has a strong emphasis on practical skills.

Practical theatre experience in acting, stage management and, particularly, direction should be gained in amateur or fringe theatre,eg through a student drama society or a youth theatre.

In addition, potential candidates will need to show evidence of the following:

- the ability to express yourself both orally and in writing and to be creative, persuasive and prepared to take risks artistically;
- creativity in solving problems and the ability to develop innovative ideas;
- an understanding of technical issues, the workings of a theatre and the process of performance and acting;
- team-working skills;
- critical analysis ability;
- leadership and people skills;
- dedication and enthusiasm.

Theatre directors must also consider issues of ethics and authorship. Understanding all types of theatre and an awareness of audiences, resources and investors is vital. Work may come from many avenues and you will need to be able to show flexibility in your approach.

Try to see as many productions as you can, from a wide range of styles and in a wide range of venues. Talk to the people who are creating the work. Often, there will be question and answer sessions with directors after a performance.

Learn more about the organisational structure of a theatre by working within the front-of-house team, perhaps as a steward. Many theatres take on stewards in both paid and unpaid positions throughout the year and this is a popular form of work experience for students.

Certain theatres offer training bursaries for young directors and it is worth doing some research to find out if any are available.

Regional arts councils may offer grants to individuals. Competition for any type of sponsorship is high.

Although it is illegal to discriminate against candidates on age grounds, in practice age may continue to be used in selection criteria by some employers.

### *Training*

Few venues or companies can afford to sponsor in-service training. Training is largely on the job and many directors have no formal training.

The skills required for directing - be it for stage, television or film - often develop in a process-led fashion. Learning from experience and personal development will be an important part of your career progression.

Many drama schools offer specialist courses. The National Council for Drama Training accredits certain courses. Details can be found in The Official Guide to Vocational Courses for Drama and Technical Training. Specific courses in theatre direction include The Channel 4 Theatre Director Scheme. Check with the Arts Councils (Arts Council England, Scottish Arts Council (SAC), Arts Council of Northern Ireland and Arts Council of Wales) to see if they are running any assistant director schemes.

A wide range of other short courses, workshop programmes, postgraduate courses and specialist training is available throughout the UK.

### *Career Development*

First appointments are usually on a small scale, either directing a small touring company or running your own company. Many directors come from self-started companies. The chance to progress to more prestigious work is determined by a combination of:

- reputation;
- obtaining funding to develop work;
- getting your work seen by people from other venues;
- flexibility;
- business acumen.

A minimum of ten years' reputable experience is normally required to apply for senior posts. Experienced directors may set up their own companies or theatre venues, others may accept residencies as associate artistic directors or artistic directors in a particular venue, where they will be responsible for the complete programme of productions in a season. These roles tend to be more managerial in nature, involving planning, budgeting and determining artistic policy. Additionally, artistic directors are usually responsible for directing one or two productions each season.

Some directors will move from subsidised theatres to the commercial sector, which can also open up opportunities in film and television directing and will involve a substantial increase in salary.

## Theatre Stage Manager

### *Job Description and Activities*

A theatre stage manager organises and coordinates rehearsals and performances, liaising with the director, technical staff and other members of stage management personnel.

The stage manager is usually supported by a deputy stage manager and assistant stage manager, but in small companies and touring theatres, the stage manager may handle all areas of the production.

The stage management team organises the production environment. They ensure the availability of rehearsal space, coordinate rehearsals, supervise access to the venue, ensure a safe working environment and arrange provision and maintenance of props and equipment.

The work also involves recording details of the production and disseminating information to colleagues.

### *Typical Work Activities*

Typical activities vary according to the role (stage manager, deputy stage manager and assistant stage manager) but in all roles responsibilities revolve around bridging the gap between the artistic and technical aspects of a production. The stage management team is responsible for:

- setting up and running rehearsal schedules;
- procuring all props, furniture and set dressings (in small companies, the team may also assist in set construction);
- arranging costume and wig fittings;
- distributing information to other theatre departments;
- managing the props and possibly the design, budgets and liaising with the production manager regarding costings;
- supervising the 'get in' to the theatre, when the set, lighting and sound are installed and the 'get out', when all the equipment is removed;
- compiling and operating prompt copy - also known as the 'prompt script', or 'the book' - noting actors' moves, changes to the set between scene changes, prompting actors and cueing technicians;
- ensuring the company's welfare and maintaining a good working knowledge of all relevant health and safety legislation and good working practice;
- running the backstage and onstage areas during performances;
- liaising with the director, stage personnel and other technical departments (*e.g.* costume, lighting, sound);

- calling actors for rehearsals and performances;
- during a long run, maintaining and replacing props and costumes as required;
- liaising with resident staff at other performance venues (if touring).

***Salary and Conditions***

- Range of typical starting salaries (as assistant stage manager): £14,500 - £17,000 (salary data collected Jan 07).
- Range of typical salaries at senior level/with experience (*e.g.* after 10 - 15 years in the role): £18,500 - £31,500 (salary data collected Jan 07).
- Freelance theatre stage managers may earn more, particularly in West End theatres.
- Salary levels vary and depend on the company and type of contract under which stage managers are employed. Self-employment skills are essential.
- Subsistence and touring allowances may be available.
- Working hours typically include regular unsocial hours as evening and weekend work and long hours are the norm.
- Most technical staff are employed on fixed-term contracts for the period of the production. Most provincial theatres have a one- to two-month lay-off period during the summer when the theatre is 'dark', but the same staff are often re-employed each year.
- Self-employment or freelance work is commonly possible. Experienced stage managers may opt to work freelance in order to gain more varied experience and earn higher rates of pay.
- Some theatre environments are dark, gloomy and hot, though open-air theatres, for example, may be just the opposite. Many arts centre venues utilise a clear area for performance.
- A good head for heights may be needed, depending on the technical area of work.

- The work is physically demanding and brings ever-changing challenges. Stage managers are commonly expected to 'muck in' and apply their skills to any given priority (especially at the beginning of their career).
- Most venues have a play in rehearsal at the same time as one in production, which may mean a constant heavy workload for technical staff.
- Stressful parts of the job include dress rehearsals, technical rehearsals, dealing with different personalities and first nights, when nerves can become frayed. On the plus side, the work affords genuine opportunities for personal and team achievements and it is often a lot of fun!
- Jobs are available in most areas of the country and there are also opportunities to work overseas.
- Directors and stage managers normally belong to Equity. Other technical staff belong to the Broadcasting Entertainment Cinematographic and Theatre Union (BECTU).
- Travel within a working day may occasionally be needed and absence from home at night is frequent. In a touring company, you may spend long periods away from home, living out of your suitcase.

***Entry Requirements***

Although this area of work is open to all graduates and Diplomates, the following subjects may increase your chances:

- performing arts;
- drama/theatre studies;
- music.

It is still possible to enter theatre stage work from any degree discipline, but candidates with relevant qualifications are often preferred. If you are interested in technical theatre, you should ensure that your degree has considerable practical content.

Entry without a degree or HND is sometimes possible. Practical experience of performance-related work and technical skills in sound, lighting or carpentry can be helpful. Some stage managers come through an acting or writing route.

A pre-entry postgraduate qualification can be advantageous, particularly if you do not have a directly relevant degree. Postgraduate courses are offered at various universities.

Increasingly, theatres prefer applicants with specific training in stage management. It is recommended that new entrants take a relevant course, particularly one accredited by the National Council for Drama Training. Membership of Equity and eligibility to join the Stage Management Association (SMA) will often be available upon graduation.

Many drama schools offer courses in technical theatre, stage management and theatre direction. Training should cover all the disciplines involved in the mounting of professional performances, including lighting, sound, design and scenic art, scenic construction, property making, wardrobe, stagecraft and stage management (*e.g.* RADA, see Technical Theatre at the Royal Academy of Dramatic Art). Administrative skills such as bookings, contracts, budgeting and licensing should also be studied. It is essential to gain practical theatre experience, particularly in relation to props, lighting and sound. Some courses may incorporate a work placement option.

Candidates will need to show evidence of the following:

- excellent communication and organisational skills;
- a sharp eye for detail;
- a sense of humour and the ability to stay calm in a crisis;
- people skills: persuasiveness, patience, tact and the ability to deal with 'artistic temperaments';
- computer skills and awareness of current technologies;
- the ability to work under pressure, especially in the run-up to a performance;
- problem-solving skills and the ability to think on your feet;
- confidence, decision-making ability and negotiation skills;
- a full driving licence, preferably clean;

- stamina, to cope with long hours during technical and dress rehearsals and for touring.

Being able to read music may be beneficial and is essential in opera, ballet and (to a lesser extent) musical theatre. Familiarity with period costume can be useful, as can sewing skills.

There is stiff competition for jobs in theatre and even experienced stage managers have periods out of work. The summer months, when there is less work, are often referred to as the 'dark period' for theatre companies.

You should contact local stage managers for advice and to find out about any available work during 'get-outs'. Gain experience as a volunteer in community productions, or through school drama, youth theatre or amateur groups.

Networking is a key factor in getting work - many jobs are filled through contacts made whilst working - so it is wise to keep a log of any contacts you make in the field and stay in touch on a regular basis.

It is now illegal to discriminate against candidates on age grounds but, in practice, age may continue to be used in selection criteria by some employers.

### *Training*

Most training is on the job. Post entry, few venues or companies can afford to sponsor in-service training and individuals will be expected to take responsibility for their own continued professional development (CPD) in technical areas.

The Conference of Drama Schools provides a list of training providers. Details of specific courses for designers can be found through the Society of British Theatre Designers.

The Stage Management Association (SMA), the professional body that supports and represents stage management in the UK, runs a number of short training courses, available to members and non-members.

These practical courses are usually designed to assist stage managers in their career development by updating or enhancing existing skills. Courses are also aimed at managers wishing to move into company management and production management.

Examples of courses offered in the past include:

- risk assessment for stage managers;
- cueing from music scores;
- relighting for stage managers;
- score reading for stage managers.

### *Career Development*

A new entrant usually starts as an assistant stage manager and, after gaining skills and experience, progresses to deputy stage manager. With further experience, the next step is to become a stage manager and then company stage manager. A company stage manager may have additional duties, such as coordinating marketing and liaising with front-of-house staff and will need knowledge of union regulations.

Some stage managers remain as assistants or deputies for their entire career (especially in larger organisations). Others may move between companies, filling roles as assistant, deputy or stage manager, as required. Managers with specialist skills may enter other areas of technical production, for example in lighting, sound, or prop-making.

Ambitious stage managers may go on to become theatre managers or producers (sometimes called production managers or production directors). They normally work in larger theatres, run significant budgets and coordinate the whole physical production of a play.

With experience and further training, some stage managers go on to become theatre directors. Others use their skills and experience gained in the theatre to work in production jobs in television or film, where they usually start as trainee floor managers. Some stage managers may move into stage management of large-scale music concerts or become events managers.

Geographical mobility is needed for career development. In order to acquire the best skills and build up substantial experience, it is usually necessary to work with a number of different companies and/or travel with a touring company to a number of different performance venues.

### *Creating the Excitement*

Sports lovers alone can't create the hoopla surrounding March Madness. Skilled advertising, public relations and Marketing specialists promote the play-offs, selling expensive TV and radio air time to companies. Web-based streaming broadcasts of the play-offs online have also generated additional advertising opportunities.

***Advertising:*** Pursuing a career in advertising means entering the fast-paced world of big city, big time New York or Los Angeles-based ad agencies. If you have a creative side, your talents are in high demand at advertising agencies, where employees create artwork, graphics and catchy slogans for campaigns. Other jobs in the industry involve selling ad space to companies and require fine-tuned business and negotiating skills. To gain a leg up on the competition, a degree in advertising is highly recommended.

***Public Relations:*** The PR business in sports revolves around advancing a team's public image, whether to sell the image, increasing viewer turnout, or influencing the politics of sports negotiations. PR managers often implement public exposure strategies for teams and players, by writing press releases, helping athletes with appropriate dress standards and speaking publicly and dealing with any public image crises that may suddenly emerge. Entry into this hot field begins with the educational training in advertising or public relations.

***Marketing:*** Marketing specialists find new markets and work with existing markets to develop promotions, produce brochures and license team logos. Marketing is often a year-round job that requires working specific duties routinely. A degree in business with an emphasis in marketing will get your foot in the door.

The competition for jobs is stiff for careers in advertising, PR and marketing, but employment in the industry is expected to grow by 22 percent from the 2004 to 2014 period, according to the BLS. Soon, you could be responsible for generating buzz about March Madness.

### *Communications*

There's no better way to watch sports than front and center from a press box or right on the sidelines. A variety of occupations in broadcasting put you in charge of writing, shooting and producing sports content to air on TV or radio stations.

***Producers:*** Producers are in charge of planning live or taped segments. They oversee the script, the setting, arrange for any necessary filming permits and direct other production staff. Producers need to have high attention to detail and work well under stress.

***Video Editors and Engineers:*** For the more technologically oriented, a variety of jobs such as video editor, sound engineer and audio equipment technician can also put you where the action is. As a cameraperson, you could be capturing the games for others to see at home. If you didn't major in film or broadcast journalism in college, a host of associate programmes offer training in technical fields. Experience is highly valued in the sports broadcast industry, so learning the trade through an internship or apprenticeship is ideal.

***Journalists:*** Many people capture the action through the written word, working as journalists for newspapers and magazines. Sports writers are expected to establish their credibility with editors and readers through strong research and reporting skills. As a sports writer you'll need to be at the games and talking to the athletes to get their stories. When you're back in the office, chances are that you'll be on the phone following up on facts to report to your readers. Most sports writers have degrees in communications, journalism or English--along with a healthy love of sports.

# Bibliography


Albarran, Alan B. and Gregory G. Pitts: *The Radio Broadcasting Industry*, Boston, Allyn and Bacon, 2001.

Albrecht, Ulrich: *A Short Research Guide on Arms and Armed Forces*, New York, Facts on File, 1980.

Alexander, James: *Internships in Communications, Ames*, Iowa State University Press, 1995.

Allman, Paul: *Careers in Video and Digital Video*, New York: Rosen, 2001.

Anders, Peter: *Envisioning Cyberspace*, New York, McGraw-Hill, 1999.

Arkin, William M.: *Research Guide to Current Military and Strategic Affairs*, Washington, Institute for Policy Studies, 1981.

Baehr, H. and Gary A.: *Turning In On: A Reader in Women and Media*, London, Arnold, 1996.

Ball, Victoria Kloss: *Opportunities in Interior Design and Decorating Careers*, Chicago, VGM Career Horizons, 2002.

Barnouw, Erik: *A Tower in Babel: the History of Broadcasting in the United States to 1933*, New York, Oxford University Press, 1966.

Baucom, Alfred H.: *Hospitality Design for the Graying Generation: Meeting the Needs of a Growing Market*, New York, Wiley, 1996.

Baxter, John: *Australian Cinema*, Sydney, Pacific Books, 1970.

Beaman, Jim: *Interviewing for Radio*, New York, Routledge, 2000.

Berkowitz, Ira: *Vault Career Guide to Advertising*, New York, Vault, 2004.

Bertrand, Ina and Diane Collins: *Government and Film in Australia*, Sydney, Currency Press, 1981.

Bliss, Edward and James L. Hoyt: *Writing News for Broadcast*, New York, Columbia University Press, 1994.

Boella, Michael John: *Principles of Hospitality Law*, London, Cassell, 1999.

Bone, Jan, & Ana Fernandez: *Opportunities in Film Careers*, New York, VGM Career Books, 2004.

Bowers, C. A.: *The Cultural Dimension of Educational Computing: Understanding the Non-neutrality of Technology*, New York, Teachers' College Press; 1988.

Boyd, Andrew: *Broadcast Journalism: Techniques of Radio and TV News*, Woburn, Focal Press, 2001.

Brown, Douglas Robert: *The Restaurant Managers Handbook: How to Set Up, Operate, and Manage a Financially Successful Restaurant.* Lauderhill, Atlantic Pub., 1991.

Brown, James and Quaal Ward: *Radio-Television-Cable Management*, New York, McGraw Hill, 1998.

Bryant, Jennings: *Television and the American Family*, Hillsdale, Lawrence Erlbaum, 1990.

Buckingham, David: *Young People and the Media*, New York, Manchester University Press, 1993.

Buckner, Robert W.: *Site Selection: New Advancements in Methods and Technology*, New York, Lebhar-Friedman Books, 1998.

Caldwell, J. T.: *Electronic Media and Technoculture*, New Brusnwick, Rutgers University Press, 2000.

Careers in Focus: *Photography*, New York, Ferguson, 2004.

Carmouche, Rita: *Behavioural Studies in Hospitality Management*, New York, Chapman & Hall, 1995.

Carroll, Victoria: *Writing News for Television*, Ames, Iowa State University Press, 1997.

Cassiday, Doris, and Bruce Cassiday: *Careers in the Beauty Industry*, New York, Franklin Watts, 1978.

Clark, Mona: *Interpersonal Skills for Hospitality Managers*, London, Chapman Hill, 1995.

Clark, Roy Peter: *A Journalist Teaches Young Writers*, Portsmouth, Heinemann, 1987.

Cockburn, C. and Ormrod, S.: *Gender and Technology in the Making*, London, Sage, 1993.

Cohler, David Keith: *Broadcast Newswriting*, Englewood Cliffs, Prentice Hall, 1990.

Cracknell, H. L.: *Escoffier: The Complete Guide to the Art of Modern Cookery*, New York, John Wiley, 1979.

Craig, James: *Graphic Design Career Guide*, New York, Watson-Guptill, 1992.

Crawford, Tad: *Starting Your Career As a Freelance Photographer*, New York, Allworth Press, 2003.

Crouse, Chuck: *Reporting for Radio*, Chicago, Bonus Books, 1998.

Davidson, M. J. and Cooper, C. L.: *Women and Information Technology*, New York, John Wiley & Sons, 1987.

Delaney, Chuck: *Photography Your Way*, New York, Allworth Press, 2005.

Dennis, Everette E. and Edward C. Pease: *Children and the Media*, New Brunswick, Transaction Publishers, 1996.

Diamond, S. Taylor's Way: *Women, Cultures and Technology*, New York: Routledge; 1997.

Donald, Ralph and Thomas Spann: *Fundamentals of Television Production*, Ames, Iowa State University Press, 2000.

Dornenburg, Andrew: *Culinary Artistry*, New York, John Wiley & Sons, 1996.

Douglas, George H.: *The Early Days of Radio Broadcasting*, Jefferson, NC: McFarland, 1987.

Easlea, B.: *Fathering the Unthinkable: Masculinity, Scientists and the Nuclear Arms Race*, London, Pluto Press, 1982.

Ellis, Elmo: *Opportunities in Broadcasting Careers*, Chicago, VGM Career Books, 2005.

Faulkner, W. and Arnold, E.: *Smothered by Invention: Technology in Women's Lives*, London, Pluto Press, 1985.

Fensch, Thomas: *Television News Anchors*, Jefferson, McFarland, 1993.

Field, Shelly: *Career Opportunities in Advertising and Public Relations*, New York, Ferguson, 2006.

Foster, Timothy R. V.: *How to Succeed As an Independent Consultant*, London: Kogan, Page, 2002.

Fox Keller, E.: *Reflections on Gender and Science*, New Haven, Yale University Press, 1985.

Gardner, Garth: *Careers in Computer Graphics and Animation*, Fairfax, GGC, 2001.

Gibbs, Jenny: *Interior Design*, New York, H. N. Abrams, 2005.

Go, Frank M.: *Human Resource Management in the Hospitality Industry*, New York, Wiley, 1996.

Goldfarb, Roz: *Careers by Design*, New York, Allworth Press, 2001.

Gordon, Sandra R.: *Great Jobs for Film Majors*, Chicago, VGM Career Books, 2004.

Graham, Duane: *The Remarkable Story of Otto Graham*, Wayne, Immortal Investments Publishing, 2004.

Green, E. and Adam, A. Virtual Gender: *Technology, Consumption, and Identity*, New York, Routledge, 2001.

Greenman, Robert: *The Adviser's Companion*, New York, Columbia Scholastic Press Association, 1991.

Griffiths, D.: *The Exclusion of Women from Technology*, London, Pluto Press, 1985.

Hall, Ken G.: *Australian Film: the Inside Story*, Sydney, Summit Books, 1980.

Hewitt, John: *Airwords: Writing for Broadcast News, Mountain View*, Oxford, Mayfield Pub. Company, 2002.

Higham, Robin: *A Guide to the Sources of United States Military History*, Hamden, Archon Books, 1975.

Hilliard, Robert L. and Michael C. Keith: *The Broadcast Century and Beyond*, Boston: Focal Press, 2001.

Hinkin, Timothy R.: *Cases in Hospitality Management: A Critical Incident Approach*, New York, Wiley, 1995.

Holloway, J. C. : *Towards a Core Curriculum for Tourism: A Discussion Paper*, London, The National Liaison Group for Higher Education in Tourism, 1995.

Horstede, G.: *Cultures and Organizations: Software of the Mind*, London, McGraw-Hill Book Company, 1991.

Hungerland, Buff: *Marketing Your Creative Portfolio*, Upper Saddle River, Prentice Hall, 2003

Jain, S. C.: *Women and Technology*, Jaipur, Rawat Publications, 1985.

Jefferson, Michael: *Breaking into Graphic Design*, New York, Allworth Press, 2005.

Jensen, Clayne R.: *Opportunities in Recreation and Leisure Careers*, Lincolnwood, VGM Career Horizons, 2000.

Jones, Sue Jenklyn: *Fashion Design*, New York, Watson-Guptill, 2002.

Kieffer, John: *The Photographer's Assistant*, New York, Allworth, 2001.

Kirkham, P.: *The Gendered Object*, Manchester, Manchester University Press, 1996.

Kissane, Sharon F.: *Career Success for People with Physical Disabilities*, Lincolnwood, VGM Career Horizons, 1997.

Kring, Robin: *Party Creations: Book of Theme Event Design*, Denver, Clear Creek Pub., 1993.

Kurzweil, R.: *The Age of Spiritual Machines*, New York, Viking, 1999.

Lavery, P.: *Tourism Marketing and Management Handbook*, New York, Prentice Hall, 1989.

Lewis, Robert C.: *Cases in Hospitality Marketing and Management*, New York, John Wiley, 1997.

MacCloskey, Monro: *How to Qualify for the Service Academies*, New York, Richards Rosen Press, 1964.

Maclay, Edgar Stanton: *A History of the United States Navy 1771-1893*, New York, Appleton Co., 1894.

Mauro, Lucia: *Careers for Fashion Plates and Other Trendsetters*, Chicago, VGM Career Horizons, 2003.

McGuire-Lytle, Erin: *Careers in Graphic Arts and Computer Graphics*, New York, Rosen, 1999.

Miller, Samuel D.: *An Aerospace Bibliography*, Washington. Office of Air Force History, 1978.

Mitchell, Leslie Scott: *Freelancing for Television and Radio*, London; Routledge, 2005.

Mogel, Leonard: *Creating Your Career in Communications and Entertainment*, Sewickley, GATF Press, 1998.

Noronha, Shonan F. R.: *Opportunities in Television and Video Careers*, Chicago: VGM Career Books, 2003.

Orlik, Peter B.: *Career Perspectives in Electronic Media*, Ames, Blackwell Pub., 2004.

Packard, Sidney: *The Fashion Business: Dynamics and Careers*, New York, Holt, Rinehart, and Winston, 1983.

Parks, Peggy J.: *The News Media*, San Diego, Lucent Books, 2002.

Paullin, C.O.: *The Navy of the American Revolution*, Cleveland, The Burrows Brothers Co., 1906.

Perna, Rita: *Fashion Forecasting*, New York, Fairchild Publications, 1987.

Rachlis, Eugene: *The Story of the U.S. Coast Guard*, New York, Random House, 1961.

Reis, Ronald A.: *Careers in Art and Graphic Design*, Hauppage, Barrons, 2001.

Rocha, Tony L.: *Careers in Magazine Publishing*, New York, Rosen, 2001.

Rubinstein, Donna: *The Modeling Life*, New York, Berkeley Publishing Group, 1998.

Satterthwaite, Frank: *The Career Portfolio Workbook*, New York, McGraw-Hill, 2003.

Seguin, James: *Media Career Guide*, Boston, St. Martin's, 2006.

Sones, Melissa: *Getting into Fashion: A Career Guide*, New York, Ballantine, 1984.

Vogt, Peter: *Career Opportunities in the Fashion Industry*, New York, Facts on File, 2002.

Wilson, Wayne: *Careers in Publishing and Communications*, Bear, Mitchell Lane, 2002.

Yager, Fred, & Jan Yager: *Career Opportunities in the Film Industry*, New York, Ferguson, 2003.

Zahler, Karen Gantz.: *Superchefs: Signature Recipes From America's New Royalty*, New York, John Wiley & Sons, 1996.

# Index

## D



## E



## F



## G



## H

## O



## P



## R

## S



## T



## U



## V

❑❑❑